London Philatelic society

The Postage Stamps, Envelopes, and Post Cards of Australia

and the British Colonies of Oceania

London Philatelic society

The Postage Stamps, Envelopes, and Post Cards of Australia
and the British Colonies of Oceania

ISBN/EAN: 9783337036461

Printed in Europe, USA, Canada, Australia, Japan

Cover: Foto ©Lupo / pixelio.de

More available books at **www.hansebooks.com**

Envelopes, and Post Cards,

OF

AUSTRALIA AND THE BRITISH COLONIES OF OCEANIA.

With Autotype Illustrations.

COMPILED AND PUBLISHED

BY

THE PHILATELIC SOCIETY, LONDON.

LONDON, 1887.

All rights reserved.

THE PHILATELIC SOCIETY, LONDON, has much pleasure in presenting subscribers to their Catalogue of *the Postage Stamps of the British Colonies of Oceania* with an Autotype Illustration of the sheet of the Registration Stamp of New South Wales. The Autotype is taken from an unused entire sheet in the collection of a well known Colonial collector, kindly lent for that purpose, and of course gives the correct arrangement of every variety of type. The enclosed sheet will therefore replace *Plate M.* previously given with the Catalogue.

LONDON,
Dec. 20th, 1888.

THE

POSTAGE STAMPS,

Envelopes, and Post Cards,

OF

AUSTRALIA AND THE BRITISH COLONIES OF OCEANIA.

With Autotype Illustrations.

COMPILED AND PUBLISHED

BY

THE PHILATELIC SOCIETY, LONDON.

LONDON, 1887.

PREFACE.

IN the season of 1881–82 the Society commenced the preparation of the Lists of Stamps of the Australian Continent, and has included in its subsequent labours those of the Colonies of Great Britain which are collectively designated Oceania. The following pages contain the results of their investigations; for the delay in the appearance of which some explanation is perhaps called for.

A perusal of the papers of the President and Vice-President will inform those members of the Society who have hitherto not been acquainted with the facts, of the difficulties of the task, and of the causes which prevented complete lists being compiled until the problems of the plates of the locally-engraved stamps had been solved. It was found advisable to entrust these specific investigations to individual members; and the prosecution of their enquiries, and the comparison and verification of the results obtained by each, have necessarily occupied much time. The Catalogues of M. Moens and of Major Evans have been freely consulted as the existing standard lists. It is believed the postponement has been attended with the result, that in the labours of the Society will be found the first systematic attempt to settle questions of the highest interest to Philatelists, and which since the earliest days of collecting have presented difficulties of an almost insurmountable nature.

The lists have been completed to the end of 1886.

Collectors will find in the remarkable Autotype illustrations a complete series of the entire plates, which, from their absolute fidelity to the minutest detail, will enable them to reconstruct their own plates, and be of essential service in detecting impostures.

LONDON, *October*, 1887.

LIST OF ABBREVIATIONS.

T.	Top.
B.	Bottom.
R.	Right.
L.	Left.
Perf.	Perforated.
Imperf.	Imperforate.
M.-Perf.	Machine-Perforated.
Pin-Perf.	Pin-Perforated.
Rou.	Rouletted.
Wmk.	Watermark.
Mm.	Millimetres.

FIJI ISLANDS.

Issue I. End of 1871.

Three values, type-printed; coloured impression on medium white wove paper; watermark, "FIJI POSTAGE," in single-lined letters, once in each sheet of stamps; white gum; shape, upright rectangular; perforation, 12½. Design: Each stamp bears the initials "C.R." ("Cakambau Rex") in script type, surmounted by a crown, in white upon ground of coloured horizontal lines within circular frame. Curved labels above and below circle, with name of country and value in words. (*Illustrations* 1, 2, 3.)

ONE PENNY. Beaded circle, with thin inner and outer lines. The upper curved label has an ornament at each end resembling a cross *pâtée*, and is inscribed with the word "FIJI" in Roman letters. The bottom label, also curved, is plain, and cut square at the ends by the frame of the stamp. It is inscribed "POSTAGE ONE PENNY" in small block letters. Both inscriptions are in coloured letters on white. In the upper spandrels are floreate ornaments, and the lower ones are filled in with triangles containing other small ornaments.

THREE PENCE. The circle, formed of alternate dice of colour and white, has a thick inner line of colour, and an outer one formed of minute dots. Labels and ornamentation of spandrels the same as in preceding value. Inscriptions in colour upon white.

SIX PENCE. Toothed circle with two thin inner and one thick outer lines of colour. The circle is dissected by a hexagon of white lines. The ornaments at the extremities of the upper label are fashioned something like nippers. Floreate ornaments in upper spandrels; beaded triangles in lower ones. Inscriptions in white upon colour.

T. "FIJI." B. "POSTAGE" and value in words.
1d., blue, very dark to light shades.
3d., green   „   „
6d., carmine (shades).

Varieties.—A series can be made, printed on distinctly yellow-toned paper. All the values also exist imperforate. Copies of these latter, however, are not known used, and they are believed to be proofs.

Issue II. 1872.

Three values. The same stamps surcharged with the numerical value above the crown, and the word "CENTS" beneath the initials "C.R." The surcharge is in black, and each word has a capital letter. Same paper, watermark, and perforation. (*Illustration* 4.)

2 cents, blue, dark and light, surcharged on the 1d.
6 „   green   „   „   3d.
12 „   carmine and rose-lake, dark and light, surcharged on the 6d.

Varieties.—All the above are also found imperforate, to which a like remark as in the unsurcharged issue applies.

Issue III. 1875.

Three values, issued after the islands had been annexed by Great Britain, on October 10th, 1874. The same stamps as the last, with the additional surcharge of "v.r.," in black, placed over the original letters "c.r." The letters "v.r." are printed in two types—plain Roman capitals, with full stop after each letter; and in ornamental Gothic capitals, with punctuation to match. Both types of surcharge are found upon the same sheet of stamps. The watermark and perforation of these stamps is the same as in the preceding issues; but the paper varies in substance. (*Illustrations* 5, 6.)

(A) *Surcharged in Roman capitals.*

    2 cents, blue and black,
    6 „ green and black, } slight shades.
    12 „ carmine-red and black,

Variety.   12 cents, carmine-red and black; surcharge "v.r." inverted.

(B) *Surcharged in Gothic capitals.*
Same values and shades.

Varieties.   (1) Surcharge "v.r." inverted.
           12 cents, carmine-red and black.

(2) The letters "v.r." punctuated by a Maltese Cross.
    2 cents, blue and black.
    6 „ green and black.
    12 „ carmine-red and black.

(3) The preceding variety, with surcharge "v.r." inverted.
    12 cents, carmine-red and black.

(4) All three values, with an inverted Gothic "A" instead of "v."
(5) 6 cents, green, Gothic "v.r." with plain instead of ornamental punctuation.
(6) 12 cents, carmine-red, Gothic "v.r.," plain period between the two letters.

Issue IV. End of 1875.

One value. Between the date of the preceding issue and 1876 provisional stamps of the value of Two Pence were formed by the additional surcharge of "2d." above that of "v.r." (*Illustration* 7.)

Two colours, red and black, were employed for this extra surcharge.

I. Surcharged on the 6 cents, green.

(A) *Surcharged in red.*
(1) Roman "v.r."
(2) Gothic "v.r."

Varieties.   (1) Roman "v.r.," with stop before the "d" of 2d.
(2) Gothic "v.r., 2d.," without punctuation.
(3) „ „ punctuated with a Maltese Cross.
(4) Roman "v.r.," no stop after r.
(5) Gothic "v.r.," inverted A instead of v.

(B) *Surcharged in black.*
(1) Roman "v.r."
(2) Gothic "v.r."

Varieties.—Same as the preceding varieties in red.

FIJI ISLANDS.

II. Surcharged in black on the 12 cents, carmine-red.
                        (1) Roman "V.R."
                        (2) Gothic "V.R."

Varieties. (1) Roman "V.R.," with stop before the "d" of 2d.
        (2) Gothic "V.R.," without punctuation.
        (3)   „   „   and 2d. surcharged twice.
        (4)   „   „   inverted A for V.
        (5) Roman "V.R.," 2d., without punctuation.
        (6) Gothic "V.R.," inverted A for V, and plain period between the two letters.

Issue V. 1876.

Three values. In this issue the currency is changed back from cents to pence. An ornamental script monogram is surcharged over the original initials "C.R." The second value is also surcharged "Two Pence" in black, in a straight line over the original value of Three Pence. The paper is thick, the perforation 12½, and there is no watermark. (*Illustration* 8.)

        1d., ultramarine, bright and milky shades,
        2d. on 3d., yellow-green, dark and light,   } black surcharge.
        6d., carmine-rose,

Varieties.—A peculiar flaw in the plate exists on certain specimens of the Penny. A kind of white patch appears in the upper left corner, either as if the details of the stamp had never been finished, or as if an injury to the plate had taken place.

Issue VI. 1878.

Four values. This issue is upon horizontally laid paper; in other respects it resembles the preceding. The fourth value, Four Pence, was formed by printing a stamp from the Threepenny die in pale mauve, and surcharging it "Four Pence" in black over the original value. (*Illustration* 9.)

        1d., ultramarine (shades),
        2d. on 3d., yellow-green (shades),
        4d. on 3d., pale mauve   „   } black surcharge.
        6d., carmine-rose   „

Varieties.—A. The same flaw, mentioned above, in the plate of the Penny exists in this issue also.

B. The Penny, Three Pence *green*, and Six Pence are found without any surcharge.

Issue VII. 1879.

One value, on white wove paper; perforation, 12½. The stamp is surcharged with the value in the same way as in the preceding issue, but is without the script monogram. The die was re-engraved, the letters "V.R.," in script type, being substituted for the initials "C.R." In other respects it resembles the preceding. (*Illustration* 10.)

        2d. on 3d., yellow-green, slight shades; black surcharge.

Issue VIII. 1880.

Three values. Die re-engraved, as above; no surcharge. The paper is wove, no watermark; perforation, 12½. (*Illustration* 11.)

        1d., ultramarine,
        2d., pale green,   } slight shades.
        6d., carmine-rose,

Issue IX. 1882.

Two values, type printed; coloured impression, on medium white wove paper; white gum. Design:

ONE SHILLING. Diademed head of Queen Victoria to left, on a background of horizontal lines, enclosed in a circle formed by a single white line. White arabesques, in spandrels on solid ground; the name of the country above, and the value in full in two lines in white block letters below the circle. The design is completed by a frame formed of a single white line.

FIVE SHILLINGS. Diademed head of Queen Victoria to left, on background of horizontal lines. This portion of the impression is printed in pale salmon-red, and is enclosed in a circle formed by a single black line. The remainder of the stamp is printed in black. The upper corners each contain the figure "5," printed in white on a black ground, and enclosed in a double-lined octagonal frame. The name of the country above, and the value, in two lines, below the central circle, are in white block letters on eccentric black cartouches. Above the upper inscription is a row of pearls, and on either side of the word "FIVE" is a five-rayed shaded star. The design is completed by a single-lined frame. Shape, long upright rectangular. Mach.-perf. 10. (*Illustrations* 12, 13.)

T. "FIJI." B. "ONE SHILLING." "FIVE SHILLINGS."
1 shilling, pale brown.
5 shillings, black and salmon-red.

Issue X. 1883 (?)

Four values. Same as the stamps of 1880. The fourpence is formed by printing a stamp from the twopenny die in dull mauve, and surcharging it "FOURPENCE" over the original value in black. Wove paper. (*Illustration* 14.)

(A) *Perf.* 10.
1d., ultramarine.
2d., pale green.
4d., mauve and black.
6d., carmine-rose.

(B) *Perf.* 10 × 12½.
1d., ultramarine.
2d., pale green.
4d., ?
6d., carmine-rose.

FISCALS USED POSTALLY.

Several values of the STAMP DUTY set have been seen postmarked. The Society does not believe they have done postal duty, but considers they have been obliterated at one of the Post-offices for the benefit of collectors.

PRIVATE STAMPS. "FIJI TIMES EXPRESS."

In 1870 the proprietors of the *Fiji Times Express*, in Levuka, issued a series of stamps to prepay the postage on their newspaper.

Issue I. 1870.

Five values, type printed on rose-coloured paper. The design is of the simplest character; consisting of an oblong single-lined frame, containing the words T. "TIMES," B. "PENNY," "PENCE," or "SHILLING," L. "FIJI," reading upwards; and R. "EXPRESS," reading downwards in Roman capitals. In the middle is the figure of value, plain in the case of the Penny, Three Pence, Six Pence, and Nine Pence, and ornamented in the case of the Shilling, which also, like the Six Pence, has the numeral larger than the other values. The stamps are separated from each other by dotted lines, and all the values are printed together on the same sheet. Shape oblong; rouletted (about) 20, on the dotted lines on *quadrillé* paper. (*Illustrations* 15, 16, 17.)

          1d., black on rose.
          3d.,   „   „
          6d.,   „   „
          9d.,   „   „
          1s.,   „   „

Issue II. 1871.

On laid *batonné* paper, same values as Issue I. A third set is catalogued by Major Evans on laid paper; but no specimens have been seen by the Society.

Reprints.—In 1876 a reprint of these stamps took place for the benefit of collectors. They may be distinguished from the originals by the design, which is smaller, and is better printed, and by the fact that they are pin-perforated, and not rouletted. A bogus set also exists on bright violet-rose paper.

OFFICIAL WRAPPER.

Issue 1884 (?)

This wrapper is employed by the Government Printing Office at Suva. It consists of plain white wove paper, size 13½ × 4¼ inches. In the upper part, to right, is the franking stamp. Design: A plain upright rectangle contains the following inscription in five lines (1st) "BY AUTHORITY," (2nd) "GOVERNMENT," (3rd) "FRANK" within a single-lined frame rounded at the four corners, (4th) "PRINT. OFFICE," (5th) "FIJI." The 1st line is in old English characters; the 2nd, 3rd, and 4th are in block letters; the 5th in lower case; and the 1st and 2nd, and the 4th and 5th, are separated by a thin line. At the top of the wrapper, in the centre, is "O.H.M.S." (On Her Majesty's Service) in Roman capitals, and some little distance below, to the left, is "*Govt. Printing Office*" in italics, directly below which is "188 ."

Without value. Black on white.

NEW SOUTH WALES.

LOCAL STAMPED LETTER-SHEET FOR THE TOWN OF SYDNEY.

Issue 1848 (?)

THE first stamp issued for this colony was a local employed in the town of Sydney. Its existence seems to have been unsuspected for many years, and the credit of its discovery belongs jointly to Sir Daniel Cooper and Mr. Pemberton. Nothing further has since transpired in reference to it, and it is simply proposed in this article to reprint the main portions of the interesting paper read by Sir Daniel Cooper, Bart., before the Society on May 29th, 1869, and published in the *Philatelist* for July, and the *Stamp Collector's Magazine* for August of the same year. In the *Philatelist* of September, 1869, appears a supplementary paper by Mr. Pemberton on the same subject, and in the *Stamp Collector's Magazine*, vol. xii. page 5, there is a short note by the author of *The Postage Stamps of British Guiana*. The only uncertainty that seems to exist is in reference to the date of issue. The last mentioned writer observes : " M. Moens erroneously gives the date 1848. The writer possesses a specimen postmarked 11th October, 1843. The authority to the Postmaster of Sydney to issue a cover franking this value will be found in the *Government Gazette* for 1838."

On the other hand, Mr. Pemberton says, "Its authenticity is unimpeachable. It is mentioned in 1849 by the Postmaster himself, and it appears in the *Government Printer's List* as '1848, embossed.'"

It is possible that what was apparently a figure 3 on the dated specimen referred to was in reality a misprinted 8, and as there are several other inaccuracies in the paper by the author of *The Postage Stamps of British Guiana*, which are fully dealt with in the following papers on the "Sydney Views," by the Vice-President, it does not seem unlikely that the writer in question was misinformed as to the date. It would certainly be a curious fact if a town like Sydney, primitive as it was in those days, had adopted stamped letter-sheets about two years before the introduction of postage stamps in England, and the balance of probability therefore appears in favour of 1848 being the correct date of issue.

Sir Daniel Cooper says, "Having passed many years of my life in Sydney, and having been a member of the 'Select Committee of the Legislative Council of New South Wales,' which passed the *Act to Establish a Uniform Rate of Postage, and to Consolidate and Amend the Law for the Conveyance and Postage of Letters* upon the stamps in question, I may be said to be an authority. Being in correspondence with Mr. Pemberton, I sent him a copy of the 'Votes and Proceedings' of the above-named Committee, which also contained the proceedings of the Select Committee, which examined and reported upon the bill named above ; and he in return asked me the meaning of the answer of Postmaster-General Raymond, in reply to question

No. 76 in the said report; viz., 'At the present moment we do not make a great many stamps for the town delivery.' To question 79 he says, 'I charge eight shillings a hundred for the present stamps, so that the vendor has fourpence profit on a hundred.' And to question 80 he says, 'I have experienced some difficulty in inducing persons to use these envelopes; for although the charge for postage when the envelope is not used is twopence, and the envelope only costs one penny, they have been very little used; of late, however, they have been much more generally used.' On a subsequent day Postmaster Raymond said, 'The charge for letters delivered in Sydney is now one penny when stamps are used; twopence without the prepaid stamps.' He further said, 'The stamps were supplied to several stationers, who paid for them as they got them; but they found they could not sell them.'

"The stamp here alluded to was to frank letters delivered twice a day within the limits of the city of Sydney. It was an uncoloured, embossed stamp, the design being the Royal Arms, encircled by the words, "GENERAL POST OFFICE, NEW SOUTH WALES," and under the arms "SYDNEY." The impression was made on wrappers or envelopes of half sheets of foolscap paper.*

"The impression was often very imperfectly struck, as the die was only an ordinary Post-office seal, and the impression taken in a powerful letterpress. In passing through the post-office, the hour of delivery, in an oblong, octagonal frame, was imprinted in black ink on the stamp to obliterate it; and the envelope was also stamped in red ink, with the word 'FREE,' the day of the month and year within a circle, surmounted by a crown.

"I had forgotten the existence of this stamp, but on receipt of Mr. Pemberton's inquiry I wrote to my friends at Sydney, and fortunately procured a used specimen. This cover, after having passed through the post-office, had been used to write an order for goods upon, filed as a voucher, and thus preserved; and by this means is authenticated by the handwritings written on the inside thereof. The date of the postmark on this envelope is 'OCTOBER 5, 1849.' Sydney being a moderate-sized town, and the chief office being the only Post-office in the city, it was generally as easy for a domestic to deliver a letter by hand as to take it to the Post-office. The awkward shape of the envelopes also caused many to fold the embossed stamps out of sight; and many letters prepaid were thus charged twopence before the stamps were discovered. For these and other reasons the stamp was very little employed, and had almost passed out of memory."

From another article upon this stamp in the *Stamp Collector's Magazine* for March, 1870, we learn that the die used for striking the stamp had been chiselled out, so that reprints were impossible.

The stamp is found struck upon medium white wove paper, and also on pale blue laid paper. The size of the sheet when open is $11\frac{3}{4} \times 8\frac{1}{4}$ inches, and the stamp is placed in about the centre of one of the half sheets. (*Illustration* 18.)

(A) *On white wove paper.*
(One Penny.) Without colour or value.

(B) *On pale blue laid paper.*
(One Penny.) Without colour or value.

* The *original* illustration of this stamp was taken from a sketch supplied by Sir Daniel Cooper, and was inaccurate, the word SYDNEY being misspelt SIDNEY. This was done intentionally, with a view of laying a trap for forgers.

THE FIRST TWO ISSUES OF THE ADHESIVE STAMPS OF NEW SOUTH WALES.

A PAPER READ BEFORE THE PHILATELIC SOCIETY, LONDON.

By T. K. TAPLING, M.P., Vice-President.

PREFACE.

It will only be necessary to refer very briefly to the circumstances which led the Society to entrust the task of preparing papers on the first two issues of New South Wales to the President and myself some two to three years ago. It was considered that in some respects we were in a better position to undertake the work than the Society as a body, the President being in possession of certain official information, and both of us having access to the finest known collections of these stamps. A word of apology is needed for the long delay in the completion of our work, which consequently, up to the present, has prevented the publication of the Society's catalogue. The arrangement was for the President to obtain all the official information possible, and to write what may be called the general history of the issues; my share being confined to study of the stamps, and to questions connected with the different plates.

At the outset we were confronted with great difficulties. I understand that even now our President has been unable, in several matters, to get at the particular information he wanted; and, as far as my task was concerned, it was not until I was fortunate enough to secure large quantities of the stamps, through the kindness of a friend in Australia, that I was able to put together anything like a connected story, or to arrive at conclusions that I fear, in one or two instances, can still only be considered approximate to the truth. When the papers are before you I think you will realize the difficulties connected with a study which depended so largely on the slow and laborious process of reconstructing the plates. Though the delay has been a long one, in reality there has been no time wasted; and with these few remarks I shall proceed to lay the results of my labours before you, and to give an account of my stewardship.

I think it is true that no two series of stamps have excited greater or more widely-spread interest among collectors than those which form the subject of these papers. At one time or another, from the very earliest days of Philately, they have received the attention of almost every philatelic writer of eminence, and have furnished the materials for numerous discussions and articles in various magazines, some of which are of great value, and to which I gladly acknowledge my indebtedness. Among them I may cite:

1. The series of papers by the late E. L. Pemberton, contributed by him to the *Stamp Collector's Magazine* for March, 1865, May and June, 1867, November, 1868, and to the *Philatelist* of January, 1868, and January, 1869.

2. Two articles by the author of *The Postage Stamps of British Guiana*, which appeared in the former journal in March, 1867, and January, 1874.

3. The paper read by Dr. Legrand before the "Congrès International des Timbrophiles" at Paris, on September 25th, 1878.

4. A paper read by Mr. Castle before the London Philatelic Society, and published in the *Philatelic Record* of December, 1884, and January, 1885.

There are numerous other notices of lesser importance, but the above-mentioned articles contain practically all the information that has to the present day been made public. It is my object in this paper to take up the story where it was left by Mr. Pemberton and Dr. Legrand. With the assistance and advice of our President and Mr. Bacon, and by means of researches conducted jointly with two distinguished collectors, MM. Caillebotte, of Paris, I am now in a position to supplement very considerably the knowledge previously acquired. To the latter gentlemen, to whose patient study was added conspicuous ability, I take this opportunity of tendering my heartiest thanks. As will appear later, they were the first to indicate to us the "right track" in several very important particulars. I am compelled to leave some minor points still open; but, in most other respects, I think, a final settlement of questions which are as difficult perhaps as any presented by our science, has at length been arrived at.

Issue I.

As everyone knows, the first issue consisted of three values only—*One Penny, Two Pence,* and *Three Pence*. I propose to take each value separately, under the four heads of—
1. Date of issue.
2. The engraving and the engravers of the plates.
3. The design, whether on different plates, or in different stamps on the same plate.
4. The various kinds of paper on which the stamps are printed.

It will be found that a consideration of one of these points involves to some extent a consideration of the others; but from the nature of the subject this is unavoidable.

ONE PENNY.

I. *Date of Issue.*—I copy the following extracts from the *Stamp Collector's Magazine* of December 1st, 1867 :

"By section 10 of an Act of Council, 13 Vict., No. 38, passed 12th October, 1849, postage stamps were directed to be prepared and issued for the colony, and to be sold to the public. The period when this was to come into effect was 1st January, 1850. By section 11 any person forging the stamps to be liable to imprisonment for such time as the court may direct, not exceeding seven years."

Sydney Gazette, 25th December, 1849, page 1927 : "Notification that at first stamps will only be issued for the subjoined values—One Penny, Two Pence, and Three Pence." The following rates of postage were fixed :

For letters not exceeding in weight ½ oz. :

Within the limits of the town of Sydney	1d.
Inland (within the colony)	2d.
Ship letters	3d.
(In addition to any inland postage.)	
All newspapers	1d.

Gazette, 15th January, 1850, page 72 : "That sums under £1 may be remitted in postage stamps." From these extracts we do not of course gather whether the finely or the roughly-engraved *One Penny* came first. The consideration of this point falls under our third question.

II. *The Engraving and Engravers of the Stamps.*—It is unfortunate that so little trustworthy information is obtainable relative to the manufacture and the manufacturers of the Sydney stamps. In the earlier days of collecting very little attention was paid to these details, which did not appear to the philatelic fraternity to possess any special significance. It is to be feared that in the case of the Sydneys the opportunity has been lost for ever of acquiring that knowledge from official sources, which alone can be relied upon. If I remember right, the Sydney Post-office was destroyed by fire in 1864. Stamps, plates, archives, in fact, everything there existing which could have thrown any light upon the subject we are considering, perished in the conflagration. Questions that might easily have been settled by application to the officials must now remain unanswered, perhaps indefinitely; and the fact that most or all of those connected with the administration of the Sydney Post-office in 1850, as far as I have been able to ascertain, are now dead, renders the hope of a complete history of these stamps being written a very remote one. Under these circumstances I can give but an incomplete answer to our second question, and can only indicate the names of certain engravers who are known to have been living in Sydney at the time, and who are said to have had a hand in the production of the stamps. For some of my information I am indebted to Mr. J. Calvert, a gentleman who lived some years in New South Wales, and who was present in Sydney when the project of postage stamps for the prepayment of letters was first entertained by the government. Mr. Calvert is a practical engraver, and though not employed by the Sydney authorities, he was frequently consulted by them towards the end of 1849 in reference to the issue of the postage stamps authorized by the Act of Council passed October 12th, 1849. He states that the first Sydneys were engraved upon wood. The designs of all were *drawn* by a Mr. Wells on separate blocks of boxwood, or stringy bark, and were then *cut* on the wood by several engravers, he (Mr. Calvert) having himself cut eight of the specimens. The separate blocks were then clamped up together in an iron frame, and proof impressions taken from them. This would be about November, 1849. A considerable number of sheets were struck off, the printing (according to Mr. Calvert) being done by boys in a small room at the back of the Sydney Post-office in George Street. Later on the stamps were printed at the Stamp Office. There can be no doubt that these specimens from wood blocks were simply essays; at any rate, no wood engraved stamps were ever issued to the public. If any were passed through the post it was done as an experiment. Mr. James Raymond, the postmaster, was apprehensive of forgery, and probably for this reason, and also on account of the perishable nature of the wood blocks, it was finally decided to have the stamps engraved on metal. A pair of the well-known, but rather uncommon, essays of the *One Penny* lies before you; and you will notice that both specimens are of the same type, though unsevered from each other. This is interesting as showing that some method of reproduction was known in Sydney at the time, though why a similar process should not have been employed for the stamps of the metal plates is a question to which I can give no answer. There is, however, as I shall show further on, some reason for thinking that the *entire* plate of the first *Two Pence* was reproduced or reduplicated early in 1850. The essays before you of the *One Penny* are said by Sir Daniel Cooper, our ex-President, who filled an important government appointment at the time in Sydney, to be lithographic transfers by an engraver named Clayton; though, the types being the same, they cannot belong to the series mentioned above as having been separately engraved by Mr. Wells. There is also a tradition of an essay of the *Two Pence* formerly existing in the collection of Count Primoli, of Paris; but this, so far as I can obtain any information, was finely engraved on metal. Putting all this together, and assuming the accuracy of Mr. Calvert's recollections, we get, first, the original essays on wood, probably of all three values, separately drawn and engraved; secondly, a lithographed stamp of the *One Penny* value only, drawn by Clayton, and reproduced by a process of transfer, of which the specimens exhibited are examples; and, thirdly, the three values separately engraved upon metal, and issued to the public on January 1st, 1850. Mr. Calvert further states his belief that, economy being an object in those days, the metal plates were merely what are called "casts" from the wood blocks. Now the characteristic of a wood block is that those parts of the block which are intended to produce coloured lines are *raised*, as in type printing, the white spaces and interstices of the design being cut away. This process is the exact opposite of that then employed in printing from engraved metal plates, where the coloured lines are cut or sunk in the plate. I do not believe that the metal plates of the Sydneys were casts from wood blocks, as the process of doing this was then unknown. If early specimens of the One Penny are examined it will be found that those portions of the design—for instance, the labels containing the words "ONE PENNY" and "POSTAGE," which at first sight appear to be of solid colour, are in reality composed of fine crossed lines. Obviously, in the case of a cast from wood, no amount of re-engraving on the metal cast could transform a label (which being of solid colour on wood, would be represented by a label of colour on metal) into a *linear* label. The lines of the labels on the metal plate are so fine that I cannot believe, with the imperfect appliances available at the time in Sydney, impressions of the merit of these stamps could have been obtained from wood engravings either by casting or transfer. It is beyond question that the Sydneys were printed from plates composed possibly of copper, more probably of "printers' metal." The latter is a soft compound of lead, antimony, and tin, and its use would account for the rapidity with which the plate of the Two Pence wore away. We are able to say, from a dated specimen, that as early as February, 1850, the plate of the *Two Pence* already showed considerable traces of use.

Stewart and Wall are said to have prepared the wood blocks, and Clayton and Dubois (or some similar name), two other engravers, are supposed to have been connected with the engraving of the metal plates. The shape of the sheets rather favours the theory that more than one engraver was employed to produce the metal plates. The *One Penny* and *Three Pence* were each printed in sheets of twenty-five stamps, arranged in five rows of five; the sheet of the *Two Pence*, consisting of twenty-four specimens, was arranged in two horizontal rows of twelve.

From information furnished through Sir Daniel Cooper we are told that the plates of the stamps used for the first issue were line engraved, each stamp being separately drawn, and thus showing separate details, though the general design was the same; and that the engraver was Robert Clayton, who was assisted in his work by his son-in-law Mason. There is some reason to think that Mason's work was limited to certain plates of the Two Pence.

I have now laid before you all the information I possess on this part of the subject, and only regret I cannot give a more definite answer to our second question.

III. *Design.*—A full description of the design of the *One Penny* will save a good deal of repetition in the cases of the *Two Pence* and *Three Pence*, so I make no apology for dealing with it here at some length.

In the left background is a view of the town of Sydney on an unshaded hill, which slopes down to the sea-coast or harbour. On the hillside are two trees. Below the hill, on what looks like a level plain, is the figure of a man and animal, apparently engaged in ploughing, or in some agricultural pursuit. On the sea, in the distance, there is a brig at anchor, heading to the right. In the left foreground there is a female figure, seated on a bale, and apparently holding a whip over the shoulder. She is very imprudently leaning against what seems to be a beehive placed upon the bale. The bale is divided into four compartments by double lines, the left lower compartment containing the numerals 17, and the right 88 (1788 being the date of the foundation of the colony). The left hand of the figure is outstretched. In the right foreground is a group of three other figures, two males and a female; the figure on the right is kneeling, probably in supplication, but possibly offering some gift which does not appear in the design. On the ground between the three figures on the right and the single one on the left lie a pickaxe and spade, to which the seated figure is apparently pointing. At the feet of the three figures there is a chain of six or seven links. Below the figures, and divided from them by a line of colour, is the legend, "SIC FORTIS ETRURIA CREVIT," in two lines on a white ground, and printed in small block capitals. The quotation is taken from Virgil (*Georgic* II., verse 533), and the translation is, "Thus grew mighty Etruria." The sky is unclouded. The whole of this portion of the design is enclosed by a white single-lined circular band, containing the words, "SIGILLUM NOV. CAMB. AUST." in coloured block capitals, and meaning, "Seal of New South Wales." I may here mention that this portion of the design is a copy of the Colonial Government seal. In the upper portion of the band, between the words "AUST." and "SIGILLUM," is a small eight-point star-shaped ornament. The spandrels are filled in with dots on a white ground. At the top and bottom of the stamp are two straight labels, with ground of horizontal and vertical lines crossed, upon which are the words, T. "POSTAGE" . D. "ONE PENNY," in white Roman capitals. The corners consist of white square blocks, containing Maltese cross ornaments. On each side, and bounded top and bottom by the corner blocks, there are two vertically-lined bands, divided from each other by a white line. The inner two, which are impinged upon by the circular band, contain a kind of trellis of white lines, and the outer ones are similarly ornamented with white spirals. The whole stamp is enclosed by a single-lined rectangular frame.

From the first, speculation was rife as to the allegorical meaning of the design, and many absurd theories were started; one particularly preposterous, according to which the three figures were "natives presenting a palm branch to some personage seated in an armchair on the seashore." I believe this account of the design was given in the *Stamp Collector's Review*, the first stamp journal ever published. According to another theory, the design represents a party of convicts just landed from the ship, whom the lady on the bale (the goddess of Australia perhaps) is exhorting to lead a new and better life by means of the pick and shovel. This explanation is not improbably correct; and I believe it used to be the custom in Australia, when convicts of either sex arrived, for them to be taken into the service of private residents, though of course they were still subject to police supervision. Taken in conjunction with the context to the quotation from Virgil, it seems quite possible that a semi-classical allusion is also intended by the design. In connection with this point I may quote the words of a lady who wrote under the *nom de plume* of "Fentonia" in the *Stamp Collector's Magazine* of April, 1866. She observes: "With regard to the fettered convicts, the allusion is classical, and therefore consistent with the supposed design. Some of the rustic slaves in Virgil's time worked in fetters, and were distinguished as *servi vincti*, while those who worked without personal restraint were called *servi soluti.*" In concluding her remarks the writer goes on to say, "Whether the theory which has been advanced by way of key to the 'picture' on the Sydney stamps be true or not, it is at least plausible. The fields (1st *Georgic*), the trees (2nd *Georgic*), the flocks (3rd *Georgic*), the bees (4th *Georgic*), together with the ship and important buildings, are highly suggestive of ancient Ostia (the old port of Rome); while Britannia seated on her commercial bale, and pointing with her left hand to the implements of labour, while she reminds her convict suppliants, 'Sic fortis Etruria crevit,' not inaptly connects the idea of Sydney being a modern Ostia to the great Australian colonies."

On the whole I am inclined to believe that something of this kind is the true interpretation of the design.

We come next to the design as modified upon the coarse or roughly-engraved plate. The hill is now shaded, there are clouds in the sky, the top and bottom labels are apparently of solid colour (though this is possibly due merely to a greater amount of ink being used in printing), and the lines generally of the stamps are coarser and thicker. With these exceptions, there is no part of the foregoing description that will not apply equally to the *course* as to the *fine* stamps. I may remark *en passant* that these differences simply amount to so much evidence of *additional* work done on the plate.

The stamps are usually divided in catalogues into—
1. Finely engraved, without clouds.
2. Coarsely engraved, with clouds.

We have now to enter into a somewhat detailed consideration of the following questions:
1. How many stamps did the plate contain, and how were they arranged?
2. Were two distinct plates engraved of this value? or
3. Was one plate a retouch of the other?
4. If there was a retouch, which was the retouched plate?

We may deal with the second and third questions, which indirectly involve the fourth also, together, as an answer to either in the negative would be to affirm the other.

1st. With reference to the first enquiry as to the size and arrangement of the sheet, I may remind you that the original theory, formally adopted by the author of *The Postage Stamps of British Guiana* in the *Stamp Collector's Magazine*, assumed forty as the number of varieties on the sheet. Dr. Legrand inclined to the same view. However, an entire proof-sheet, which I have great pleasure in presenting for your inspection, passed into my possession some months ago, and from it the fact is proved beyond doubt that there were twenty-five stamps engraved on the plate, and that they were arranged in five rows of five. It is only right to say that previously to the acquisition of this sheet MM. Caillebotte, of Paris, who had access to all the finest collections there, which in two notable instances contained accumulations of these stamps dating from the very earliest days of collecting, had arrived at precisely the same conclusion, and had even been able, by means of unsevered and overlapping pairs and blocks of stamps, to replace the varieties of type in their original order. The assumed discovery of Dr. Legrand of a twenty-sixth type is now admitted by him to have been an error; and, without a single exception, MM. Caillebotte's arrangement of the varieties is completely confirmed by this entire sheet. It also gives a *quietus* to the old idea that the fine and the rough stamps were engraved on the same plate; the theory being that as he went on the engraver improved in his work while constructing the plate. Mr. Pemberton was easily able to disprove this in the *Stamp Collector's Magazine* of May, 1867. He recognised the different style of workmanship in the two kinds of stamps; but arguing probably from single specimens, and, like Dr. Legrand, with an imperfect knowledge of the constitution of the sheet, he fell into the error, adopted more recently by Mr. Castle, of assuming that there were two distinct plates. This brings us to the consideration of our second and third questions.

2nd and 3rd. On page 6 of the *Stamp Collector's Magazine* for 1874 the author of *The Postage Stamps of British Guiana* remarks: "The plates of the *One Penny* and *Two Pence* were renewed and retouched at a later stage, when is not precisely indicated." This seems to be the first hint we get of the possibility of the plate having been repaired or renewed owing to wear of the die, until the able article by Dr. Legrand, read by him before the "Congrés International des Timbrophiles" on September 25th, 1878, and afterwards printed in the "Memoires."

In it the theory is for the first time brought definitely forward, with certain arguments that I must be excused for calling inconclusive. Inconclusive, not that I doubt for a moment that a retouch took place, but because the reasons given seem to me scarcely sufficient to prove either the retouch or the further point on which Dr. Legrand insists; viz., that the finely-engraved plate was a retouch of the other.

At the time the paper was written Dr. Legrand had not succeeded in getting together complete sheets of the varieties in both stages, though in all probability his were more advanced than those in any other collection. I must point out to you that to prove the retouch of any plate with certainty it is absolutely necessary, in the absence of official documents, not only to possess all the varieties of type in both stages, but also to be able to prove a *portion* at any rate of their arrangement. This done, it becomes possible to compare the same stamps; *i.e.* those occupying the same position on the two sheets, and to indicate exactly which parts of the stamps were left unaltered and which were retouched. The proof of the arrangement of the varieties on the two sheets is obtained from the following list of pairs and blocks, &c. :

Plate I.   Finely engraved, without clouds.

An entire sheet exists in my own collection.

Plate I.   Retouched.

Nos. 1, 2, 3, 4	are in Mr. Tapling's collection.	
1, 6	„	„
6, 7, 8, 11, 12, 13, 16, 17, 18	„	„
8, 9	„	„
9, 10	„	„
5, 10	„ Mr. Rodd's	
9, 14	„ Mr. Tapling's	„
14, 15	„	„
18, 19	„	„
18, 23	„	„
21, 22, 23, 24, 25 . .	„ Mr. Garth's	„
19, 20	„ Mr. Tapling's	„

The MM. Caillebotte and I have examined many hundreds of specimens of the coarsely-engraved stamps, but we have never found more than the twenty-five varieties of type, and you may take it as absolutely beyond all doubt that the sheet consisted of this number of specimens. I have thus given you a detailed proof of the arrangement, and have indicated the collections where, to my own knowledge, the various pairs and blocks are to be found. Now, if the two sheets of finely and coarsely-engraved specimens are placed side by side, a remarkable similarity will be at once observed in several particulars, which I will proceed to indicate. You will notice that the words of the legend, the abbreviated words in the circular band, and, further, the letters of each word, all vary considerably on each stamp of the same sheet in their relative positions to each other, and to the other portions of the design. It is not possible to find two stamps alike in these respects on either sheet. But when a comparison is made between the two sheets, stamp by stamp, we find that the relative positions of the words and letters, and, in some cases, even the very shapes of the letters themselves, are absolutely and identically the same. Precisely the same thing occurs in the relative positions of the two dots which follow the words "NOV." and "CREVIT;" though, as between stamps on the same sheet, they also vary very greatly. And, lastly, the shapes of the white lines forming the trellis work and the spirals at the sides will be found to tally exactly with each other, if a slight allowance is made for the touching-up of the interstices. We are therefore left with this conclusion: We find that the engraver of one plate (assuming either one to be the first) was unable to produce two stamps alike on the same sheet; yet we are asked by the upholders of the theory of two distinct plates to believe that in twenty-five different instances another engraver was able to *exactly* copy the work of his predecessor, not only in the difficult details I have mentioned, but in many others I have not alluded to. It would be easy to accumulate evidence from any given stamp on the two sheets, but I think you will consider this unnecessary. I will mention one further instance only. Nos. 4 and 10 are the only two stamps on the plate with the word "NOV." placed so low in the circular white band as to be at some distance from the perpendicular band at the side, which is cut by the circle. This and the other coincidences of type occur on both sheets, and I have proved that they occur in the same position.

The sheets are before you, and each member present can verify the facts I have stated. Summarising briefly, my conclusion is that one plate is a retouch of the other.

4th. We have, lastly, to decide which plate was the retouched one, and I may shortly state my opinion that the coarsely-engraved stamps are from the same plate as the others, but represent the results of a retouch or repair executed upon it. My reasons are as follows:

(a) I believe I am correct in saying, that it is not possible to so alter coarse workmanship on an engraved plate, that stamps presenting the appearance of being finely engraved could be printed from it. Traces of the deeply-cut lines, due to the heavier hand of the engraver, would necessarily remain long after the finer work of his successor had worn away and disappeared with use of the plate. It would be easy to fill in more details, and possibly to improve or modify the shape of some of the lines; but anything of this kind would only be in the nature of additional work on the plate, and could never entirely disguise its former characteristics. It would obviously be impossible to narrow the width or lessen the depth of a coarse or deeply-cut line, and I have failed to find on the finely-engraved *One Penny*, in any stage of wear, the slightest trace of coarse lines. It is a fact that on specimens of the finely-engraved *One Penny*, in the earliest stage, there is not a vestige of the lines that are intended to represent clouds. It is equally true that on the coarsely-engraved One Penny, in the latest stages of use, traces of these lines can always be detected. In other words, it might be possible to add lines on a plate, but not subtract from it, without removing or erasing the engraving already there. I have shown that in several important respects the stamps were practically unaltered, and, as I previously remarked, the differences that do exist can all be ascribed to additional work on the plate, and are, in fact, just what one would expect from it.

(b) I have never yet come across a copy of the coarsely-engraved stamps that could fairly be described as much worn, whereas the others are met with in almost

NEW SOUTH WALES.

every conceivable stage. This being so, we may fairly ask, Where was the necessity of retouching the coarsely-engraved plate?

(c) I submitted the two sheets without a word of comment to a skilled engraver in the employ of Messrs. Waterlow and Co. He at once recognized the intimate connection between them, but could only say for certain that the coarsely-engraved sheet was either a retouch or transfer from the other. His opinion was rather in favour of the latter, and he thought it likely that the best possible impression having been taken from the plate in its worn state, it was transferred while still wet to a fresh plate covered with a thin layer of wax, or some other special preparation. What remained of the old lines could then be recut through the wax on the fresh plate. A similar result might have been obtained by means of "transfer paper," and the points of similarity and difference between the two sheets would be thus accounted for. This is of course possible; but though hesitating to set my opinion against that of an engraver with technical knowledge of the different processes of engraving and printing, I adhere to my belief that the coarsely-engraved stamps are the results of a retouch and not of a re-engraved transfer. Before dealing with this question, you will excuse my digressing for a moment to another point, which will explain my reason more clearly. In order to explain the differences between the two sheets, yet another theory has been propounded. It has been suggested that the centre part of the design of each stamp, the view of Sydney, &c., was cut out, and that a species of plug, of similar design, but freshly engraved, was inserted in each case. I have shown that even if this were so, the legend "SIC FORTIS ETRURIA CREVIT" was not touched; but it is not difficult to prove that no part of the plate was cut away, and that the centre portions of the stamps, like the other portions, were simply re-engraved either by retouching or transfer. The principal things to notice are the relative positions of the whip held by the seated figure and the houses towards the word "AUST.," and the position of the bowsprit of the ship in respect of the letters of "SIGILLUM." The bowsprit and the whip in particular point in very different directions on stamps of the same sheet; but if the same stamps on the two sheets are compared together they will be found to tally exactly in these particulars, just as I previously showed they agreed in others. There are certainly fewer houses on what I call the retouched plate, and one would naturally have expected to find the contrary; but on the *early* specimens of the coarsely-engraved stamps on the sheet before you, you will still be able to trace between the retouched houses the *faint remaining lines* of the houses as they were originally engraved. Now it is these faint traces of old lines that convince me a retouch and not a transfer took place. It is quite true that in any process of transfer everything in the shape of a line that remained on the original plate would be found on the layer of wax or upon the transfer paper. But it seems impossible to believe that in re-engraving the transferred impression upon a fresh plate a new engraver, and one evidently possessed of less skill, would go to the trouble of renewing old lines, which, as they appear on the specimens before you, are mere meaningless scratches. Again, I have already quoted a reference to a *repair* of the plate of the *One Penny*, and it is scarcely likely that the word "repair" would have been used if a transfer had taken place. I was not acquainted with these facts when I had the interview with Messrs. Waterlow's engraver, and I have since had no opportunity of a fresh discussion with him on the subject. Whichever theory, retouch or transfer, seems most probable, everything tends to prove the intimate connection between the two sheets, and my own opinion is still the one I first arrived at.

(d) The fourth reason for thinking the finely-engraved stamps came first is the fact that all the early copies were printed upon a soft, yellowish paper, which, from dated specimens I have examined, I can prove was used early in 1850. The roughly-engraved are never found upon this paper. They were printed upon hard white, slightly blued, or blue papers, which I shall be able to show were used at a later date.

(e) All the best English catalogues place the finely-engraved *One Penny* first.

(f) We have, on the authority of Mr. Pemberton, the testimony of a member of the Legislative Council of New South Wales, our ex-President (Sir Daniel Cooper), who belonged to the Select Committee which considered the Postal Bill in August, 1849, in Sydney, and who says that in 1850 all the *One Penny* and *Two Pence* were of the fine type.

(*g*) Taking, lastly, the dated specimens, I have seen an unsevered pair of Nos. 3 and 4 of the finely-engraved stamps on a letter, dated January 14th, 1850. As the stamps were only issued on January 1st, 1850, this seems tolerably conclusive.

These reasons appear to me to establish beyond doubt the question of the order of these two stages of the plate of the *One Penny;* and, summing up briefly, I think we may conclude that the *One Penny* stamps were first printed from a finely-engraved plate, that the coarsely-engraved specimens are the results of a retouch, or possibly of a transfer, and that in each case there were twenty-five varieties of type on the plate, arranged in five rows of five. I am in some uncertainty as to the exact date at which the retouch took place. You will notice a pair among my specimens on a letter, dated August 21st, 1850, of the coarsely-engraved stamps. Arguing from this, and for certain reasons connected with the employment of the blue paper, in conjunction with the wear of the plate in its first stage, I think I shall not be far wrong in naming the end of July or the beginning of August, 1850, as an approximate date for the renewal or retouch. I have mentioned that each stamp was separately engraved, and that there are consequently as many varieties of type as there are stamps to the sheet. It would be easy to give the differences in detail, or such a description of each variety that would enable you to identify any particular stamp. This, however, would be a mere waste of time, and the photographs which accompany this paper will be a better guide than pages of description. The most prominent variety is No. 15 of the retouched plate, which is without clouds.

IV. We have, finally, to consider the different kinds of paper on which the stamps were printed ; and here, to some extent, the observations I have to make would apply equally to the *Two Pence* and *Three Pence*, though, for the sake of clearness, it will be best to consider the values separately.

I have shown that the finely-engraved *One Penny* came first. There are equally strong reasons, as will be explained a little later, for thinking that the *Two Pence* with vertical lines was the first plate of that value, and I can produce early specimens of the *Three Pence*. All these stamps, in an early stage of the die, are invariably found on a soft, yellowish paper, somewhat spongy in texture. I conclude, therefore, that it was the first paper used, and in this I am confirmed by Mr. Pemberton (*Stamp Collector's Magazine*, June, 1867), who went exhaustively into the whole subject, and who in the same journal of November, 1868, gives as the result of his study two kinds of paper for the first One Penny, and no less than seven for the second. Some of the distinctions he makes of the latter appear to be rather finely drawn, and I would suggest the following classification as being sufficiently comprehensive for most purposes :

The finely-engraved *One Penny* is found upon—
1. The soft, yellowish paper.
2. Harder paper, white or slightly blued.
3. Paper white, but finely ribbed, producing the appearance of closely-laid lines.

The worn impressions are nearly always upon the blue paper.

The roughly-engraved *One Penny* is found upon—
1. Medium paper, blue or slightly blued.
2. Hard paper, thick white or slightly yellowish, varying in substance.
3. Stout paper, white or slightly yellowish, deeply ribbed, and presenting the appearance of broad laid lines.
4. Same as the last, but slightly blued.

I have taken these in the order given by Mr. Pemberton with one exception. This is in the case of the retouched *One Penny*. I am inclined to think that the blue, or slightly blued, wove paper should come first, as we find it used for the finely-engraved *One Penny* at a period which could not have been long anterior to the retouch of the plate. The earliest specimens I have seen of the finely-engraved *One Penny*, on the bluish paper, are on a letter dated Sydney, July 18th, 1850. You will see this pair among my specimens, and I think I shall not be far wrong in saying that the yellowish paper was used for about five or six months only in 1850, and that May or June of that year is the earliest date for the employment of the blue paper. The latter, and the white paper used subsequently, are probably one and the same, the tinge of blue being due to some chemical property either in the colour of the stamp or in the paper itself. How far these variations in the paper may be due to some natural chemical process of bleaching I cannot say, though this is a point that seems to merit the attention of amateurs.

The ribbed or laid paper, white or slightly bluish, I place last in both stages of the plate. There is no evidence to constitute it a separate issue, and it seems more probable that its employment was an accident, due to the temporary exhaustion of the stock of ordinary paper. The earliest specimen in my possession is dated March 3rd, 1851, and is an example of the deeply ribbed paper.

It is worthy of note that the ribbed paper, used for the finely-engraved *One Penny*, is much finer (that is, the ribs in the paper are much closer) than that employed for the retouched *One Penny*. Specimens of the first are very uncommon. The gum used for all specimens of the 1d. was yellowish, and it is almost superfluous to add that they were unperforated.

THE TWO PENCE.

I now approach the most difficult, though not the least interesting, part of the subject—the question of the *Two Pence* in its various stages. Here, for some time, I was led into error by the old theory of forty or fifty stamps to the plate, and certainly the arrangement of the sheets that has at length been arrived at is about the last that would, *à priori*, occur to anyone taking up the study of these stamps for the first time. I shall have occasion to go more fully into this a little later, and in the meantime it will be best to consider the stamps under the same heads as those adopted for the *One Penny;* viz., date, design, and papers.

I. *Date.*—The stamps from the first plate of the *Two Pence* were issued on January 1st, 1850, together with those of the *One Penny* and *Three Pence*. I need only refer you to the extracts previously quoted from the *Sydney Government Gazette* to prove that this date is the correct one. The question of the order of issue of the different plates naturally falls under this heading. I shall, however, defer any consideration of it until the distinctions between the plates have been fully dealt with. It would be useless to discuss data referring to the order in which the plates appeared, before their characteristics had been explained in a way which will enable you to appreciate the arguments I shall lay before you.

II. *Engraving and Design.*—The difficulties began here, and the amount of research involved would have seemed almost beyond belief to anyone not engaged in the study. It has only been after a prolonged examination of hundreds of specimens, extending over several years, and after making innumerable notes of everything that seemed important, that I have at length arrived at a solution of some of the most perplexing questions that ever fell to the lot of a philatelist to investigate.

Following the plan adopted for the *One Penny*, the case may be most conveniently stated in the form of questions, which are as follows:

1. How many distinct plates existed, and were any or all of them transfers from the previous plates?
2. How often were these plates retouched, wholly or in part, and what were the distinctions between the retouches?
3. What was the number of stamps on the plates, and how were they arranged?
4. What order should the plates and the retouches be placed in, and what were the approximate dates of their being put into use?
5. Was more than one plate employed at the same time?

It will be noticed that one or two of these questions involve the consideration of the others. But before proceeding to deal with them, it will be advisable to state, in the first place, the conclusion at which I have arrived; viz., that there were three distinct plates, and three only, of the *Two Pence;* Plate II. being a re-engraved transfer from Plate I., and Plate III. from Plate II., all other varieties being assignable to different processes of retouch or repair on the actual plates themselves; and, secondly, to fully describe the design, on the modifications of which the distinctions between the various stages in the history of these stamps mainly depend. For the moment I must beg the question of the order of the plates, and designate as Plate I. the stamp that is ordinarily known as the *Two Pence* with vertical lines.

Plate I.—The design is similar in character to that of the *One Penny,* and, as far as the central portion is concerned, the description given for the *One Penny* will apply equally well to the Two Pence, with the following unimportant exceptions: The bale is divided into four compartments by single lines, the upper two of which contain the inscription " NO ⊕ " (evidently intended to represent a shipping mark), and the lower two " 17, 88." The hill is shaded in all early copies, and sometimes there are four trees at the base, sometimes none. The ship is heading to the left, and is three-masted. The abbreviated words "CAMB. AUST. SIGILLUM, NOV." are printed in small *Roman* capitals. Between the words "AUST." and "SIGILLUM" is a small ornament of shaded lines, and between "CAMB." and "NOV." there is a shaded fan of seven segments. The remainder of the design is quite different to that of the *One Penny.* The spandrels, and the space above and below the circular band, are filled in with straight and wavy vertical lines crossed. One variety on the sheet has crossed vertical wavy lines only. At the sides, and bounded top and bottom by the white blocks mentioned below, there are two white single-lined perpendicular bands. These are filled in with a series of interlacing reticulations, which form pointed ovals, and are cut by the white circular band. At the top and bottom there are two labels of solid colour, containing the words, T. "POSTAGE" B. "TWO PENCE" in white Roman capitals. The corners are composed of white square single-lined blocks, containing Maltese cross ornaments, with dot in centre, and the design is completed at the top and bottom by a single line of colour, which meets the outer lines of the square blocks and the perpendicular bands. Whether or no this plate was reduplicated is a matter I shall have something to say about in dealing with the third and fourth questions.

Plate II.—This plate in reality is very similar to Plate I., and to save repetition I will merely indicate the differences between the two. The most important distinction is in the spandrels. On Plate II. these are filled in with straight and wavy *horizontal* lines crossed. The abbreviated words in the circular band are printed in small block capitals. The bale is generally divided by double lines, and there are sometimes two, sometimes three, trees at the base of the hill. The corner blocks are filled in with eight-rayed stars, with a small dot in the centre, and there are rather fewer reticulations in the bands at the sides. Speaking generally, Plate II. is much inferior in execution to Plate I., and in style strongly reminds one of the retouched *One Penny.*

Plate III.—To all intents and purposes the design is the same as that of Plate II. The following are the only distinctions of importance: The bale is not dated, and is divided into four compartments by single lines; the fan is unshaded; there is no dot in the corner stars, the rays of which are somewhat thinner, and present the appearance of being more separated from each other. There are trivial differences in the lines of the spandrels and reticulations, and a few other unimportant modifications, of which description is unnecessary, and which you will easily ascertain from the photographs of the two sheets.

It will be noticed that all three plates are divided into twenty-four compartments by means of three horizontal and thirteen vertical ruled lines, giving two horizontal rows of twelve stamps, each in its own compartment. The thirteen vertical lines meet and stop at the upper and lower horizontal lines, intersecting the middle one, and the three horizontal lines stop in the same manner where they meet the two end vertical lines. A glance at the accompanying diagram will make this more clear. We have been able to prove the position of every variety on the three plates, and this somewhat *bizarre* arrangement of the sheets was only arrived at after much trouble. These ruled lines, as will be seen presently, have an important bearing on some of the questions we are considering; and, further, it was by their means that I was enabled to make a start in the arrangement. The four corner stamps were thus ascertained without much difficulty; but, of course, specimens with good margins were necessary. At one time I was inclined to believe that the stamps were each engraved on separate blocks, which were clamped up together to print from, and it was suggested that the compartment lines would be printed from thin pieces of brass, or what are called "metal lines," which printers use in such cases to fix blocks tightly together. This theory would explain a point in connection with certain specimens bearing *double* ruled lines in the margin, which I shall speak of further on, and which has greatly puzzled me. It is negatived, however, by the fact that the lines intersect one another. It would not be possible to make separate pieces of "metal lines" fit as accurately as they appear on the specimens before you, and the only possible inference is that these lines were ruled upon the metal plate.

These "compartment" lines are characteristic of the *Two Pence* only, and this fact corroborates the theory that more than one engraver was employed in the manufacture of the plates.

1. I stated my conclusion that there were three distinct plates only of the *Two Pence*, though I am aware that this theory, at least in the particular form I have adopted it, is opposed to those of all previous writers on the subject. The foreign catalogues recognize three, and the English four plates, but I shall have no difficulty in showing that the classification given of the so-called Plates II., III., and IV. relates in reality to different stages of, or transfers from, one matrix plate. The foreign catalogues, of which M. Moens' is by far the best, fall into the error, in one instance, of attributing to use of the die peculiarities found on certain specimens which really belong to a distinct plate; and in another of constituting, as a separate plate, what is merely a retouch of a previous one. Dr. Legrand makes the same mistakes in the article he wrote for the "Congrés International des Timbrophiles." He remarks: "We admit therefore the existence of three plates for the Two Penny Sydney. One can see by Mr. Pemberton's articles that he recognizes four; but evidently his third plate, which only differs from the second by the absence of certain details of the design, can only be called an impression from a worn plate." Dr. Legrand goes on to say that in his opinion the specimens with a pearl in the fan were, without doubt, printed from a distinct plate, and his arrangement therefore is as follows:

Plate I. Two Pence, with vertical lines in the spandrels.
Plate II. ,, ,, horizontal ,, ,, ,,
Plate III. ,, ,, ,, ,, ,, ,, and pearl in the fan.

Mr. Pemberton's articles in the *Stamp Collector's Magazine* are of great value, and reflect the highest credit on the critical acumen of the author, who was working in the dark, entirely without official information. Viewed in the light of later discoveries, it is plain that he was travelling in the right direction, the only mistake being that of considering the varieties with a pearl in the fan as proceeding from a fresh plate. Mr. Pemberton classifies the stamps in the following order:

Plate I. Two Pence, with vertical lines in the spandrels.
Plate II. ,, ,, horizontal ,, ,, ,, bale dated, dot in corner stars.
Plate III. Two Pence, bale not dated, no dot in corner stars.
Plate IV. ,, fan with pearl.

The above is a brief summary of the results arrived at by the two principal writers on the subject, and before proceeding further I will deal with the two mistakes just alluded to.

(*a*). Dr. Legrand's remark as to the differences between Mr. Pemberton's second and third plates is correct, but the conclusion he draws is wrong. A single instance only is necessary to disprove his theory. The position of variety No. 13, the left bottom corner stamp, has been definitely ascertained on both sheets. No. 13, on

Plate II., is the well-known variety with the word "CREVIT" wanting. An early copy of No. 13, Plate III, on the sheet before you, has "CREVIT" perfectly distinct, and a little examination will show you that there are many other differences in small details between the two stamps. Obviously, therefore, the variety on Plate III. cannot be a worn impression from Plate II. It may be objected that if a retouch or repair of Plate II. took place this error would naturally have been rectified, and the specimen may still be said to have been printed from the same plate. Admitting this as possible, it has really nothing to do with Dr. Legrand's theory that the absence of the date on the bale and the dots in the corner stars, characteristic of Plate III., is due to wear of the die. If early specimens of Plate III. and worn ones from Plate II. are placed together (the comparison of course being made between stamps occupying the same places on the sheets), lines will be found on the former which do not exist on the latter, and *vice versâ*. It would be easy to accumulate evidence in disproof of this theory from every stamp on the two sheets; but the very marked illustration I have drawn your attention to in the case of variety No. 13 will, I think, render this unnecessary.

(*b*). Both writers fall into the error of supposing that the stamps with the pearl in the fan were printed from a distinct plate. I need not anticipate my remarks on the retouched plates, but in the meantime I may state that it can be proved conclusively that these specimens were the results of a *second retouch* of Plate III. There can be little doubt that these two errors arose from the fact that neither Dr. Legrand nor Mr. Pemberton had been able to reconstitute the entire sheets with the varieties of type in the right order.

I have already given the distinctions between what are recognized as the distinct plates, which are, in fact, nothing else but the first three of Mr. Pemberton's classification. There can be little doubt that the specimens with vertically-lined, and those with horizontally-lined, spandrels were printed from distinct plates. Had Plate II. been merely a retouch or repair of Plate I., we should naturally have expected to find certain traces remaining of the work of the first engraver, as in the case of the *One Penny*. After a prolonged examination of the same specimens on both sheets in an early stage, I have been unable to discover on Plate II. the slightest trace of any of the old lines of Plate I. (I am speaking here of the stamps themselves, and not of the *compartment* lines previously noticed). This fact, taken in conjunction with the inferiority of execution of Plate II., seems to warrant the conclusion that they were two distinct plates. There are, however, one or two coincidences that seem to point to the theory of Plate II. being in reality a re-engraved transfer from Plate I. In my remarks upon the *One Penny* I dealt with one or two of the different methods of transfer that might possibly have been employed at Sydney in the year 1850, though it is not possible now to say which of them was selected. In this case I believe that the best possible impression by transfer having been obtained from what remains of the design on Plate I., the old lines were re-cut on the fresh plate, and the rest of the design filled in according to the idea and fancy of the new engraver. It is quite evident that very little remained of the original design beyond a few of the straight lines of the stamps, a little of the lettering, and the lines of the compartments; in fact, one or two of the impressions on the sheet before you are almost illegible. My reason for thinking that a transfer of some kind took place is mainly connected with the ruled lines previously referred to, which divide the sheet into the twenty-four compartments. Now these ruled lines are not always quite straight, and the stamps are sometimes engraved at irregular distances and irregular heights within their respective compartments. The accompanying sketch of the right hand portion of Plate I. will better illustrate my meaning. It is certainly a curious coincidence that the same irregularities occur in the same places on Plate II., as we are able to prove by specimens with good margins, whose position on both sheets has been ascertained. Thus variety No. 10 is slightly higher in its frame than No. 9; the top frame line of No. 12 bends slightly inwards towards the top right corner of the stamp; No. 24 is placed very close to the right outer frame line, which in the lower part bends away from the stamp; No. 23 is nearly 1 millimétre longer than No. 24. In other parts of the sheet it would be easy to point out similar coincidences, as, for instance, in the case of Nos. 14 and 15, which are placed higher than Nos. 13 and 16. A glance at the photographs of the two sheets will show that the stamps themselves offer also in numerous cases certain rough points of resemblance, notably in the relative position of the inscription "TWO PENCE" to the white corner blocks. Now these peculiarities and irregularities occur in the same places on both sheets. You will recognize their importance from the fact that they only became apparent after we had obtained, quite independently of their means, the arrangement of the varieties on both plates by overlapping pairs and blocks of stamps. All this is perfectly consistent with the theory of a transfer. A point I shall have occasion to refer to presently in speaking of a repair or renewal that was executed upon Plate I. about February, 1850, will, I think, show conclusively that if there was any connection at all between the two plates it took the shape of a transfer, and not of a retouch. In the face of this evidence of apparently *designed* coincidence, circumstantial it is true, but almost conclusive, it seems impossible to doubt that some kind of transfer took place. The engraver would thus obtain a rough outline to work upon, the result being what is commonly called Plate II., with horizontal lines in the spandrels and bale dated.

The points of resemblance between Plates II. and III. are far more numerous and strongly marked, but the question of retouch or transfer is difficult to determine. It is not without some hesitation that I adhere to the opinion that Plate III. is a re-engraved transfer from Plate II. In my remarks on the retouched *One Penny* I pointed out that in the case of early specimens from a *repaired* plate we should almost inevitably find traces of the previous work; that any alterations would be of the nature of additional work, and that the stamps would naturally have a somewhat coarser and heavier appearance. After a careful examination I can detect nothing of this kind on Plate III. Mr. Pemberton very truly remarked that on the worst copies from Plate II. there were always to be found some traces either of the date on the bale or of the dots in the corner stars, and it is a curious fact that this should always be the case. If this plate, therefore, had been merely retouched, some sign of these details of the design would have remained, but not a fragment of either date or dots can be discovered on Plate III. In certain details there is a great similarity between the two plates, to which I shall refer directly, but on the earliest copies I have examined from Plate III. I can find no trace either of old or thickened lines. It is evident that if a line cut on a plate produces a blurred impression through its edges becoming worn with use, it can be again made clear and sharp by re-cutting it deeper and wider. On early specimens, however, of Plate III. the lines of the engraving, while beautifully clear and distinct, are no thicker than, if as thick, as those on Plate II. The later copies from Plate II. were extremely blurred and indistinct, and in speaking of impression some allowance should possibly be made for defective printing; but arguing generally from the style, Plate III. is, in my judgment, the work of a lighter hand.

I must now draw your attention to the points of resemblance between the two plates, which seem to prove beyond doubt that if it is not a retouch Plate III. is a re-engraved transfer from Plate II. In the first place we find exactly the same irregularities of position of the stamps and their surrounding lines that were described in the case of Plates I. and II., occurring in exactly the same places on Plate III. A few minutes' examination and comparison of the sheets, stamp by stamp, will show you many other similarities quite as strongly marked. The relative positions of the words in the circular band to other portions of the design—those of the words "POSTAGE" and "TWO PENCE" in respect of the corner blocks, and in some cases even the shape of the letters and the oval reticulations at the sides—are almost identical on both plates. These coincidences occurring on stamps occupying the same position appear to place beyond doubt the intimate relation between the two plates, and it would be wasting time if I entered into further details. Of course these points of resemblance would fit in equally well with the theory of a retouch; but, in my opinion, the reasons to the contrary I previously laid before you negative the supposition. And, lastly, I may quote an extract from the *Sydney Government Gazette* of April 2nd, 1851, stating that the governor had approved of the repair of the *plates* of the *Two Pence*. There is good reason for believing that one of these plates was Plate III.; and if, as I hope, I am able to show, this was the last one made, then its existence as distinct from Plate II. becomes morally certain.

We have now dealt very fully with our first question. Some of the theories advanced will, I fear, appear to you to rest on somewhat slender foundations. The unfortunate fire which destroyed all records at the Sydney Post-office has put it out of my power to either substantiate or disprove, from official documents, conclusions which have only been arrived at by study of the stamps themselves, and which every effort has been made to verify.

2. The consideration of our second question, which relates to the retouches and repairs executed on the plates, involves to some extent that of our third also, since it was the investigation into the number of stamps on the plates that led to the discovery that certain varieties were, in reality, printed from retouched and not from distinct plates, as was previously supposed. As before, I will first of all briefly state my conclusion that a portion of Plate I. was retouched once, Plate II. (to the best of my knowledge) remained unaltered, and Plate III. was retouched twice. Putting this into the form of a synopsis, we get—

    A. Plate I.
    B. Plate I., retouched.
    C. Plate II., being a transfer from Plate I.
    D. Plate III.   ,,   ,,   Plate II.
    E. Plate III., first retouch.
    F. Plate III., second retouch.

Or six different states of the Two Pence.

In dealing with the retouches and repairs that were executed on the different plates we are on firmer ground. To show the course of the researches it may not be without interest to quote an extract from a letter I received from MM. Caillebotte, of Paris, as far back as 1884. At that time I and they were under the impression that Plate I. contained forty or fifty stamps, which was confirmed by the acquisition of an uncut strip of six specimens, proving that there were more than five in a row, and also, as we thought, that this sheet was larger than that of the *One Penny*. Having found far fewer varieties of type of Plate II., we concluded that it and the succeeding plates, like the *One Penny*, probably contained twenty-five specimens, especially as we were only able to muster, with our united collections, some twenty varieties of the plate with the pearl in the fan, which we had always considered the last and distinct from the others. Plate III. greatly puzzled us. We found considerably more than twenty-five varieties, and there was no apparent reason why this plate should have been larger than those which preceded and followed it. It was not until MM. Caillebotte pointed a way out of the difficulty that we were able to arrive at a satisfactory conclusion. Their letter is dated June 20th, 1884, and in speaking of our united collections of varieties of Plate III. they remark: "There is some complication here. If we add your stamps and ours together we find thirty-four different types. Our opinion is that there are two sheets, each containing twenty-five stamps, and that one is a retouch of the other." They go on in the same letter to give the proofs of this assertion, and the distinctions between the two sheets. Every word they wrote has since been completely substantiated, except that there are twenty-four stamps to the sheet, and not twenty-five. This discovery of MM. Caillebotte was of great importance, and, as you will now see from my previous remarks, it was practically the key to the whole question. The idea of a retouch having been started, of course threw a new light on the subject, and the difficulties that so much perplexed us disappeared one by one. A short examination made independently soon after the receipt of this letter showed conclusively that the specimens with the pearl in the fan, hitherto considered to have been printed from a distinct plate, were also printed from a retouch of Plate III., and were the results of a *second* retouch. Absolute certainty was arrived at when we were at length able, with pairs and blocks, to prove a portion of the arrangement of the stamps on the sheets; and we think that, with the sheets and photographs before you, you will have no difficulty in adopting our theory as correct. Our attention was next turned to Plates II. and III. Mr. Castle, in his article in the *Philatelic Record* of December, 1884, suggested that the latter was a retouch of the former, arguing generally from the style. I have already given the reasons for thinking that it was a transfer, and have nothing to add to my previous remarks. In reference to

Plate I. I mentioned that for a long time we were under the impression that there were forty or fifty stamps to the sheet. It was not until after the whole arrangement of the sheet had been ascertained that there was no longer any room to doubt that it consisted of twenty-four only, and consequently that the other varieties of type we were acquainted with at the time, numbering ten or twelve specimens, must have been printed either from a distinct or from a retouched plate. Guided by our experience in the other cases we instituted a careful comparison, and were at length enabled to satisfactorily establish the fact that this plate also was retouched.

I must now explain the distinctions between these various stages of the plates.

Plate I., retouched.—The first plate of the *Two Pence* wore away very rapidly, and in February, 1850, a repair or retouch was found necessary. The earliest specimen I have seen is on a letter dated "Maitland, Feb. 24, 1850." The engraver employed, perhaps from want of skill or experience, seems to have done very little to the plate, and to have confined himself principally to deepening the straight lines of the stamps, such as the outer rectangular frame, the lines below "POSTAGE" and above "TWO PENCE," and the inner lines of the perpendicular bands at the sides. On one stamp (No. 16) he apparently tried to improve the lines of the circular band; but, as you can judge from the specimen before you, he did it rather clumsily. On others he engraved a double line above "TWO PENCE," which you will see did not exist on the plate as originally engraved; and here and there may be detected slight touches and alterations in the concentric reticulations at the sides, and in the wavy perpendicular lines of the spandrels. The deepened or double lines, however, above "TWO PENCE" and below "POSTAGE" are the chief characteristics of this retouched plate. It is a curious fact that, as far as the stamps are concerned, the bottom row only was retouched, the top row remaining unaltered. We have examined so many specimens from the top row in every stage of wear, that if a retouch had been effected in that part of the plate it is absolutely impossible that we should not have found traces of it. But you will notice, on the sheet before you, two or three vertical pairs of stamps, the lower specimens in each case showing the deepened lines, while the upper ones are without the slightest trace of retouch, though they evidently required repairing as badly as the others. I am quite at a loss for an explanation, and can only mention the undoubted fact. Something else, however, *did* occur in connection with the top row, which leads me to the consideration of a point of great difficulty to which I have previously referred incidentally—the question of whether this plate was *reduplicated* wholly or in part, and whether it was in consequence of an intended reduplication that the retouch was executed. A *double ruling* was made of the upper horizontal compartment line. I must draw your attention to three specimens of Type No. 1, two of No. 3, two of No. 5, one of No. 4, and four of No. 10, photographed on a separate sheet, and lettered respectively A, B, C, &c.* Each of the three specimens of No. 1 has the upper horizontal compartment lines differently drawn. In the first stage there is a single line, in the second two parallel lines, and in the third two lines which converge and meet. On B the lower, and on C the upper of the two lines represent the original single line; that is to say, they are drawn in exactly the same position, the doubling of the line therefore taking place in a different position. You will notice that B is in an earlier stage of wear than C. Taking next the two specimens of No. 3, lettered D and E, you will observe that on E there are two parallel compartment lines, which might very well be the continuation of the parallel lines on B, but for the fact that the original line is the *upper* one, the new line (which is the thickest) being *within* the old one. On variety 4, lettered F, there is au entirely fresh line, which almost touches the stamp, and consequently cannot be a continuation of any of the lines I have been describing. The two specimens of variety 5, lettered G and H, are very curious. H has a double compartment line, the new one being drawn parallel to and above the original line, at about double the distance between the parallel lines previously referred to. An examination

* Owing to several of these lettered specimens forming portions of unsevered pairs and blocks, it was considered unadvisable to separate them. They will be found on two different sheets; viz., the first plate of the *Two Pence* and the plate of the *Three Pence*. This arrangement is inconvenient, but was unavoidable without cutting up the blocks. I should add, that the different specimens were taken off the sheets, and accurately tried and fitted with their neighbours.

with the microscope will show that H is printed from a plate in a later stage of wear. There are, lastly, the four specimens of No. 10, lettered I, J, K, L. I and J are from the same original plate, though in different stages. K, though in a much earlier state than J, has the compartment line drawn much closer to the stamp. L is a worn impression of K. On C, F, H, L, there are traces of what look like perpendicular compartment lines, starting from the horizontal lines and running upwards, as if another row of compartments for stamps had been drawn on the plate. Taking the dates of such of the specimens as we have seen on letters, we get—

    E, postmarked "Sydney, Feb. 21, 1850."
    K,   "   "Windsor, March 19, 1850."
    B,   "   "Sydney, March, 1850."
    H,   "   "Tamworth, May 2, 1850."
    G,   "   "Sydney, June 24, 1850."

At the risk of being considered tedious I have given an accurate description of all the specimens with double compartment lines that have come under my notice, and you will easily understand how perplexed I have been to imagine what really *was* done with this mysterious plate. Everything would have explained itself if we could have adopted the theory of separate blocks for the stamps, clamped up and fixed together by metal lines. In such a case some of the blocks might have got loose, and additional metal lines been found necessary to tighten them. As was explained before, this theory is inadmissible, and I can only indicate to you what I think may *possibly* have been done. The original plate was divided into compartments by single ruled lines, and very probably it soon became apparent that sufficient stamps could not be printed from it alone to satisfy the requirements of the Post-office. The idea might then have been entertained of adding another row, perhaps two rows, of stamps to the plate. The traces I mentioned above of lines probably intended for fresh compartments strengthens this supposition. This plan being found impracticable, or unadvisable perhaps, on the score of the expense of engraving fresh stamps, it was decided to reduplicate the plate. This might have been done by means of a double cast in metal, which would give the reverse sunk impression necessary to print from. Previous to taking this double cast, or to whatever process of reduplication was employed, the stamps of the lower row were retouched. This point is proved by the vertical pairs I mentioned above. For some inscrutable reason a second compartment line was added to the top row of the reduplicated plate, and possibly a slip on the part of an engraver attempting to re-rule the line on the original plate will account for the third set of double lines.

These remarks are of course mere conjecture, but the lengthened examination I have made has convinced me that they are not far from the mark. The different sets of double lines point beyond doubt to four, if not to five, stages in the history of this first plate of the *Two Pence;* but which specimens belong to reduplicated and which to re-ruled plates, and whether there was a reduplication on the same plate of copper, are questions to which I can give but an incomplete answer, and which I have puzzled over in vain. We have unfortunately not been able to get together sufficient specimens of any one set of double lines to reconstitute an entire upper row. For some reason or other these specimens are very uncommon, though their scarcity is probably due to the former bad habit of clipping off the margins of stamps. Anyhow, until this is done, nothing can be said with certainty. A little study of the specimens I have drawn your attention to will show you that double compartment lines exist on certain varieties in a comparatively early stage of wear, of which there is no trace on specimens in a rather later stage, the varieties of type being the same in both cases; and there is evidence before you to prove that the plate with the lines, as originally drawn, was printed from down to the very last stage of wear, and even in its last stage shows traces of the original compartment lines. On the block of four in the retouched sheet, varieties 11, 12, 23, 24, the traces are still visible of the original compartment lines, but there is no sign of the double lines that we know were added about February, 1850. All this tends to show that there was certainly one, if not two, reduplicated plates. It is curious that the middle and lower horizontal compartment lines were never altered, but are exactly the same on the plate in every one of its stages. To summarize briefly,

I conclude that, as far as the stamps are concerned, the lower row of this plate was retouched once, but that in several different processes of re-ruling or re-duplication the upper compartment line was doubled. I take leave of a difficult and interesting question, which I regret must remain unsettled for the present. I have placed the facts fully before you, have propounded the theory, and must now leave it to some succeeding writer to give a solution of the difficulty, which, with every care, I have been unable to arrive at.

Plate III., first retouch.—Passing to this subject, I may remark that the credit of the discovery was entirely due to MM. Caillebotte. The distinctions between Plate III. and the retouched plate lie in the corner stars and the bale. The lines on the bale were redrawn and *doubled*, and a small circle was added within the rays of the corner stars. Other slight alterations were effected in the reticulations, and here and there the lettering appears to have been touched up; but apart from these differences, stamps printed from the plate in its original and in its retouched stage are practically identical. You will notice that these distinctions, as in the other cases, represent additional work, and consequently there can be no doubt that the specimens are from a *second* stage, and do not represent the plate in its original state. A comparison of the sheets and photographs will show how little alteration was made, except in the details I have described. As a rule, the retouched stamps are printed in rather a fuller shade of blue than the others; but their characteristics are briefly the double lined bale and the circle in the corner stars. One variety, No. 10 of Plate III., has a double-lined bale, but has no circle in the corner stars.

Plate III., second retouch.—This is very similar to the first retouch, but the handle of the fan is replaced by a pearl, and the horizontal wavy lines of the spandrels are rather further apart, and there are fewer of them. The reticulations, the lettering, and, speaking generally, all the other details of the design, are almost identical with those of the first retouch. We can prove a good portion of the arrangement of the stamps of these three states of Plate III. independently of each other; and as we find the same varieties occurring in the same places, the fact is placed beyond doubt that what we have called *retouches* are simply different stages of the same original plate. It is not possible that our retouched plates can be re-engraved transfers, as in the case of Plates I., II., and III. Faint traces of some of the lines of Plate III., in its original state, which had nearly disappeared and which were not re-engraved, can still be distinguished on the first retouch; and the same remark applies to certain details of the second retouch in connection with the first. Nothing, however, we have said about the retouches of Plate III. would be inconsistent with the theory of their being retouched reduplications of Plate III. Once grant the possibility of some process of reduplication being known in the colony at the time (and this is proved by the essays of the *One Penny*), it becomes by no means improbable that it was employed for the plates of the *Two Pence*, the demand being greater for this value than for the others. The similarities, as well as the differences, between these three stages of the third plate are thus easily accounted for. There is, however, but little evidence in connection with this theory of a retouched reduplication to be obtained from study of the stamps themselves, and there is only a slender inference to be drawn in its favour from the dated specimens, which will be described in dealing with our fifth question. Many of the dated letters overlap; for instance, specimens of Plate III., in its first stage, are found used at a date long after the plate had been retouched; and, similarly, specimens of the first retouch are found used after the second had been executed. Of course nothing can be inferred with certainty from these overlapping dates, as the earlier specimens might easily have been kept back in small country offices which had not exhausted their stocks, and which therefore did not require a fresh supply from the plates in their later stages. This frequently occurs in England at the present day, obsolete stamps being often procurable at branch offices long after a new series has been issued. However this may be in the case of the Sydneys, these overlapping dates, and the mention by the governor of the repair of the *plates* of the *Two Pence*, are the only evidence we possess of distinct reduplicated and retouched plates being in use at the same time.

E

3. Our third question deals with the number and arrangement of the stamps on the plates, and I have already referred to the error we were at first led into in supposing that there were twenty-five specimens, in five rows of five. I should be wearying you if I entered into details of the laborious process of reconstruction, or of the method of measurement of the lines, &c., which enabled us to arrive at the truth. But I may say briefly that the compartment lines I have spoken of so much first set us in the right direction, and by their means we soon found out that there were more than five stamps in a row. One or two vertical pairs, with sufficient margin above and below to show that the vertical compartment lines ceased where they met the upper and lower horizontal ones, settled the fact that there were two rows of stamps only, and the examination of many hundreds of specimens, conducted by MM. Caillebotte in Paris and myself in England, showed conclusively that there were only twenty-four specimens on each plate. Of course they *might* have been printed in two panes of twelve, but we could never come across more than four corner stamps (the position of which was proved by the compartment lines) to each plate. If the arrangement of panes had been adopted there would have been of course eight corner stamps, but we soon decided that they were printed in two rows of twelve. The rest was simply a matter of time, and some six months since we came across a pair which settled the last doubtful point, and enabled us at length to place every stamp of all the plates in its right position. The following is the proof in detail of the arrangement, the different pairs, &c., being located in different collections:

Plate I.

No. 1 is the top left corner stamp (Mr. Firth's collection).
    12 „ „ right „ (MM. Caillebotte's collection).
    13 „ bottom left „ (Mr. Tapling's „).
    24 „ „ right „ („ „)

Pairs and blocks.

Nos. 1, 2, 5, 13, 14, 15, 16, 17, 18 are in Mr. Tapling's collection.
    2, 3, 4 . . . . . „ Mr. Rodd's „
    5, 6 . . . . . . „ Mr. Tapling's „
    7 is in the top row of the sheet . Mr. Rodd's „
    7, 8 . . . . . „ „ „
    8, 9, 10 . . . . „ Mr. Tapling's „
    10, 11, 12 . . . . „ Mr. Garth's „
    18, 19 . . . . . „ Mr. Rodd's „
    20, 21 . . . . . „ „ „
    9, 21 . . . . . „ Mr. Tapling's „ retouched plate.
    10, 22 . . . . . „ „ „ „
    11, 12, 23, 24 . . . „ „ „

Plate I., retouched.—The arrangement of course is the same, and can be ascertained from the plate in its original state.

Plate II.—I give as much of the arrangement as has been arrived at independently of Plate III. and its two retouches. The remainder of the stamps have been placed according to the arrangement of Plate III. This was not done without considerable difficulty and a very minute and careful examination; but, as I explained before, there are numerous points of resemblance between the specimens on the two sheets, just sufficiently marked to enable me to place them in the same order. I do not pretend to infallibility, and there *may* be a mistake in the arrangement; but I have recently seen more than one fresh pair from Plate II., and each one has fully confirmed the arrangement I made some months ago by means of Plate III. The pairs, &c., are located as follows :

No. 1 is the top left corner stamp in my own collection.
    12 „ „ right „ „ „ „
    13 „ bottom left „ „ „ „
    24 „ „ right „ „ „ „ and MM. Caillebotte's.

Pairs and blocks.

Nos.						
1, 2	.	.	.	are in Mr. Tapling's collection.		
3, 4				„	A Parisian	„
5, 6				„	Mr. Tapling's	„
7, 8				„	Mr. Rodd's	„
8, 9				„	„	„
9, 10				„	Mr. Tapling's	„
11, 12				„	A Parisian	„
3, 15				„	Mr. Tapling's	„
14, 15				„	„	„
19, 20				„	„	„
20, 21				„	„	„
23, 24				„	„	„
12, 24				„	Mr. Firth's	„

A little study of these particulars and of the accompanying diagram will show you that the position of seven specimens only is absolutely certain at the present moment, apart from the arrangement of Plate III. The other pairs and blocks, the arrangement of which you may consider arbitrary, prove this much at any rate, that certain varieties of type *did* exist side by side on Plate II. When therefore we find the same coincidences in the types, &c., occurring side by side on Plate III. (the complete arrangement of which is proved independently), it becomes morally certain that the specimens are correctly placed on Plate II. As I pointed out, there is a possibility of error, but I do not believe this is likely.

Plate III. Ditto, first retouch. Ditto, second retouch.—It will save time if I give the proof of these together. They are so nearly alike, that no doubt can exist that they are simply stages of the same plate :

No. 1 is the top left corner stamp (Mr. Tapling's collection), Plate III.; ditto, first and second retouch.

12 is the top right corner stamp (MM. Caillebotte's collection), Plate III.
13 „ bottom left „ (Mr. Tapling's „), „ second retouch.
24 „ „ right „ (Mr. Rodd's „), „ first retouch.

Pairs and blocks.

Nos.							
1, 2, 3	.	.	are in Mr. Tapling's collection, Plate III., second retouch.				
3, 4			„	Mr. Firth's	„	„	first retouch.
4, 5			„	A Parisian	„	„	„
5, 6			„	Mr. Tapling's	„	„	„
6, 7			„	Mr. Rodd's	„	„	„
7, 8			„	Mr. Tapling's	„	„	„
9, 10, 11, 12			„	„	„	„	„
1, 13			„	„	„	„	
13, 14, 15			„	„	„	„	second retouch.
16, 17			„	„	„	„	
18, 19			„	„	„	„	
19, 20			„	„	„	„	
20, 21			„	Mr. Wilson's	„	„	first retouch.
21, 22			„	MM. Caillebotte's	„	„	second retouch.
22, 23			„	Mr. Tapling's	„	„	first retouch.
23, 24			„	„	„	„	
12, 24			„	Mr. Firth's	„	„	

A large portion of the arrangement of these three stages of Plate III. could be proved independently, but this is not necessary. I have not come across specimens of Nos. 16 and 17 connected with any of their neighbours, but a glance at the sheet will show that there is no other place to put them in.

The process of reconstruction of the three plates of the *Two Pence* has been, as you can judge, long and tedious, and necessitated a great deal of reference to several different collections. Until it was completed nothing could be written, and to the difficulty of obtaining or examining a sufficient number of uncut blocks and pairs must be attributed the delay in presenting these papers for the consideration of the Society.

4. I have all along been assuming the order of the plates and their various stages of retouch or transfer, and it is now time to give some reasons for the

arrangement that has been adopted. When this paper is printed, and you are able to carefully examine into and criticise the theories I have ventured to lay down, with your own collections of the stamps before you, you will, I think, be convinced that there is internal evidence in several cases in support of the order I have suggested. For instance, the only distinction between Plate III. and Plate III. first retouch is that certain details do not exist on the former which are found on the latter, the two sheets in other respects being identical. Obviously therefore these details were *added*, and no question of priority can arise. We have the confirmation of Mr. Pemberton, Dr. Legrand, and all the best English and foreign catalogues as to the order of what I have styled Plates I., II., and III.; and lastly, though there is little official information, we have the confirmation of dated specimens. Of these I have examined a large number, and give a list of the oldest, which are of course the only ones that can be relied upon as showing how early a plate or any stage of it was in existence.

Two Pence.

Plate I.	Specimen, dated Sydney, Jan. 9th, 1850. Very early stage of impression; colour, pale dull blue (in my own collection).
Plate I.	Retouched. Dated Maitland, Feb. 21st, 1850 (in my own collection).
Plate II.	Specimen, dated Sydney, April 20th, 1850. Very early stage of impression; colour, pale ultramarine (in Mr. Rodd's collection).
Plate III.	Specimen, dated Oct. 23rd, 1850 (in Mr. Castle's collection).
Plate III.	First retouch. Specimen, dated Jan. 20th, 1851 (in Mr. Rodd's collection).
Plate III.	Second retouch. Specimen, dated Paramatta, May 10th, 1851. Very early stage of impression (in Mr. Rodd's collection).

These are the earliest dates I have seen, and the specimens are important because they enable us to say in what order the plates and the retouches should be placed, and to assign, within a month or two, a correct date to each. Thus about three months after the stamps were first issued a new plate of the *Two Pence* was found necessary, a probable interval of four or five months separating it from the third. The retouches seem to have followed at about the same intervals of time, the last one with pearl in the fan being executed in April, 1851, and continuing in use till about the end of July or the beginning of August, when the first *Two Pence laureated* was issued. The postal authorities evidently had great difficulty in meeting the increasing demand for stamps, or at any rate in supplying stamps that were sufficiently presentable. From the State Book of March 11th, 1851, we learn that authority was given to J. C. C. Boyd and A. H. Manning to destroy a quantity of damaged postage stamps. These were probably the *Two Pence*, as on April 2nd, 1851, the governor sanctioned the repair of the *plates* of the *Two Pence*. This brings us to the consideration of our fifth and last question as to whether the different plates were in use at the same time.

5. I have already alluded briefly to this point, which after all is not of great importance, except as confirming my previous conclusion that Plates I., II., III. were really distinct and separate plates, and not retouches of one another. The entry just quoted as to the repair of the plates can hardly refer to anything but Plates II. and III., and possibly to a re-engraved reduplication of the latter. That a larger sized sheet of stamps was absolutely necessary is proved by the fact that there were fifty specimens on each plate of the *Two Pence laureated*, and it is very probable that, pending the preparation of the last-named stamps, the authorities printed as best they could from more than one of the plates of the Sydneys, the worn out state of which necessitated the repairs authorized by the governor. These repairs were certainly not executed upon Plate II., which, as I previously remarked, was not retouched or altered; and judging from the worn state of some of the specimens before you, it seems likely that the engraver found the plate was not worth the trouble of repairing, or that an efficient repair was out of the question.

Anyhow, the only results of the repairs that were done in April, 1851, were the stamps with the pearl in the fan, and the use of the word "repair" in the entry seems to negative the idea that a re-engraved reduplication of Plate III. in its retouched stage took place. That more than one plate still existed is however quite evident; that the first retouch of Plate III. took place some months previously is proved by the specimen dated January I mentioned above; and we are left consequently with the conclusion that if the first retouch is not a re-engraved reduplication, the entry in question must refer to Plates II. and III.

Plate I. may, I think, be left out of consideration, as the repair upon it was executed early in 1850, and I have never seen a specimen used later than the autumn of that year. Perhaps I should mention that the whole of the correspondence of a firm in Sydney was examined on my behalf, and if impressions from Plate I. had been taken and issued in 1851, I should almost inevitably have received specimens. The stamps came on this correspondence in a very regular order; and I had so many sent me, that it was easy to trace almost month by month the state of wear of the plates and the different kinds of paper that were adopted from time to time. I found numerous specimens of Plate II. used in almost every month from April, 1850, to as late a date as November, 1851. Of course they may all have been kept back, as I mentioned previously; but this continuous use, and the fact that almost every specimen was in a different stage of wear, point rather strongly to the probability of Plates II. and III. being in use at the same time after about September, 1850. It is also worthy of remark that the pair of stamps dated November, 1851, in fact all the specimens used in 1851, are printed upon a peculiar grey paper, which does not appear to have been used before that year. My experience of the comparative rarity of the specimens strengthens this supposition, as, with the exception perhaps of Plate I., specimens from Plate II. are more common than any of the others. However, as I remarked before, dated specimens can only be relied upon to prove how early a plate was in existence, and are but little guide as to the length of time it was used, though in this case the overlapping dates are far longer than those I referred to in considering the possibility of a re-duplication of Plate III. We can only make a conjecture, and the arguments which were insufficient in one case cannot be considered conclusive here.

In concluding this portion of the subject, I may add a word or two as to the differences of style that may be traced between the two stages of the *One Penny* and the three plates of the *Two Pence*. One cannot criticise the drawing of a postage stamp like the style of a literary composition, and it is only those who, like some of us, have devoted much time to the study of these stamps that are able to affirm, by a sort of intuitive perception, that any two given plates are or are not by the same hand.

No reason can be given for what Mr. Pemberton called the "imperceptible sense;" and yet, from my own study, I feel convinced that the original plate and the retouch of the *One Penny* were not done by the same engraver. Apart from the coarser workmanship, there is a difference of style that cannot be mistaken, and which reminds one very strongly of the engraving of Plate II. of the *Two Pence*. The little dot in the corner stars occurs on both plates, and is a very characteristic detail of style. If I may hazard a guess, I should say that the first *One Penny* and *Three Pence* were drawn by the same engraver, the first *Two Pence* by a second, and the retouched *One Penny* and Plate II. of the *Two Pence* by a third. I do not believe that Plate III. of the *Two Pence* was drawn by the engraver of Plate II.; but, of course, all this is pure speculation, and I can bring forward no arguments in support of my opinions.

III. We have lastly to consider the various kinds of paper which were used for specimens of the *Two Pence*. To a great extent they are the same as those employed for the *One Penny*, and seem to have come into use about the same time. All the earliest specimens of Plates I. and II. were printed upon the soft yellowish paper; in fact, Plate I. is found upon no other, though this paper occasionally absorbed a little of the ink of the impression, which gave it a slightly bluish appearance. It can easily be distinguished, however, from the hard bluish paper which succeeded it, and which must have been used soon after Plate II. came into existence, as comparatively early copies from this plate are found printed upon it. The earliest specimen I have seen of the *Two Pence* on the bluish paper is dated June 3rd, 1850. A third kind of paper seems peculiar to Plate III., and Plate III. second retouch, and, as I mentioned previously, to certain specimens of Plate II. It is hard, of medium thickness, and in colour grey or dirty white. In my opinion, it is distinct from the hard bluish paper, though it is possible that this paper, originally white, has become tinged in some cases with the colour of the impression, which in these two stages of Plate III. is of a greyer shade of blue than that of the first. On the other hand, it is possible, as you can see from an unsevered block in my collection, that the yellowish gum may have had something to do in changing the colour of the paper. I may say, however, that as far as my experience goes, no specimens of the *One Penny* or *Three Pence* are found upon this grey paper; but in any case the point seems of little importance.

Specimens of the first and second retouch of Plate III. are also found upon the ribbed or laid paper, identical with that used for the *One Penny*. There can be no doubt that it was used intermittently, pending a supply of the ordinary paper. The earliest specimen I have seen upon this paper is dated February 27th, 1851.

Mr. Pemberton went very carefully into the question of the different papers employed in days when the distinctions between the plates were not so well understood as they are now. His enquiries were made mainly with the view of showing that there were three distinct plates of what he called the roughly-engraved *Two Pence;* and having found certain kinds of paper peculiar to certain varieties of the stamps, he very reasonably argued that the latter must have been printed from separate plates. That he was partly right and partly wrong in his conclusions I have already shown; but his researches all tend to confirm the order I have adopted for the plates in their different stages. I recognize then four different kinds of paper for the Two Pence:

1. The soft yellowish paper, occasionally tinged with blue.
2. Hard bluish paper, varying in substance.
3. Hard grey or dirty white paper.
4. Ribbed or laid paper, white or slightly bluish.

I omitted to mention that in the case of the *Two Pence* on laid paper the laid lines are always vertical, those of the *One Penny* and *Three Pence* being horizontal. I have some recollection of a specimen being mentioned on horizontally laid paper, but this I have not been able to verify.

Three Pence.

My remarks upon this value will be brief, as it presents absolutely no point of any difficulty. It was issued on January 1st, 1850, and continued in use until December, 1852, when it was superseded by the *Three Pence laureated*. It was not used to anything like the same extent as the other values, and consequently we never meet with very worn copies. You will learn with satisfaction that only one plate of the *Three Pence* was prepared, and though the varieties of type are very difficult to identify, there are no perplexing questions of retouch or transfer to trouble us.

Design.—As far as the centre portion is concerned, it is practically the same as that of the *One Penny* and *Two Pence*, with double lined and dated bale, the only difference being that the legend "Sic fortis," &c., is printed in three lines instead of two. There are two white perpendicular bands at the sides (impinged upon by the centre white circular band), filled in with horizontal coloured ovals, which sometimes touch and sometimes interlace each other. The spandrels are composed of straight and wavy horizontal lines crossed, and the corners of white square blocks, containing Maltese crosses, with four-point star centre. Straight linear labels above and below, containing the words, T. "POSTAGE," D. "THREE PENCE" in coloured block capitals. The design is completed by a single rectangular coloured line, and as in the *One Penny* value there were no divisional or compartment lines to the plate. Mr. Pemberton was under the impression that there were three distinct plates, and his divisions were as follows:

1. Without clouds.
2. With clouds, side ovals touching each other.
3.   ,,   ,,   interlacing each other.

With regard to the two latter, you will see by the sheet before you that they are simply varieties of type occurring on the same plate, and I am inclined to think that specimens without clouds, if they really exist, should be merely considered as similar varieties, or should be attributed to wear of the plate. The colour employed for this value was often very ineffective, and it is sometimes difficult to trace out the other details of the design in addition to the clouds. It is a fact that the well-known proof impressions in myrtle green and the earliest copies on the yellowish paper show the clouds perfectly distinct; and I believe therefore that if any specimens without clouds exist, they are simply varieties of type, similar to the single specimen on the retouched plate of the *One Penny*. It is probably the analogy of the two editions of the latter value that has given rise to the error. At any rate, on the complete sheet before you, of which the position of every stamp has been ascertained, there are only one or two specimens which afford any reason for doubt as to the presence or absence of clouds. The sheet consisted of twenty-five stamps, each separately engraved, and arranged, like the *One Penny*, in five rows of five. The varieties of type are minute, and, owing to the colour, much more difficult to identify than those of the *One Penny* and *Two Pence*. However, every care has been taken, and I believe the arrangement before you is the correct one. It is proved as follows :

Pairs and Blocks.

Nos. 1, 2, 3, 6, 7, 8 are in	. . .	Mr. Tapling's collection.
7, 12, 17 „	. . .	„ „ „
17, 22 „	. . .	„ „ „
1, 6, 11, 16 „	. . .	MM. Caillebotte's „
16, 17, 21, 22 „	. . .	„ „ „
3, 8, 13 „	. . .	Mr. Tapling's „
13, 18, 23 „	. . .	„ „ „
3, 4 „	. . .	„ Rodd's „
4, 9 „	. . .	„ Tapling's „
8, 9 „	. . .	„ „ „
9, 10, 14, 15 „	. . .	MM. Caillebotte's „
24 is in the bottom row in	. .	Dr. Legrand's „
25 is in the right bottom corner in	„	„ „
19, 20 „	. . .	„ „ „

No. 5 is unaccounted for, not having been met with in a pair or block; but as there is only one space left, it is of course correctly placed. The same remark applies to No. 24, there being only one vacant place left in the bottom row.

The *Three Pence* is found upon four different kinds of paper, similar to those already described for the *One Penny* and *Two Pence*. They are briefly :

1. Soft yellowish paper.
2. Hard bluish „
3. White laid or ribbed paper.
4. Bluish „ „

I have not seen a sufficient number of dated specimens to be able to say with any certainty at what period these papers were used, but in all probability their employment was contemporaneous for all three values. As you are no doubt aware, specimens of the *Three Pence* on the laid paper have become exceedingly scarce, and I have never seen an unobliterated copy. There is little further to add in reference to the Sydneys. The four strongest collections of these stamps I am acquainted with are those of Herr von Ferrary, MM. Caillebotte, Dr. Legrand, and my own; and I can only once again express my acknowledgments for the opportunities of reference that have been afforded me by these gentlemen and others, and for the information that has been freely placed at my disposal. You are now in a position to judge of the difficulties we have had to contend with, and how far they have been successfully surmounted. I can only hope that the Sydneys may not now be altogether looked upon in the light of a "sealed book," and that some succeeding writer, more fortunate in obtaining access to official information, may succeed in giving a solution of the questions I have left unanswered in these papers.

Issue II.

The second series, commonly known as the laureated issue, presents comparatively little difficulty, and has been very fully dealt with in the four following articles:

1. "Notes on the Second Series of the Stamps of New South Wales," by the author of "The Postage Stamps of British Guiana." (*Stamp Collector's Magazine*, 1867, page 33.)
2. "A Contribution towards the History of the Stamps of New South Wales." (Same Author and Magazine, 1874, page 5.)
3. "The Laureated Stamps of New South Wales," by E. L. Pemberton. (*Philatelist*, 1868, page 3.)
4. The article by Dr. Legrand in the *Memoirs of the Congrès International des Timbrophiles*.

I have little to add to or correct in these articles, which contain what is practically a complete history of the issue. Since they appeared, however, some additional information has been obtained relating to the arrangement of the varieties on the plates; and, with the exception of the *Eight Pence* and the registered stamps, we have been able to completely reconstruct all the sheets of each value as they were originally printed. It is almost superfluous to remind you that, like the Sydneys, each stamp on the plates was separately engraved, thus giving as many varieties of type as there were stamps to the sheet. Following the course adopted in the case of the first issue, I shall consider each value separately under the same headings of date of issue, design and engraving, and paper. This adds a little to the length of this paper, but it is desirable for the sake of clearness, and is certainly more logical. The different values were issued at different times, but it seems more convenient to take them in order of value rather than in order of issue, though this is a matter of individual taste. There are five values—*One Penny, Two Pence, Three Pence, Six Pence, Eight Pence.*

One Penny.

I. *Date.*—From the *Sydney Government Gazette* of December 23rd, 1851, we learn a notice was issued to the effect "that stamps of the Queen's head with laurel wreath, of the value of One Penny, will immediately be issued." The *One Penny* value was therefore issued on or about this date.

II. *Engraving and Design.*—One plate only of this value was prepared. In the *Stamp Collector's Magazine* of 1874, page 7, it is stated that this value was engraved on steel by John Carmichael, Kent Street, North Sydney, and consisted of fifty stamps arranged in five horizontal rows of ten. Carmichael was in the habit of putting his name at the foot of the different plates he engraved, but I have never seen a specimen of the *One Penny* with sufficient margin to show whether he did so in this case or not. Mr. Pemberton states that this plate was engraved by Carruthers, but which of the two authorities is correct I cannot say. The writer of the article just referred to remarks, "By February, 1854, a new plate of the *One Penny* was ready; it was engraved on copper by Carmichael, and contained fifty stamps, all separately engraved, as in former instances. The *One Penny* and *Two Pence* values were, in the month of February, 1854, printed and issued on paper watermarked with double lined figure of value." This is evidently a mistake into which it is surprising that the well-known collector who wrote the article, and whose name I forbear to reveal, should have fallen. The *colour* of the stamps, printed on watermarked paper, is a bright orange, and is certainly very distinct from the red or lake shades used in the earlier stages of the issue; but a comparison of the two sheets before you, on unwatermarked and watermarked paper, will show conclusively that, as far as the design is concerned, they are absolutely

identical in every detail. There is not even a question of a retouch, and I
can only conclude that the remarks I have quoted were evolved from the inner
consciousness of the author. I have alluded to this mistake simply because
I have directed your attention to these earlier articles, and therefore it became
necessary to obviate the possibility of error arising in your minds. The design of
the stamps on this plate may be described as follows:

Laureated profile of Queen Victoria to left, on a background of straight and
wavy vertical lines crossed, enclosed in a rectangular frame. Above the head there
is an arched label of colour, containing the word "Postage" in white block capitals.
Straight white labels above and below, containing the words, T. "SOUTH," B. "ONE
PENNY," in coloured block capitals, the bottom label being an octagonal oblong.
The top label contains three leaf ornaments on each side of the word "SOUTH."
The sides are composed of interlacing pointed oval reticulations, broken in the
middle by two white labels, containing the words, L. "NEW" reading upwards,
R. "WALES" reading downwards. The corners are composed of white square blocks
containing Maltese cross ornaments, and the design is completed by a single
outer line of colour. Shape, upright rectangular, yellowish gum; imperf. This
plate continued in use until the *One Penny*, with the diademed head of Her
Majesty, was issued. Its arrangement is settled by the following list of pairs
and blocks, &c.; and you will see that here, as in the case of several other values,
I am largely indebted to MM. Caillebotte for the information they have collected
and kindly placed at my disposal:

Nos. 1, 2, 3	are in Dr. Legrand's collection.	
3, 4	„ Mr. Tapling's	„
5, 6	„ Dr. Legrand's	„
6, 7	„ Mr. Tapling's	„
8, 9, 10 are in the right upper corner in	„	„
7, 17	are in Dr. Legrand's	„
8, 18	„ MM. Caillebotte's	„
11, 12	„ Dr. Legrand's	„
12, 13	„ Mr. Tapling's	„
15, 16, 25, 26	„ Dr. Legrand's	„
16, 17	„ „	„
17, 18	„ „	„
19, 20	„ MM. Caillebotte's	„
20, 30	„ Dr. Legrand's	„
11, 21	„ Mr. Tapling's	„
21, 22, 23, 24, 25, 31, 32, 33, 34, 35	„ A Parisian	„
25, 26, 27, 28, 29, 30 . . .	„ Dr. Legrand's	„
14, 24	„ Mr. Lincoln's	„
26, 27, 36, 37	„ Mr. Tapling's	„
28, 38	„ Dr. Legrand's	„
29, 30, 39, 40	„ M. S. de Wilde's	„
37, 38, 39, 40	„ A Parisian	„
35, 36	„ M. S. de Wilde's	„
31, 41	„ Mr. Burnett's	„
41, 42	„ Dr. Legrand's	„
42, 43	„ Mr. Lincoln's	„
43, 44	„ Mr. Wilson's	„
44, 45	„ Mr. Tapling's	„
45, 46	„ „	„
35, 45	„ Mr. Lincoln's	„
47, 48, 49, 50	„ Dr. Legrand's	„

An examination of these details, and of the photograph, will show you that
every stamp is accounted for, and that no other arrangements of the sheet is
possible. There are two or three prominent varieties of type on the plate that
are worth noticing:

No. 7 has no floreate ornaments on the right of "SOUTH."
No. 9 is the error "WALE."
No. 15 has one floreate ornament missing.
No. 21 has no floreate ornaments on the right of "SOUTH,"

and on one or two specimens the corner stars are imperfect, evidently having been
left unfinished by accident.

III. *Paper.*—The *One Penny* is found upon four different kinds of paper—
1. Blue paper unwatermarked, the tinge of blue varying considerably in depth.
2. Stout white unwatermarked paper.
3. Blue paper, laid vertically.
4. Thinner white paper, watermarked with numeral of value.

These varieties call for no particular remark. Judging from the state of the impressions, it is impossible to doubt that the blue wove paper was the first used. I am unable to say whether the white wove paper preceded the blue laid paper or not, but I am inclined to think the latter was only used temporarily, during the exhaustion of the ordinary stock, and pending the arrival of a fresh supply. We learn from the *Sydney Government Gazette* of January 31st, 1854, that the watermarked paper was first to be put in use on February 1st, 1854.

Two Pence.

This was the first value of the series to appear, and there seems to have been a far greater demand for it than any of the others, as no less than three plates, each containing fifty stamps, were prepared and printed from between 1851 and 1856. I alluded to the fact of this value being in such request in an earlier part of these papers, and since writing I have come across some remarks of Mr. Pemberton's, which are to be found in the *Philatelist* of 1868, page 3. He observes: "Until the 15th of July, 1851, Victoria was a dependency of New South Wales; but though commencing an independent existence of its own in that year, it still seems to have used some of the higher valued stamps of the parent New South Wales, in addition to its own primitive set known as the *half lengths*. Before its independence Victoria (and the other Australian colonies till a later date) was amenable to New South Wales in postal matters, using the stamps issued by the Sydney office, which may, in some manner, account for the incomprehensible number of stamps (and varieties) issued, as it supplies a reason for the wear of the plates, at first quite inappreciable, if owing simply to demand for stamps in New South Wales."

Two Pence was the inland rate for letters, and the necessity for the large number of different plates of this value is thus accounted for, and is indirectly rather a striking proof of the great internal development of the trade of the Australian colonies. I shall deal with the distinctions between the plates and their constitution a little further on, and will now give you the ascertained facts as to the dates of issue.

I. *Date.*—From the *Sydney Government Gazette* of July 24th, 1851, we get a notice to the effect that "it has been found necessary to provide new plates, bearing the Queen's head instead of the present design (view of Sydney). That a new design of the Queen's head, with a laurel wreath, has been already engraved, value Two Pence, and that this stamp will be immediately issued to the public." I may remark, *en passant*, that in 1849 there was a somewhat disloyal section in Sydney who objected to the Queen's head appearing on the stamps of the first issue; but the difficulties were apparently overcome by the time the laureated *Two Pence* was issued, when, I believe, Major Christie had become postmaster.

We learn from the *Stamp Collector's Magazine* of 1874, page 6, that a second plate was put in hand directly the first one was completed, and the date of issue for this is given by M. Moens as December, 1851, when the *One Penny* first made its appearance. We are also told in the same article that "on the 8th August, 1853, authority was given to H. C. Jervis to engrave another plate of this value, which he did on *copper*, fifty stamps to the plate. This plate was afterwards used for printing on paper watermarked with the figure of value." The only difficulty that presents itself here is in connection with the second plate. If it was in use as early as December, 1851, it evidently ought to have had a lengthened existence. It is a fact, however, that specimens of this plate, which I shall show directly were what are known as the *six-rayed star* stamps, are extremely uncommon, and in reality are as rare as any of the Sydneys. The only explanation I can offer is that in one instance Jervis, who engraved this plate, is known to have worked upon copper. If this was a copper plate, and it has every appearance of being so, its rapid deterioration and early withdrawal are easily accounted for. I have never seen a specimen dated earlier than 1854, but in the *Stamp Collector's Magazine* of 1867, page 33, we find a specimen mentioned as existing on a letter dated December, 1852. On the whole, therefore, I am inclined to think that December, 1851, is very probably the correct date for the second plate.

II. *Engraving and Design.*—We have here, fortunately, the fullest information. The first plate of the *Two Pence* was engraved on steel by John Carmichael, and contained fifty stamps, each separately drawn. The second was engraved (probably on copper) by H. C. Jervis, of Pitt Street North, Sydney, and was similarly constituted. As you can see from the sheets before you, each engraver signed his name at the foot of the plates. Jervis evidently possessed nothing like the skill of Carmichael, his work being much rougher, with a very distinct and characteristic style. As I mentioned previously, Jervis engraved the third plate on copper in August, 1853, though in this instance he does not appear to have signed his name. From the *Sydney Government Gazette* of August 8th, 1853, it appears that he had instructions at the same time to repair the steel plate. This, however, he does not seem to have done, as, in my experience at any rate, no retouched specimens of the first plate exist. There is, however, a very close connection between Plates I. and III., and I shall be able to prove without difficulty that the latter is beyond doubt either a retouch of or a transfer from the former. This question involves the consideration of the only point of any difficulty in connection with the *Two Pence;* viz., the order of issue of the three plates. But before dealing with it, it will be more convenient to explain the distinctions between them.

Design. Plate I.—If we substitute the words "TWO PENCE" in the bottom label for "ONE PENNY," the description I have just given for the *One Penny* will apply equally well to the *Two Pence*, though, of course, as each plate was separately engraved, they differ from each other in the same way as the individual stamps. Speaking generally, the design is the same, and I have only to direct your attention to the background, which is composed of five straight and wavy vertical lines crossed, and to the stars in the corners, which are multi-rayed. The stamps are finely engraved, and are good specimens of workmanship. The plate contained fifty specimens, and is without division lines or frames.

Plate II.—Similar to the preceding, but of much inferior workmanship, almost resembling etching work. All the details are poor copies of Plate I. except the stars in the corners, which are six-rayed, and this will be found the easiest point of distinction. The plates contained fifty specimens, each separately drawn, and the rows are divided, like the two Sydneys, by horizontal and vertical compartment lines.

Plate III.—Very similar to Plate I., but the background is composed of horizontal and vertical lines crossed. The plate is divided into compartments, as in the previous case, and the crosses are Maltese crosses, similar to Plate I. The remainder of my remarks on this value may be most conveniently stated in the form of answers to the following questions:

1. Was any plate a retouch of or transfer from another?
2. What order should they be placed in?
3. The number of the stamps on the plates and their arrangement.

1. A very short examination will convince you, when the sheets are placed side by side, that Plate III., though much rougher in execution, is either a retouch of or a re-engraved transfer from Plate I. I would direct your special attention to the lettering of the words "SOUTH" and "TWO PENCE," and to the reticulations at the sides. There is considerable irregularity in the relative positions of these words to other portions of the design, and in the shape and size of the lettering. You will notice the unusually small size of "SOUTH" on the two specimens of No. 19, and the variations in the white interstices of the reticulations on Nos. 8 and 36. The same varieties are found on both sheets, and we can prove that they occur in the same position. Coincidences could be described if necessary on every stamp on the two sheets; but the photographs will enable you to judge for yourselves as to the truth of what I am saying. It is also worth remarking that the spaces between the rows vary very considerably, and the stamps themselves are sometimes not placed quite in line. As far as I have been able to ascertain from vertical pairs and blocks, the spacing of both sheets was identical. The space between the two bottom rows in particular is much wider than the others. These facts are, of course, quite consistent with the

theory of a retouch, and the authorization to Jervis, in August, 1853, to *repair* the steel plate rather points to this conclusion. It is known that at that date he did one of two things: he either repaired the steel plate or constructed a fresh one on copper. My own opinion is, that Plate III. is a transfer from Plate I., re-engraved on a fresh copper plate. In the first place, no trace of the finer work of Carmichael can be detected upon it; but there is another, and, to my mind, far more conclusive reason. As you can see by my specimens, Carmichael signed his name under the bottom row in the middle. There is no sign of a signature on Plate III., which a specimen with a large margin on my plate proves clearly. If Plate I. had been merely repaired or retouched, some trace of the signature would certainly have remained, unless it had been erased by Jervis, which seems unlikely. Bearing in mind that Jervis had orders to engrave a new plate, it seems morally certain that, to save himself trouble, he took a transfer from Plate I., and then re-engraved the design upon a fresh copper plate. One other point will probably occur to you when you have an opportunity of considering these papers in print; viz., that the order to engrave a fresh plate may possibly refer to what I have called Plate II., the plate with the six-rayed stars. Against this we may place the following facts: As soon as Plate I. appeared, in July, 1851, instructions were given for another to be put in hand. It is known that Carmichael, when pressed, employed Jervis to help him, and having to get the plate of the *One Penny* ready, which he did by December, 1851, there is every probability that it was on that account that Jervis was entrusted with the task of engraving Plate II.; and, as I mentioned before, it is stated that a second plate of the *Two Pence* appeared in that month with the *One Penny*. There is also the specimen dated December, 1852, and it is obvious that, if we can rely on the statement of the writer in the *Stamp Collector's Magazine*, this dated specimen of Plate II. proves conclusively that this plate was in use long before the order was given to Jervis in 1853. And, lastly, if Plate II. was not engraved before August, 1853, we should have expected to find specimens of it on the watermarked paper; but none such are known to exist.

2. *Order of Issue.*—I have already mentioned several matters connected with the order in which the plates appeared; but the paper by Major Evans, which you will find in another part of this work, proves beyond doubt that what I have designated Plate I. was the first one issued. The notice in the *Sydney Government Gazette* proves that the plate which was afterwards printed from on watermarked paper was the last, and it follows of course that Plate II. was intermediate.

3. *The Number and Arrangement of the Stamps.*—For the sake of brevity we may take Plates I. and III. together, the proof of the arrangement being as follows:

        No. 1 is the top left corner stamp . Mr. Tapling's collection.
        Nos. 1, 2, 3, 4   .   .   .   are in Mr. Thornhill's ,,
             4, 5, 6   .   .   .   ,,   Mr. Tapling's   ,,
             6, 7, 8   .   .   .   ,,   Mr. Thornhill's   ,,
             8, 9, 10, 18, 19 .   .   .   ,,   Dr. Legrand's   ,,
             11, 21, 31, 41   .   .   .   ,,   ,,   ,,
             11, 12, 13, 14   .   .   .   ,,   Mr. Tapling's   ,,
             15, 16, 17   .   .   .   ,,   ,,   ,,
             17, 18   .   .   .   ,,   Dr. Legrand's   ,,
             18, 28, 38   .   .   .   ,,   Mr. S. de Wilde's ,,
             19, 20   .   .   .   ,,   Dr. Legrand's   ,,
             21, 22   .   .   .   ,,   Mr. Tapling's   ,,
             22, 23   .   .   .   ,,   MM. Caillebotte's ,,
             23, 24   .   .   .   ,,   Dr. Legrand's   ,,
             24, 25   .   .   .   ,,   MM. Caillebotte's ,,
             15, 16, 25, 26   .   .   .   ,,   Dr. Legrand's   ,,
             26, 27   .   .   .   ,,   Mr. Tapling's   ,,
             27, 28, 29   .   .   .   ,,   ,,   ,,
             29, 30   .   .   .   ,,   Dr. Legrand's   ,,
             31, 32   .   .   .   ,,   MM. Caillebotte's ,,
             32, 33, 34   .   .   .   ,,   Dr. Legrand's   ,,
             35, 36, 46   .   .   .   ,,   Mr. Tapling's   ,,
             37, 38, 39, 40   .   .   .   ,,   Dr. Legrand's   ,,
             41, 42, 43, 44, 45, 46, 47   ,,   ,,   ,,
             47, 48   .   .   .   ,,   ,,   ,,
             48, 49, 50   .   .   .   ,,   ,,   ,,

Plate II.—The entire constitution of this plate has not yet been definitely ascertained. Specimens are very scarce, and it is difficult to meet with any number of them in pairs or blocks. Enough, however, has been proved to show that the arrangement indicated below is not far from the mark. I should add that the sheet before you is complete as far as the varieties of type are concerned; it is only the position of one or two specimens about which there is any doubt. Like the other two, there are fifty stamps to this plate.

No. 1 is the top left corner stamp	.	Mr. Tapling's collection.	
10 ,,	top right ,,	.	,,	,,
41 ,,	bottom left ,,	.	,,	,,
50 ,,	,, right ,,	.	,,	,,
Nos. 2, 3, 4 are in the top row in	.	,,	,,
5 is in the top row	.	.	,,	,,
6, 7 are in the top row in	.	,,	,,
7, 8, 9, 17, 18, 19 are in	.	,,	,,
20 is on the right side	.	.	,,	,,
11 ,, left ,,	.	.	,,	,,
2, 12 are in	.	.	.	,,	,,
12, 13 ,,	.	.	.	,,	,,
13, 23 ,,	.	.	.	,,	,,
23, 24 ,,	.	.	.	,,	,,
24, 25 ,,	.	.	.	,,	,,
14, 15 ,,	.	.	.	Dr. Legrand's	,,
29, 30 ,,	.	.	.	Mr. Wilson's	,,
30 is on the right side	.	Mr. Tapling's	,,
21, 22 are in	.	.	.	,,	,,
22, 32 ,,	.	.	.	,,	,,
31, 32 ,,	.	.	.	,,	,,
31, 41 ,,	.	.	.	,,	,,
41, 42 ,,	.	.	.	,,	,,
27, 28 ,,	.	.	.	,,	,,
28, 38 ,,	.	.	.	,,	,,
35, 36, 37 are in	.	.	Dr. Legrand's	,,
37, 38 ,,	.	.	Mr. Tapling's	,,
38, 39, 40 ,,	.	.	,,	,,
38, 48 ,,	.	.	.	,,	,,
33, 43 ,,	.	.	.	,,	,,
43, 44 ,,	.	.	.	MM. Caillebotte's ,,
44, 45 ,,	.	.	Mr. Tapling's and MM. Caillebotte's collection.
46, 47 ,,	.	.	,,	collection.
49 is in the bottom row	.	.	,,	,,

From these details you will see that very little more information is wanted to enable us to place every stamp in the right order, and it will be simply a matter of time to ascertain the places of the one or two specimens whose position at present is doubtful. The only prominent variety is No. 23, with the well-known error "WAEES" instead of "WALES." All three plates of the *Two Pence* wore away considerably with use, and may be found in several distinct stages. To use of the plate must be ascribed the spotted appearance frequently seen on specimens from Plate I.

III. *Papers.*—These vary considerably. Plate I. is found upon blue, greyish or slightly blued, and white or toned paper, unwatermarked, and also upon closely-ribbed paper, the ribs or lines being horizontal. Plate II. is only found upon the blue paper. Plate III. exists on blue, greyish or slightly blued, both unwatermarked, and also upon the white watermarked paper. The blue and greyish papers seem to have continued in use till the early part of 1854, when we find a notice in the *Sydney Government Gazette* to the effect that "in future all stamps would be printed on paper bearing a watermark." As far as I am aware no specimen of the *Two Pence* exists upon the vertically-laid paper, which seems peculiar to the *One Penny*.

THREE PENCE.

There is no difficulty in connection with this value, of which only one plate was prepared. From the *Sydney Government Gazette* of December 7th, 1852, we learn that "stamps of the value of Three Pence, of the same design as the One Penny, Two Pence, and Six Pence now in use, have been prepared, and will immediately be issued." The engraver was Carmichael, and I think I am correct in saying that he signed his name at the foot of the plate as in previous cases. There were fifty stamps to the plate, each separately engraved, and arranged in five horizontal rows of ten. The design is very similar to that of the *One Penny* and *Two Pence*, Plate I., the only difference being that the concentric pointed ovals at the sides are replaced by vertical, wavy, reticulated, and interlacing lines. The sheet before you is complete, and the proof of the arrangement of the varieties is as follows:

Nos.		
1, 2	are in Mr. Tapling's collection.	
3, 4, 5, 6, 7, 8, 9, 10, 13, 14, 15, 16, 17, 18, 19, 20	„	MM. Caillebotte's „
11, 12	„	„ „
12, 22, 32, 42	„	„ „
21, 22	„	„ „
15, 16, 17, 25, 26, 27	„	Mr. Tapling's „
14, 24	„	„ „
23, 24	„	„ „
27, 28	„	Mr. Thornhill's „
9, 10, 19, 20, 29, 30	„	Mr. Tapling's „
28, 29	„	Dr. Legrand's „
21, 31	„	MM. Caillebotte's „
33, 34, 43, 44	„	Mr. Tapling's „
35, 36, 45, 46	„	„ „
37, 38, 47, 48	„	„ „
38, 39, 40, 48, 49	„	„ „
41, 42, 43, 44, 45	„	MM. Caillebotte's „
46, 47, 48, 49, 50	„	„ „

The most prominent variety of type on the plate is No. 37, the so-called error "WACES." This is merely due to the letter "L" of "WALES" being badly drawn. The engraver accidentally added a stroke to the top of the letter, something like the top stroke of an "E".

The paper employed is practically the same as that used for the Two Pence. We get first the unwatermarked paper blue and slightly blue varying to greyish and almost white, and next the white paper watermarked with a double-lined numeral of value.

SIX PENCE.

On March 16th, 1852, authority was given to Carmichael to engrave a plate of the *Six Pence;* and in the *Sydney Government Gazette* of April 30th, in the same year, we find a proclamation by the Governor-General that in pursuance of the Act 15th Victoria, No. 12—"an Act to amend the laws for the conveyance of postage mails"—a plate has been provided for stamps of the value of Six Pence, of the same design as the One Penny and Two Pence stamps now in use. The Six Pence stamps of this design will immediately be issued. I have seen specimens with margins bearing traces of the words "Engraved by J. Carmichael," so there can be no doubt that he carried out his instructions. We should have expected to find this sheet the same size as the others with fifty stamps, but for some unexplained reason the plate contained twenty-five only, without division lines or frame.

The design is very nearly the same as that of the *One Penny* and the first *Two Pence*, the only difference being that the floreate ornaments are more numerous, the lettering of the value and of the word "SOUTH" is rather larger, and the value fills up the label between the Maltese crosses in large block capitals at the foot.

Two plates of this value were prepared, the second being easily distinguished from the first by the coarseness of the lines of the background and of other details of the design. There is very little doubt that the second plate was the work of Jervis, and was either a retouch of or a re-engraved transfer from the first. Reasoning by the analogy of the two plates of the *Two Pence*, I am inclined to the latter opinion, though at present there is no direct evidence either one way or the other. A comparison of the two sheets will show very strong points of resemblance, though there seems no trace on the second plate of the finer work of Carmichael. A specimen or two from the bottom row with a large margin would probably settle the matter, but the style of the engraving is so like that of the *Two Pence*, Plate II., and the *Eight Pence*, both of which are known to have been prepared by Jarvis, that there really can be little doubt as to this plate being his work. The question of the date of Plate II. is more difficult to determine. Mr. Pemberton mentions May 16th, 1853, the date of the *Eight Pence*, as being the probable date of the second plate. I am rather inclined to think that as the original plate of the *Six Pence* only contained twenty-five stamps, a second plate would have been found necessary at a somewhat earlier date. Upon this point, however, there is absolutely no evidence, as far as I am aware. Each plate contained twenty-five stamps arranged in five rows of five. The arrangement of the second has been obtained from the first, and though there may be an error in the placing of the types, no pair or group has invalidated it up to the present time. The proof of the arrangement of Plate I. is as follows:

Nos. 1, 2, 3, 4, 5, 6, 7, 8, 9, 10 . . are in Mr. Tapling's collection.
. 11, 12, 13, 14, 15, 16, 17, 18, 19, 20 „ „ „
7, 12 . . . . „ „ „
21, 22, 23, 24, 25 . . . . „ „ „
20, 25 . . . . . . „ Mr. Lincoln's „

The *Six Pence* is only found upon blue unwatermarked paper, the tinge of blue varying, and upon stout white unwatermarked paper; the latter in my experience being peculiar to Plate II. The most prominent variety of type is the well-known error "WALLS," which exists only on the finely-engraved plate.

EIGHT PENCE.

On May 16th, 1853, a notice appeared in the *Sydney Government Gazette*, to the effect that a plate of stamps of this value had been prepared and approved, and that the stamps would be immediately issued to the public. The plate contained fifty stamps, each separately engraved, and was the work of Jervis, who signed his name at the foot. We have unfortunately been unable to ascertain the position of a single variety on the sheet, and it is consequently impossible to give even an approximate idea of the arrangement. Pairs and blocks of this value are extremely uncommon, and I fear it will be a work of time and much difficulty to place the varieties of type in the right order. There is, however, no reason to doubt that, like the other values, the stamps were arranged in five horizontal rows of ten; but beyond the fact that certain specimens, judging from their large margins, belonged to the top, bottom, or side rows, I have absolutely no information to give you.

The design is practically the same as that of the *Six Pence*, Plate II., but the lettering is rather smaller. There are none of the dividing compartment lines which have proved so useful in other cases; and, as far as I am aware, there are no errors, and no varieties of type of any special significance. The photograph, of course, represents a provisional arrangement only, which will no doubt have to be much modified when the real arrangement has been ascertained. I ought to have mentioned that MM. Caillebotte and myself just make up the fifty varieties, and that the photograph represents our united collections.

The *Eight Pence* is only found on the blue unwatermarked paper.

In conclusion, I may say that you are now in full possession of all the knowledge obtainable at the present time of the first two issues of New South Wales. The study has been a long one, and the amount of research involved very considerable. I can only hope that my share of the work may meet with your approval, and I ought to add that I should welcome any criticism from any member whose special knowledge would better qualify him to speak than myself. I trust the subject may not be allowed to rest at the point I quit it, and that the questions I have been compelled to leave in some obscurity may be taken up and settled by some writer with more opportunities of access to official information. If this should prove to be the case, I shall be quite satisfied with the knowledge that an effort on my part has been the means of inducing further study and research, and of aiding in a solution of some of the most difficult questions presented by the science of Philately.

NOTE.—Since these papers were written, I have received a friendly criticism from Mr. W. T. Wilson, to whom I have already been indebted for several valuable hints. For the most part we are entirely in accord, and there are really only two points of any importance about which there is any difference of opinion between us. In reference to the Sydney *Two Pence*, Plate I., retouched, Mr.

Wilson remarks, "The mysterious lines above and intersecting the upper frame line are undoubtedly where the engraver commenced to engrave another row of stamps, so that more stamps could be printed from the plate. Doubtless this could not be carried out because the plate was so much in use, and it was therefore found best to engrave fresh plates. I draw this conclusion from the fact that the upright divisional lines start upwards from the new horizontal base lines, and that they constitute pretty equally-sized compartments, although not true to the old stamps already on the plate." This is not unlikely, but a reference to my remarks will show that it by no means explains the whole difficulty. For instance, how is it we find three or four different sets of ruled lines on specimens which are the same variety of type, and which consequently occupy the same position on the plate? If Mr. Wilson's explanation is correct, it strengthens my theory that the other sets of double lines were executed on another plate probably reduplicated from the first. I can, however, add nothing to what I have already written on this part of the subject.

Mr. Wilson goes on to say, "The material point upon which I differ from you is that I consider the *Two Pence* Sydney, Plate III., first retouch and second retouch, are really re-engraved transfers from Plate III., and not retouches. Your own argument, as applied to the retouch of the *One Penny* Sydney, tells against you here, as you say that a retouch cannot be finer in detail, but coarser. My reasons for this opinion are that Plate III., second retouch, is so finely engraved as to conclusively disprove in my mind all idea of a retouch. The material alteration to the fan also supports this view. My reason for saying they are re-engraved transfers is the fact that variety No. 20, showing six segments only to the fan, as against seven on all other specimens on these plates, is found on all three plates—viz., Plate III., Plate III., first retouch, and Plate III., second retouch—taking them by your description. Another strong point in my favour is that on neither of the last-named plates are any traces of old engraving to be found."

I frankly admit that a recent prolonged and careful examination has convinced me that there is some foundation for this theory of Mr. Wilson's. He is, however, in error in thinking that no traces of the old engraving of Plate III. in its first stage can be found upon Plate III., first retouch. On several specimens on the sheet before you such traces are clearly distinguishable, but as regards Plate III., second retouch, I must confess I made a mistake (as far as my own sheets are concerned), and I cannot now point to a specimen on this plate showing indisputable traces of the old work on Plate III., first retouch. I may, however, still be right in my theory. Very few of my specimens on the sheet are in an early stage of impression, and it is obvious that traces of old work would soon wear away and disappear. It is also the fact that the Governor in the entry previously quoted merely authorized the *repair* of the plates, and made no mention of the construction of a fresh plate. On the whole I am rather inclined to believe Mr. Wilson is right in respect of this last plate, but there are unfortunately no means of speaking definitely either one way or the other, and after all the point is perhaps not one of very great importance. I am also indebted to Mr. Wilson for drawing my attention to two articles (which I overlooked) by Mr. Pemberton in the *Philatelist* of 1869, pages 86 and 97. From them it appears that Mr. Robert Clayton was employed to prepare the plates of the Sydney stamps. Mr. Pemberton mentions a copy of Mr. Clayton's tender to furnish "Press, dies, and plates for the sum of £36, covering the whole expense necessary for the full completion of the work required for the General Post-office establishment."

I have already given my reasons for thinking that the plates were not all the work of one hand; and if Mr. Pemberton's information is correct (and he seems to have had access to official evidence), it is probable that Mr. Clayton employed some of his subordinates to help him. In the other article Mr. Pemberton mentions that the three lower values of the laureated series were engraved, the *One Penny* by Carruthers, the *Two Pence* by Jervis, and the *Three Pence* by a deaf and dumb engraver named Carmichael. I mentioned that I had seen no signature on the plate of the *One Penny*, so I think we may accept Mr. Pemberton's statement as correct.

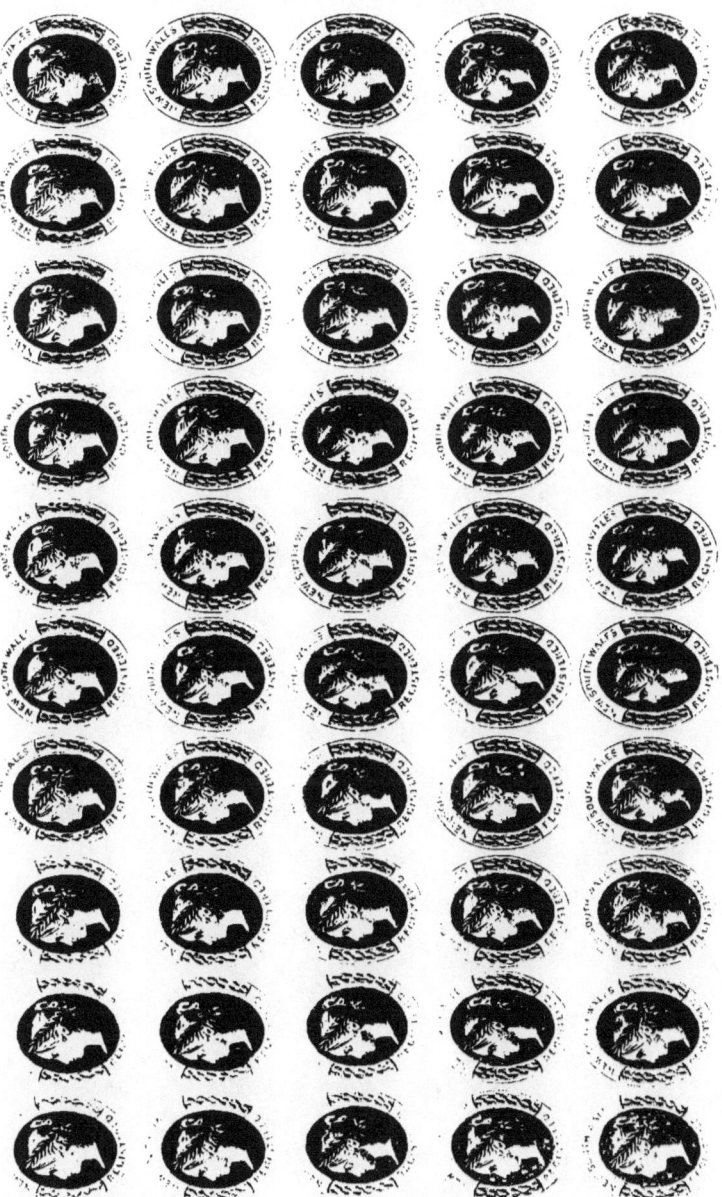

UNIV. OF
CALIFORNIA

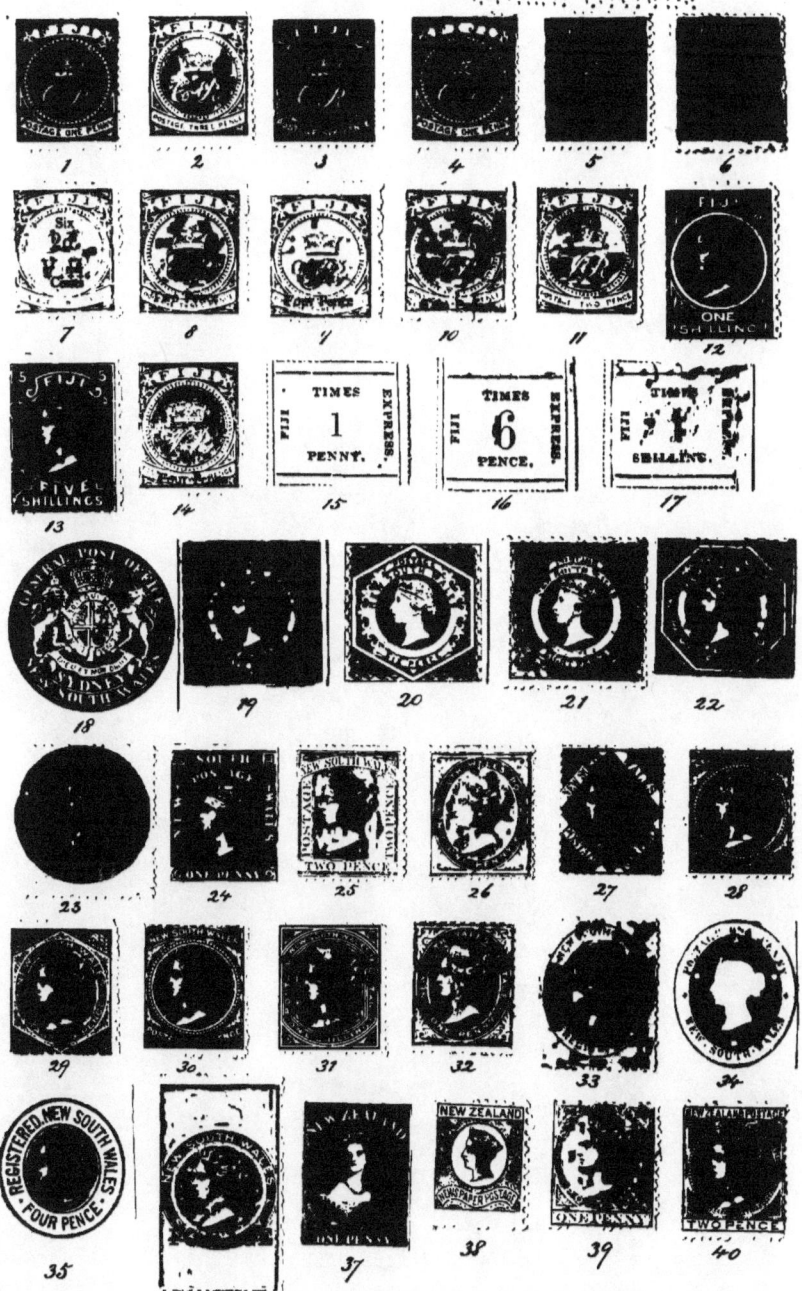

41

42

43

44

45

46

47

48

49

50

51

52

53

54

56

57

55

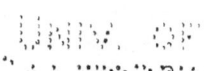

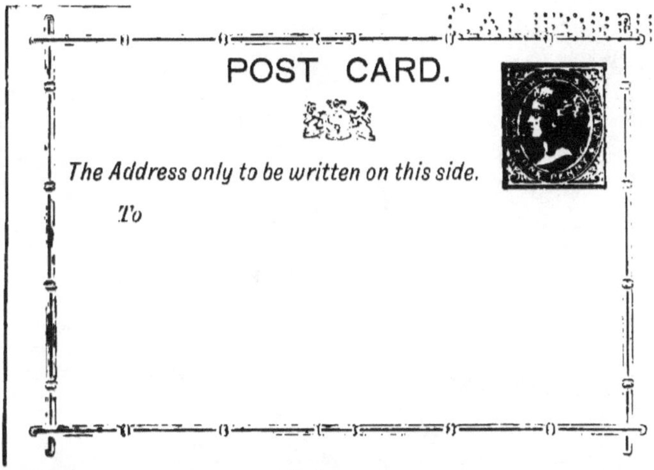

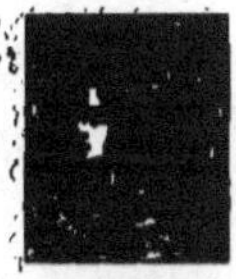

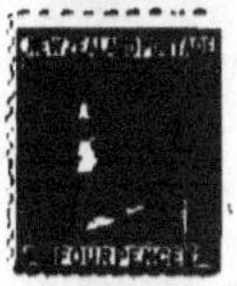

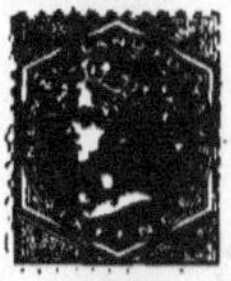

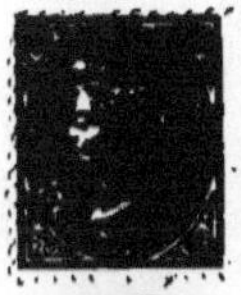

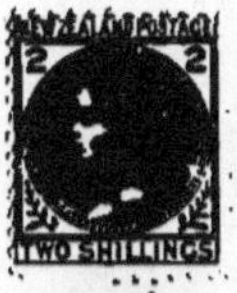

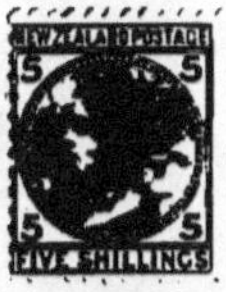

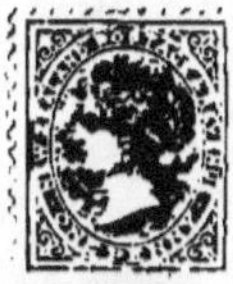

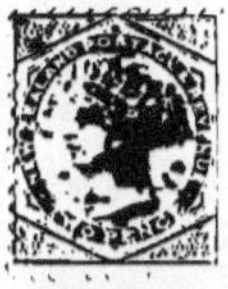

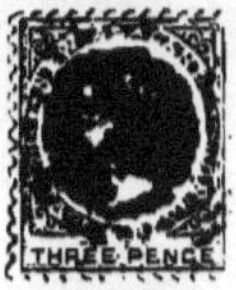

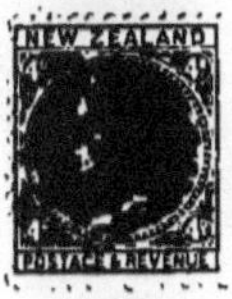

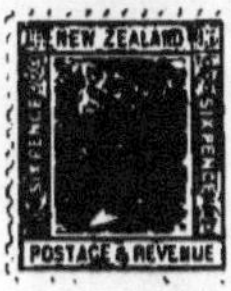

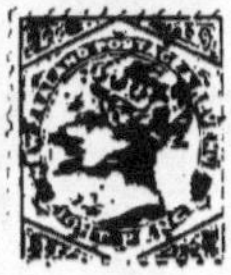

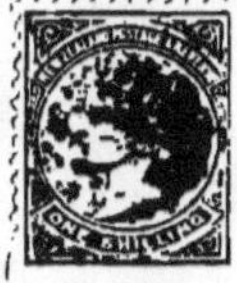

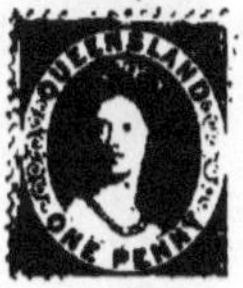

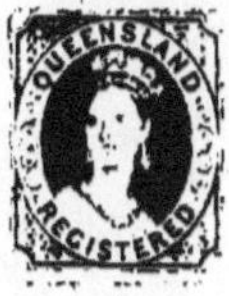

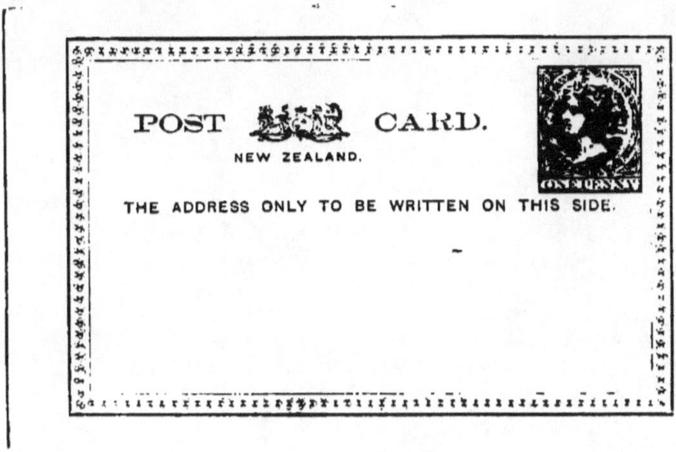

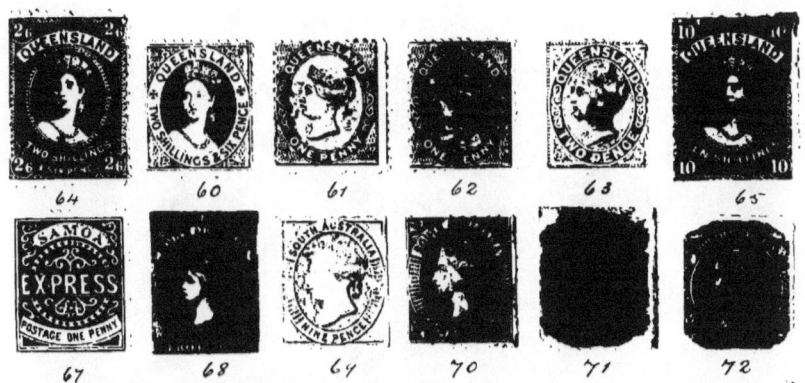

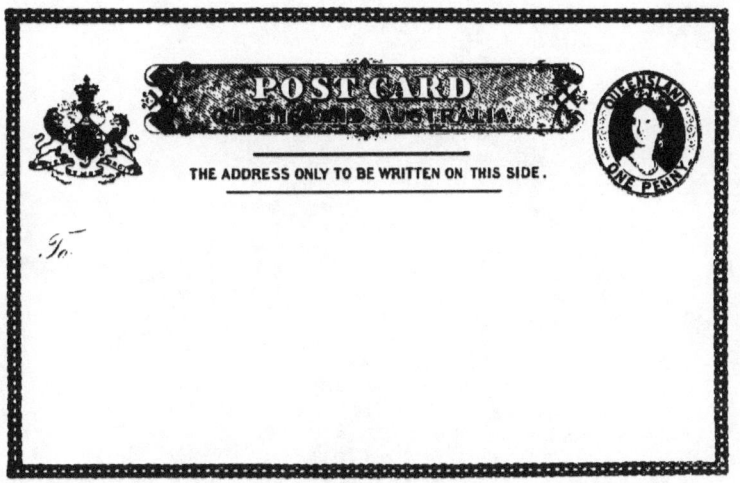

66

 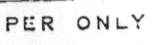 

73

74

80

75 76 77 78 79 81
82 83 84 85 86

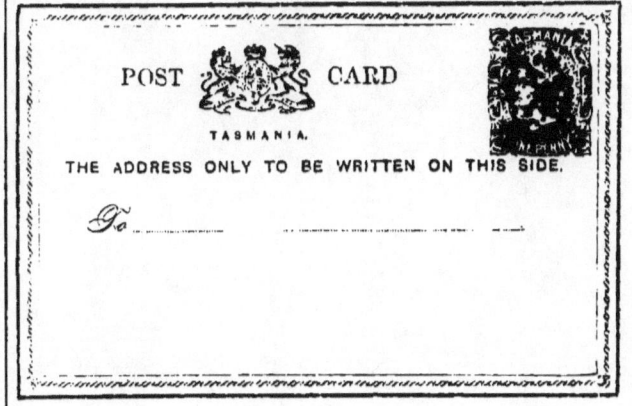

87

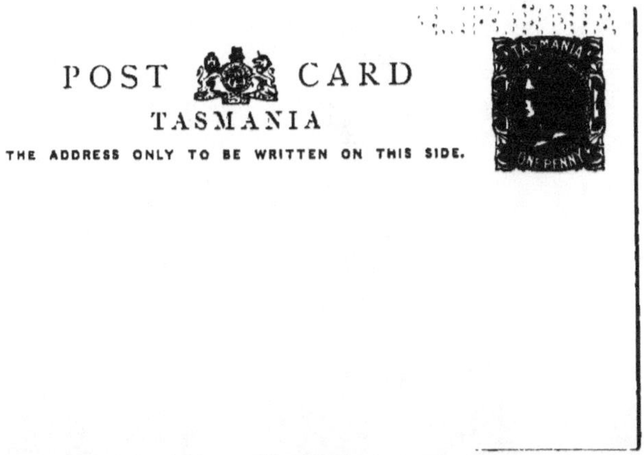

88

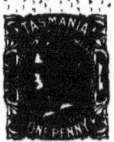

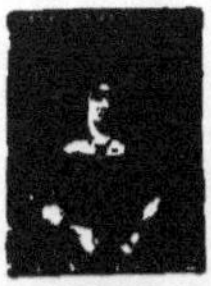
89

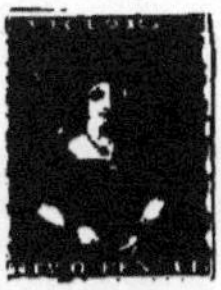
90

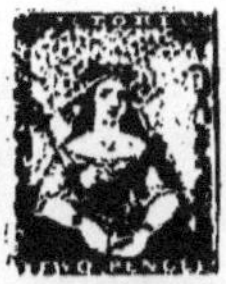
91

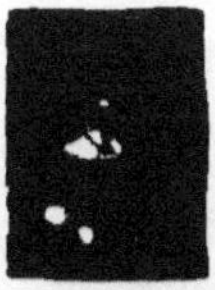
92

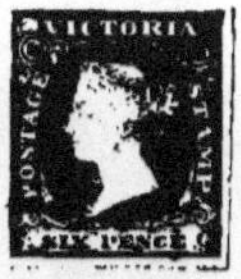
93

94

95

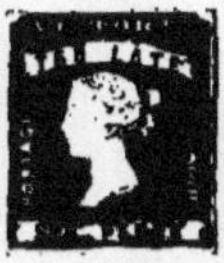
96

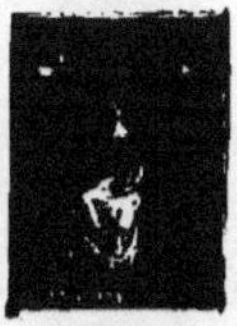
97

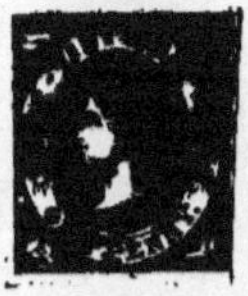
98

99

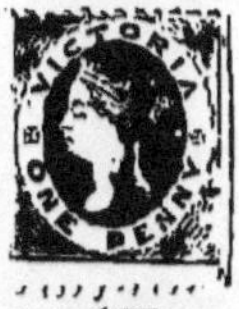
100

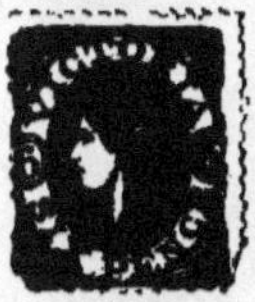
101

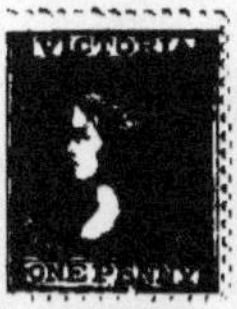
102

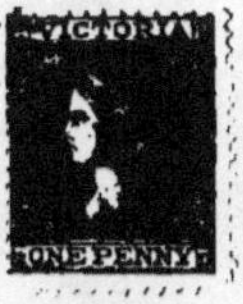
103

104

105

106

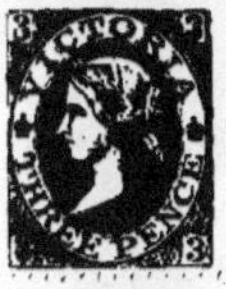
107

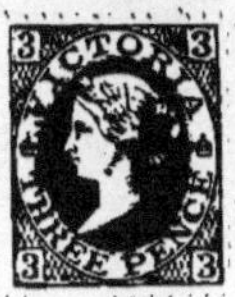
108

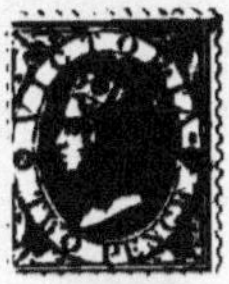
109

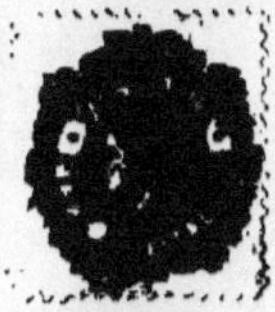
110

111

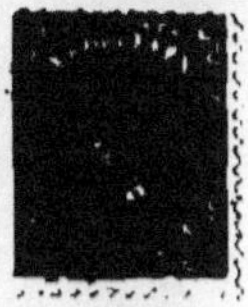
112

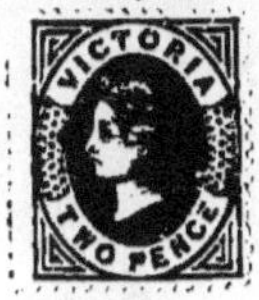
113

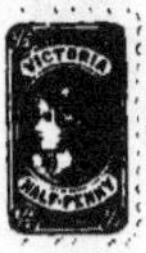
114

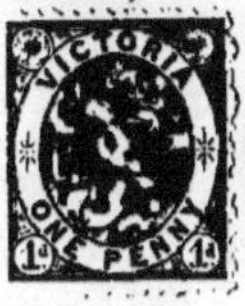
115

116

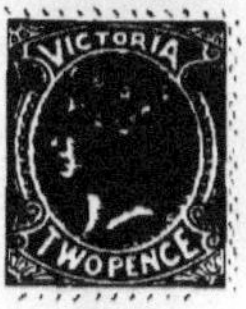
117

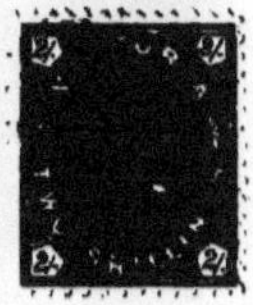
118

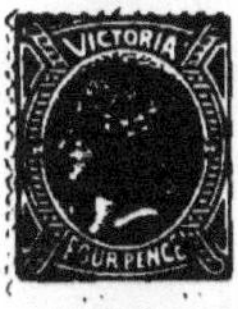

119

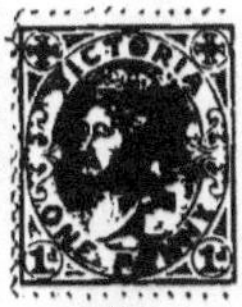

120

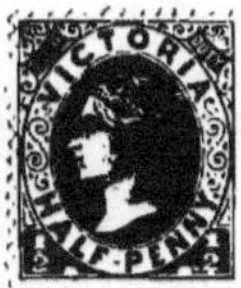

121

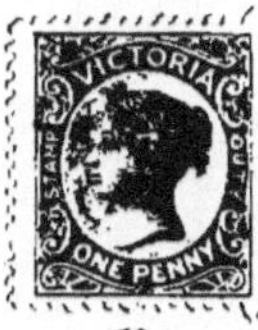

122

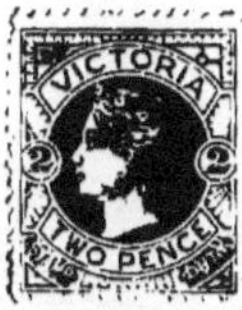

123

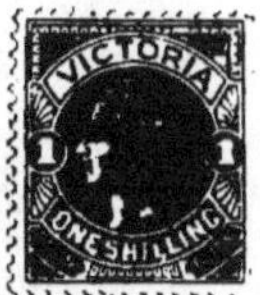

124

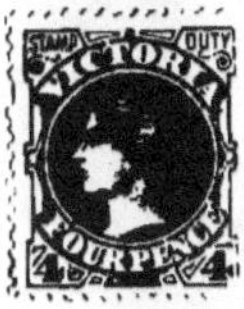

125

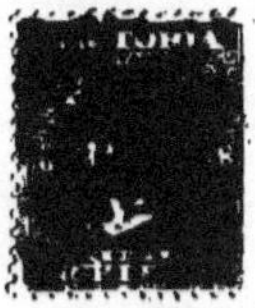

126

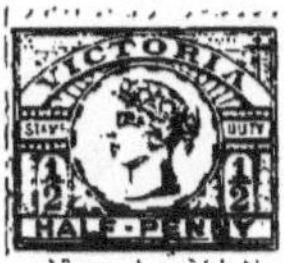

127

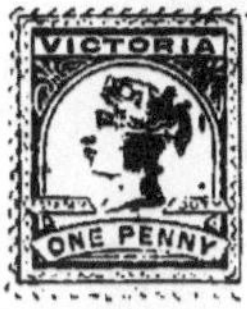

128

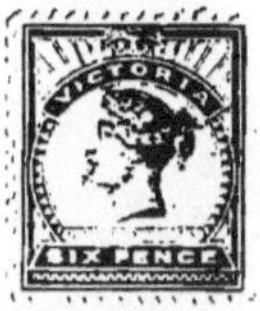

129

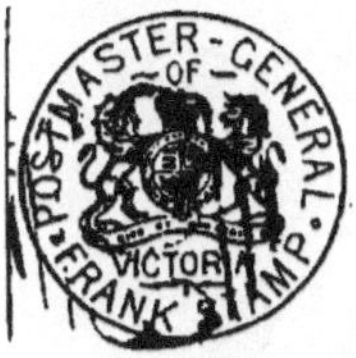

130

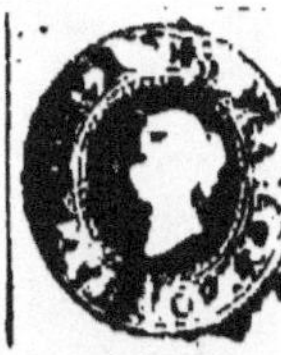

131

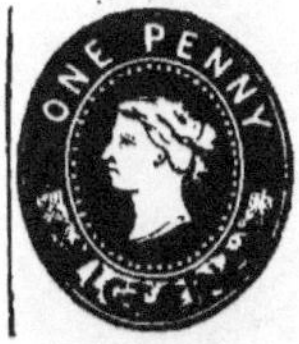

132

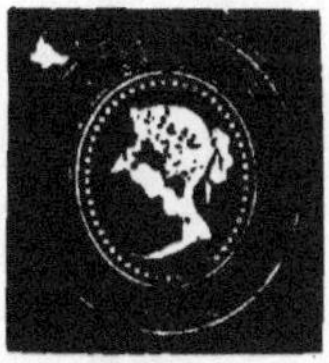

133

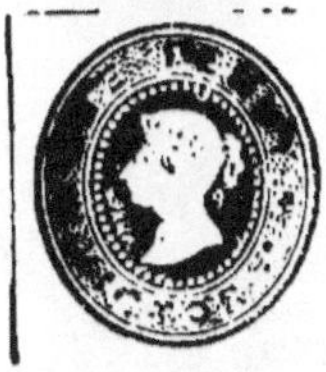

134

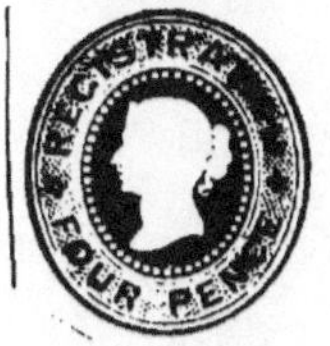

135

136

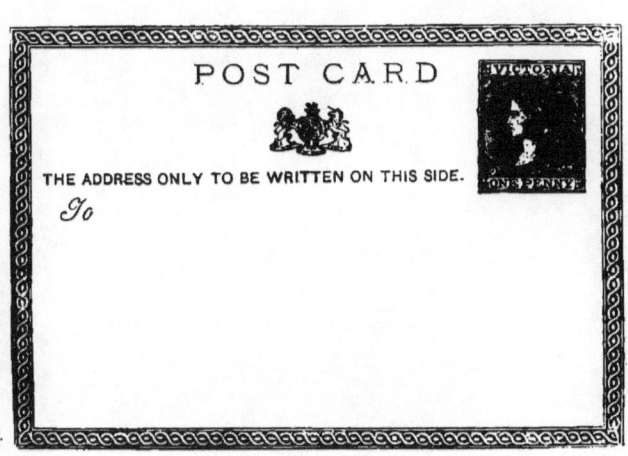

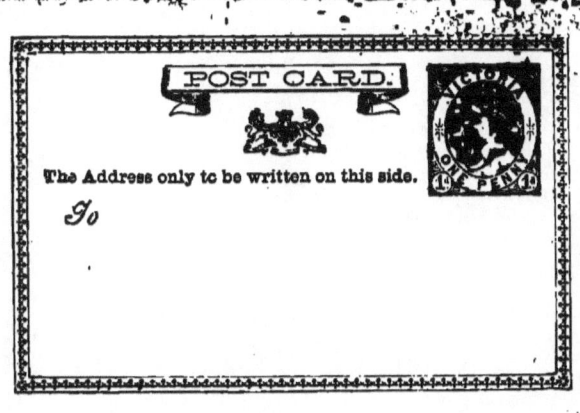

737

138

739

141   142   143   144   145

146   147   148   149   150

151

CALIFORNIA

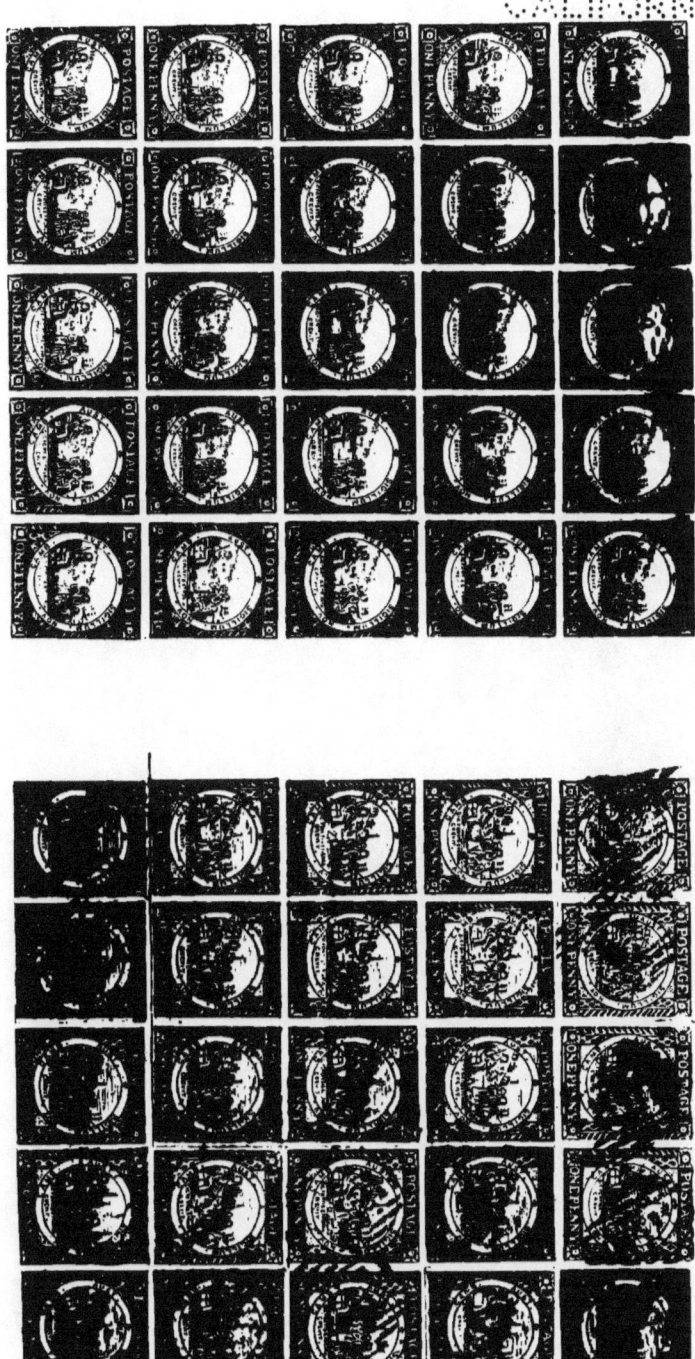

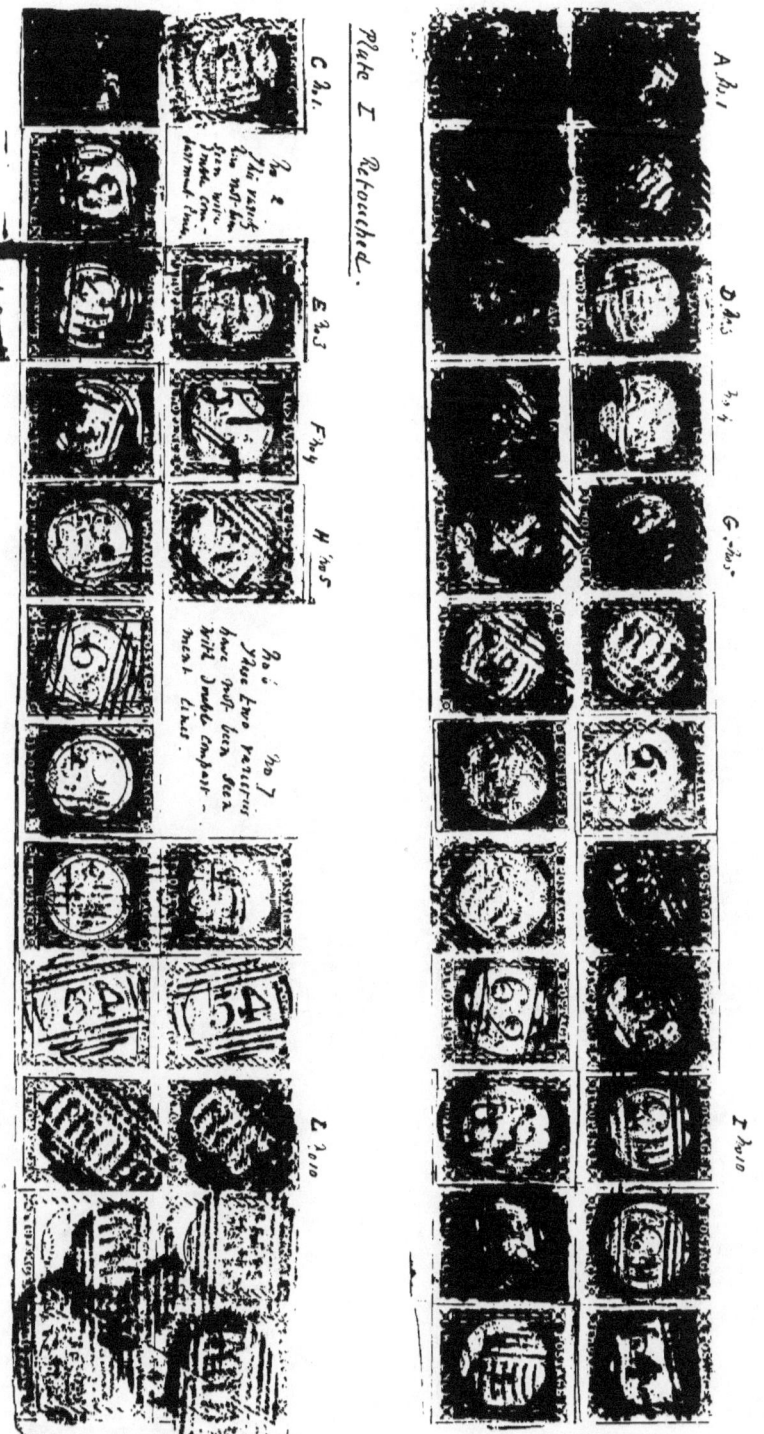

Plate III

Plate IV

PLATE C.

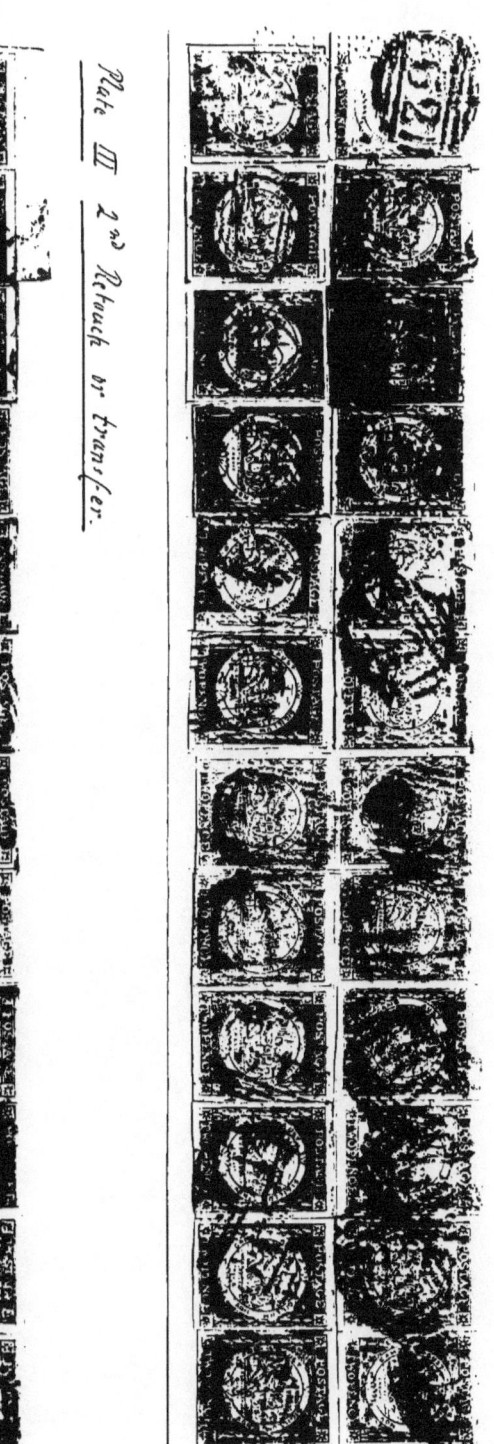

Plate III   2nd Retouch or transfer.

Three Pence One Plate only.

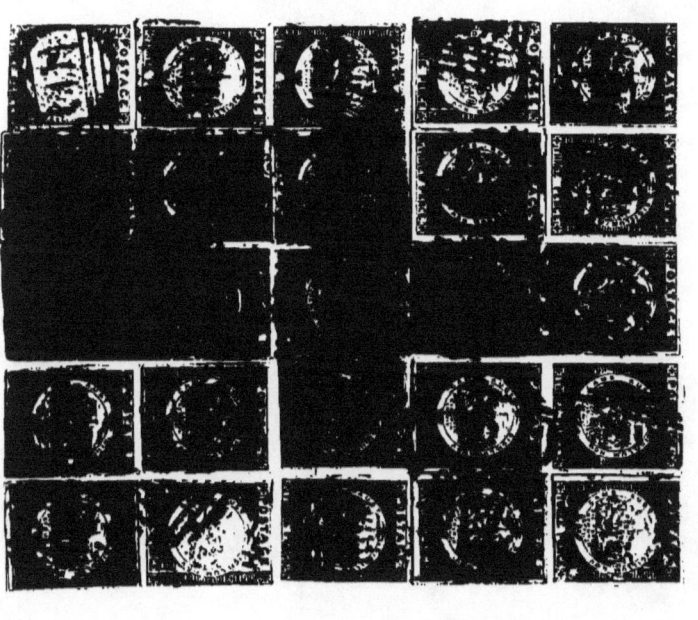

Plate I. & Plate I Retouched PLATE E.
B. No. 1   J No. 10   K No. 10

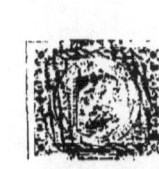

Sketch of the right hand ^position of Plate I
of the Two Pence shewing the
irregularities of the positions of the
stamps, & the compartment lines &c.
This sketch is only approximately accurate.

PLATE F.

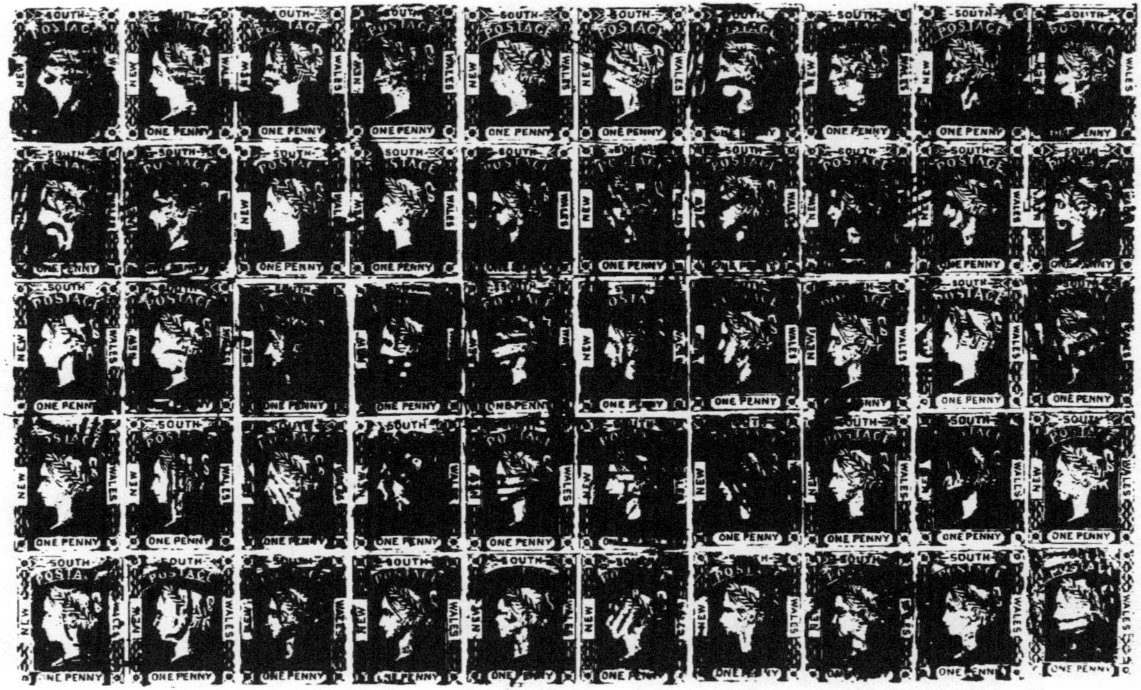

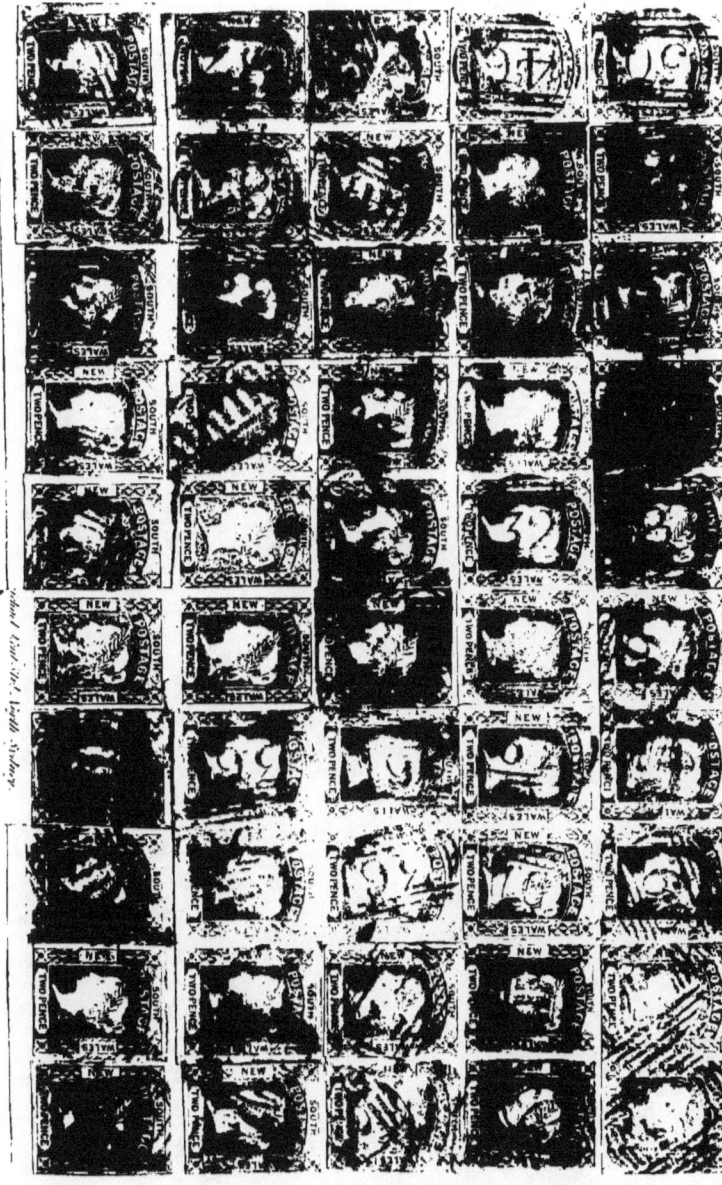

PLATE G.

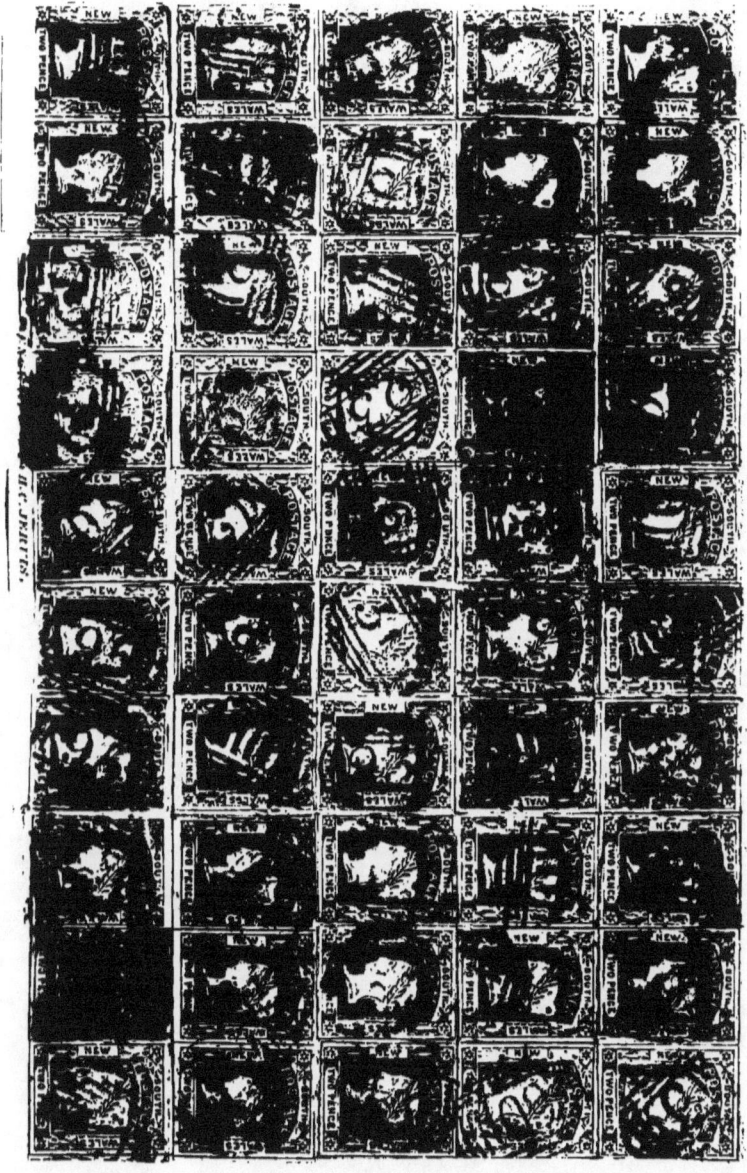

PLATE H.

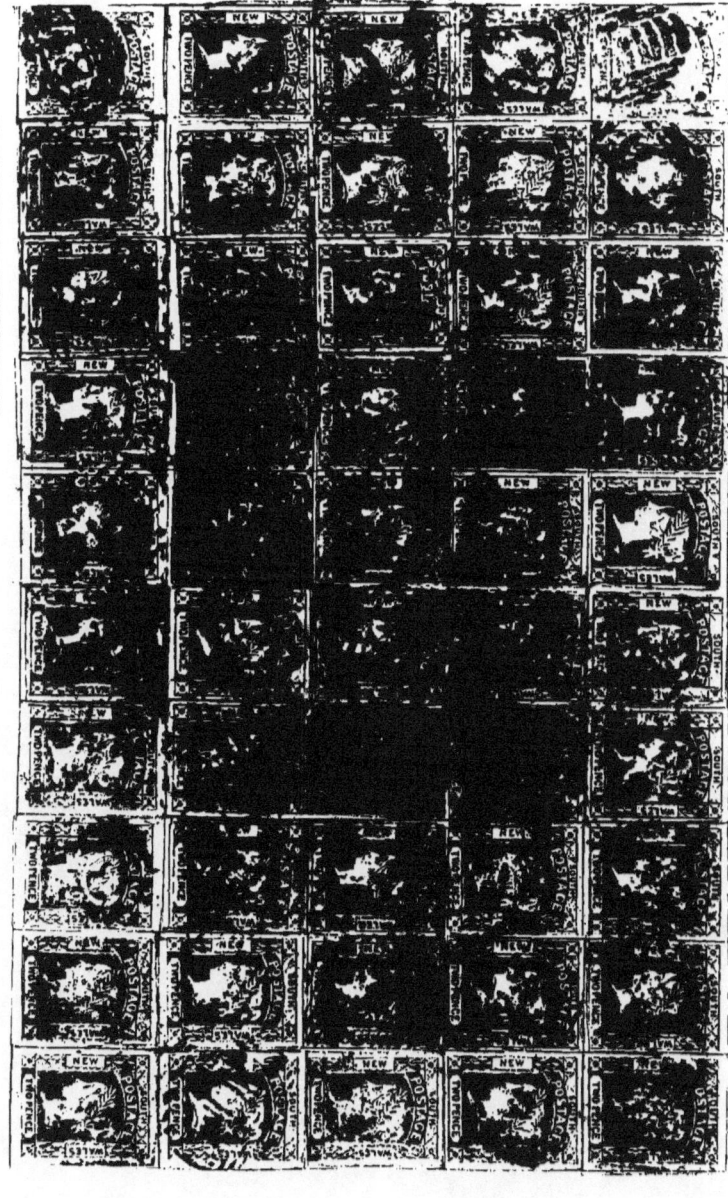

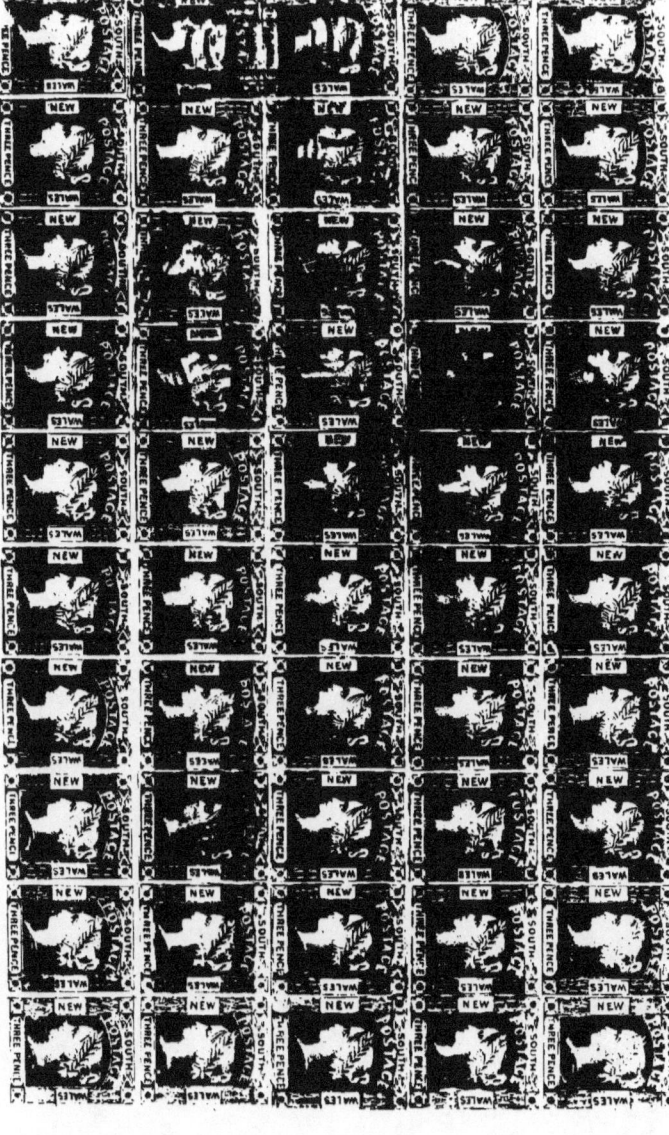

Three Pence One Plate.

PLATE J.

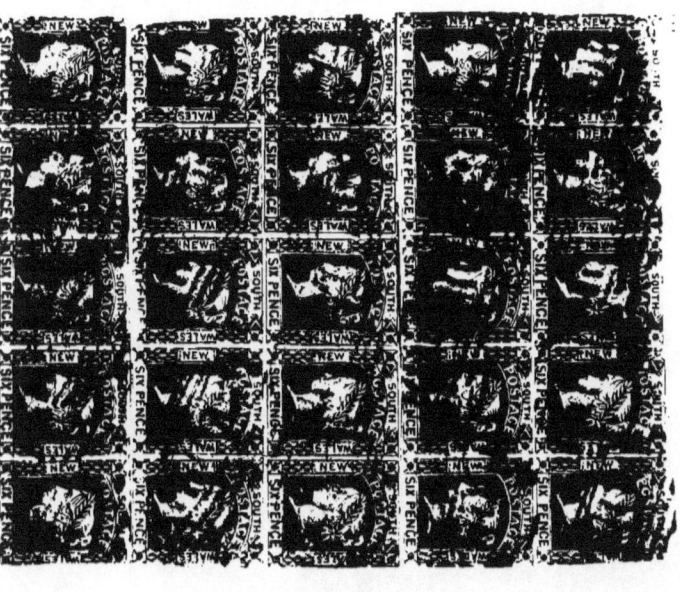

Six Pence. Original Plate

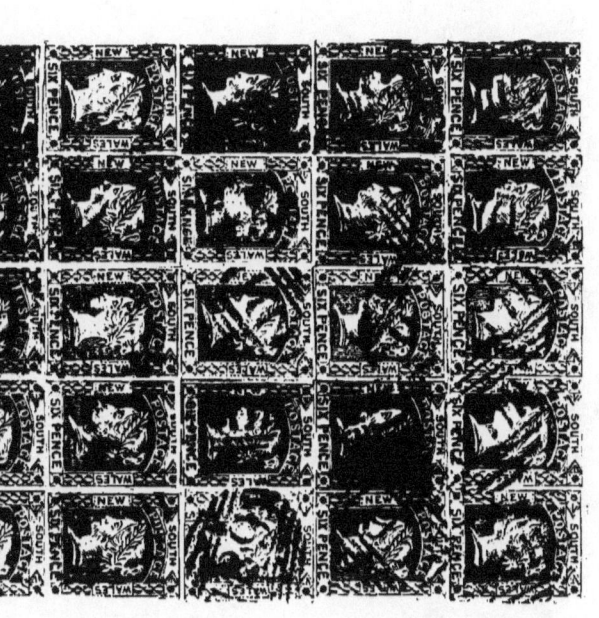

Retouched or reengraved Plate. PLATE K.

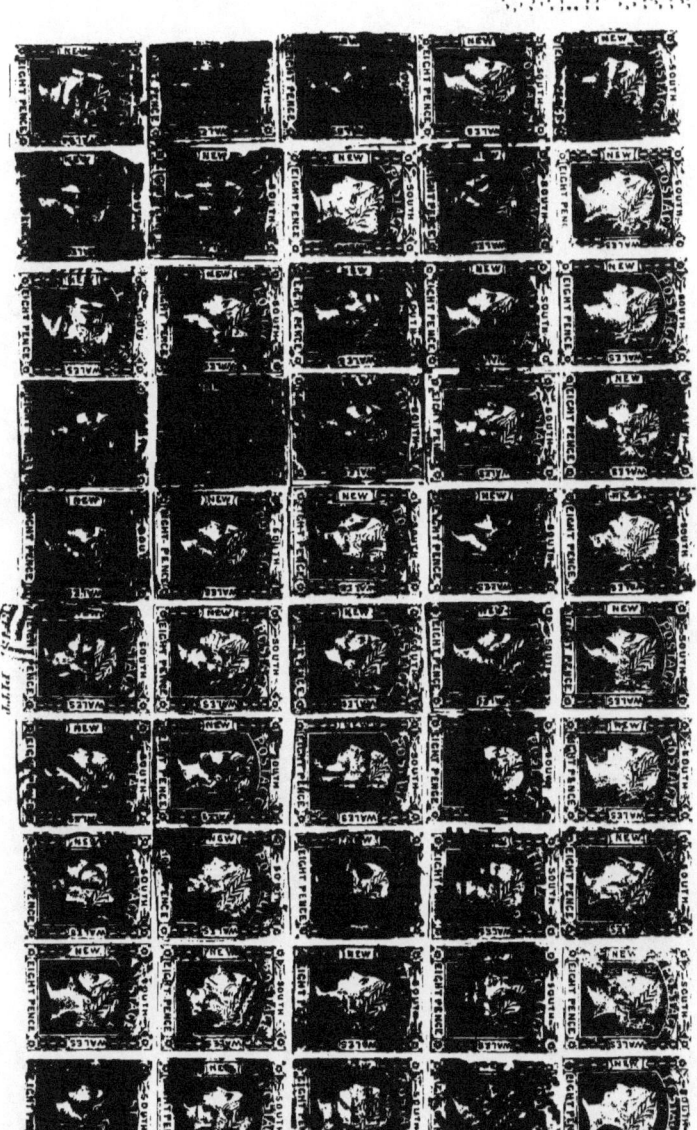

Eight Pence

One Plate.

PLATE L.

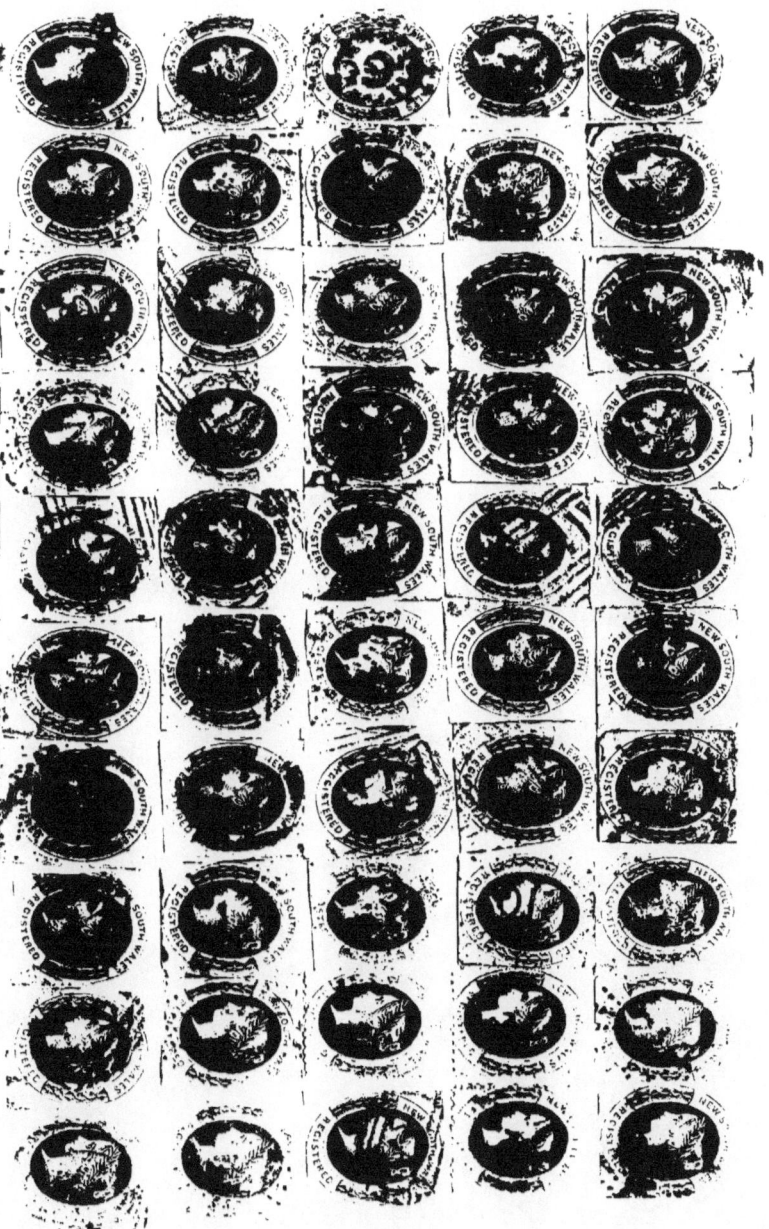

PLATE N.

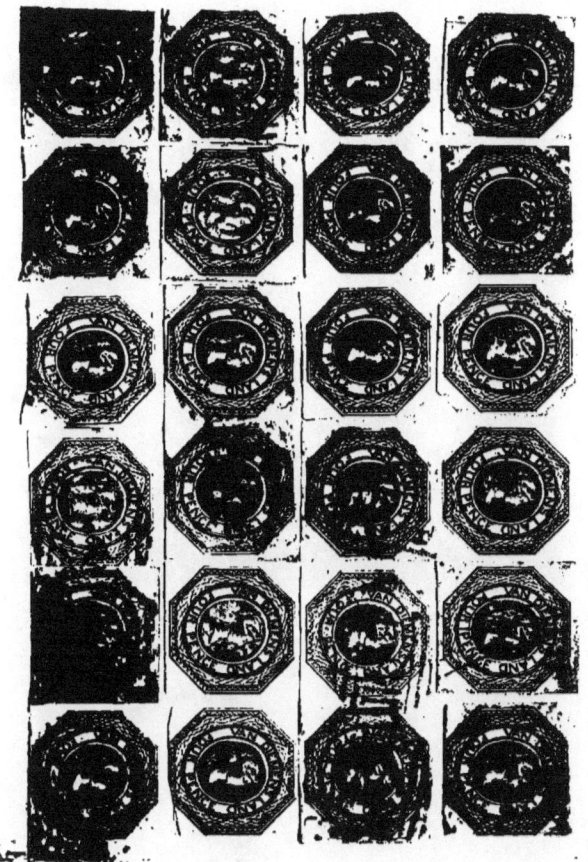

PLATE O.

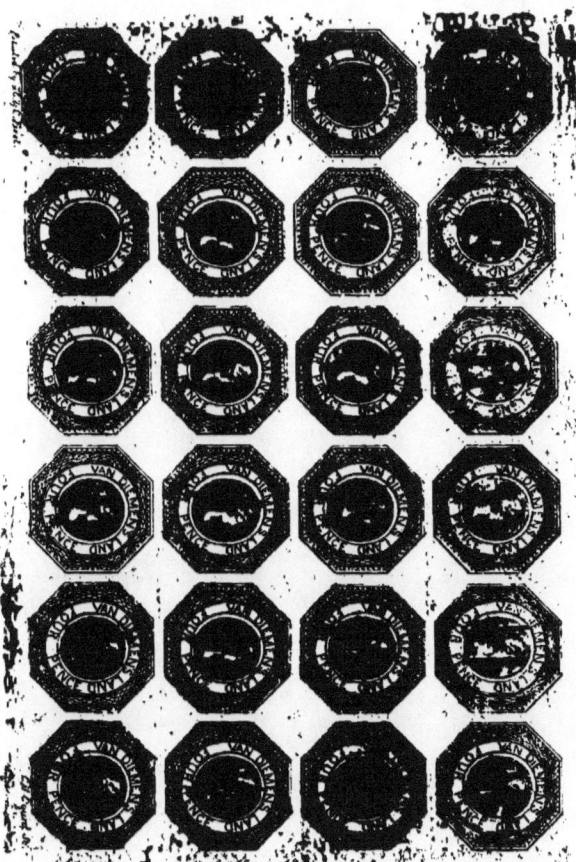

PLATE P.

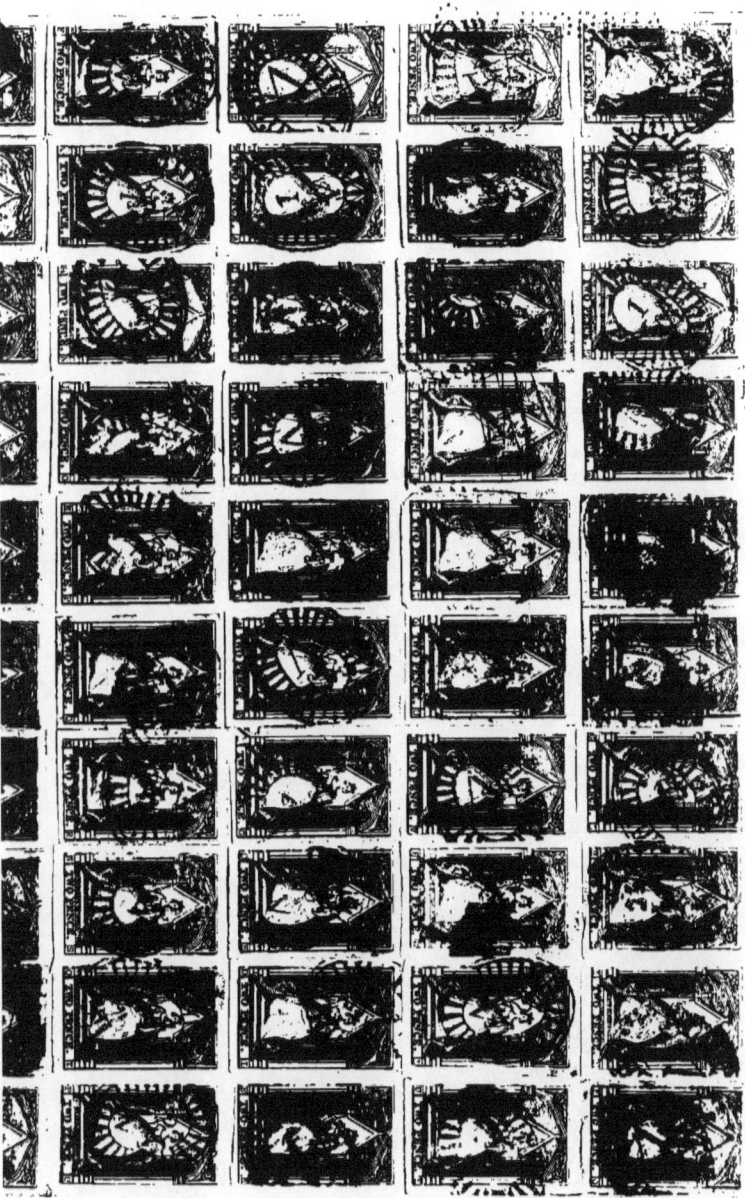

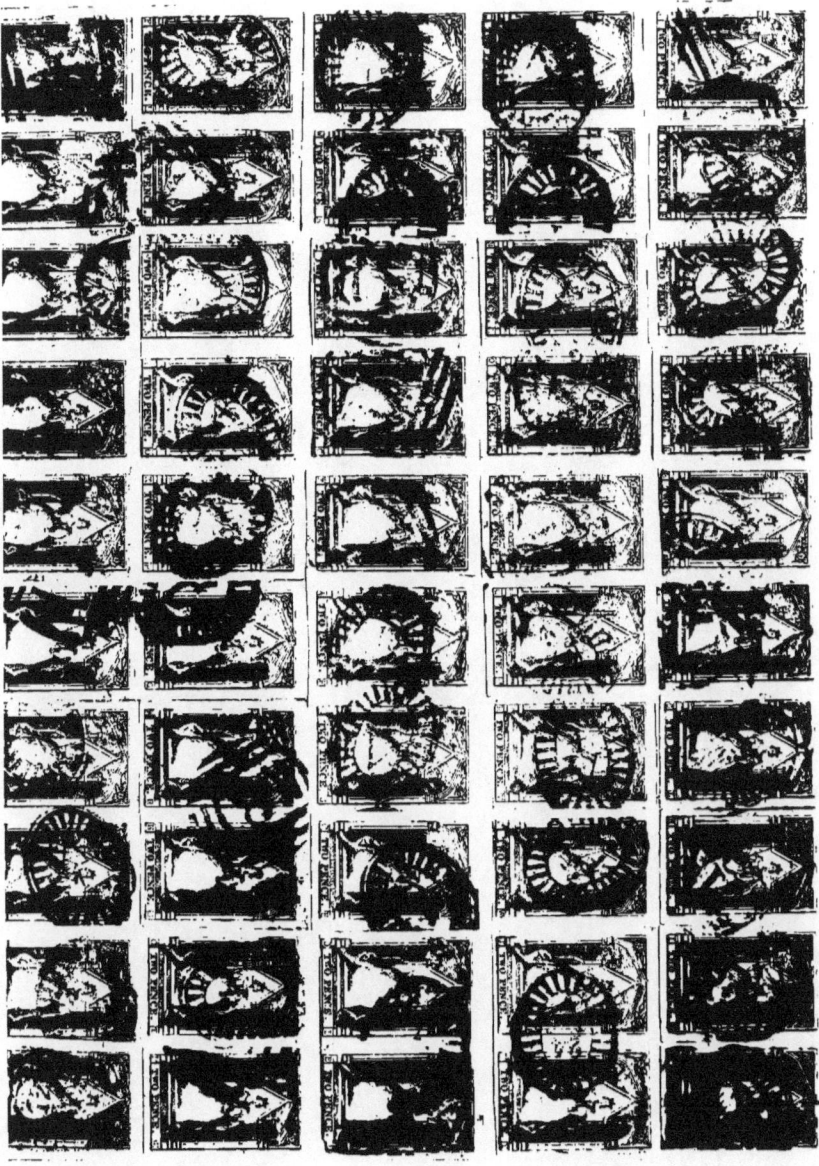

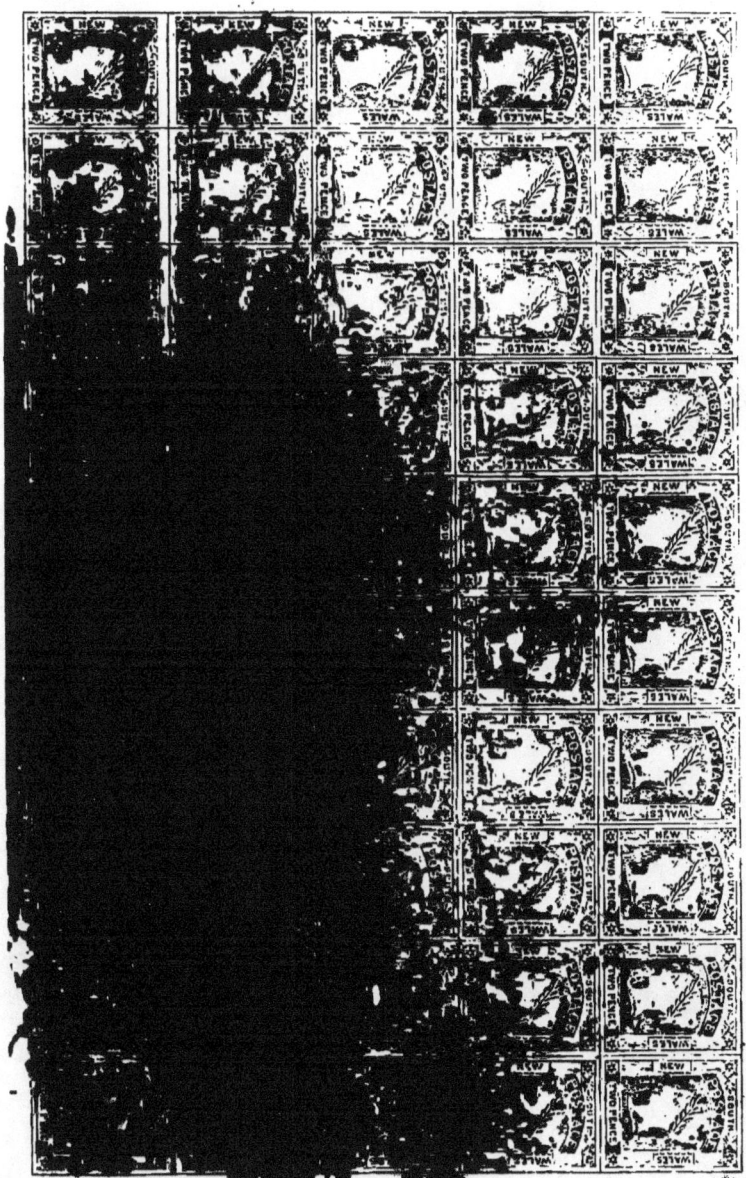

PLATE H.

PLATE K.

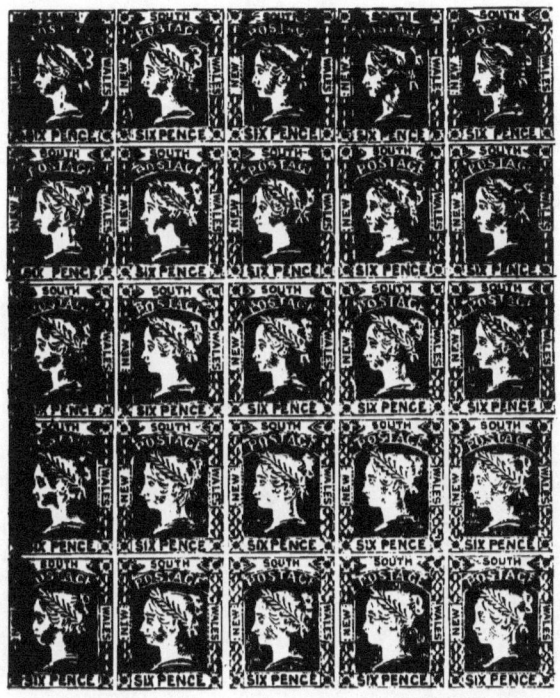

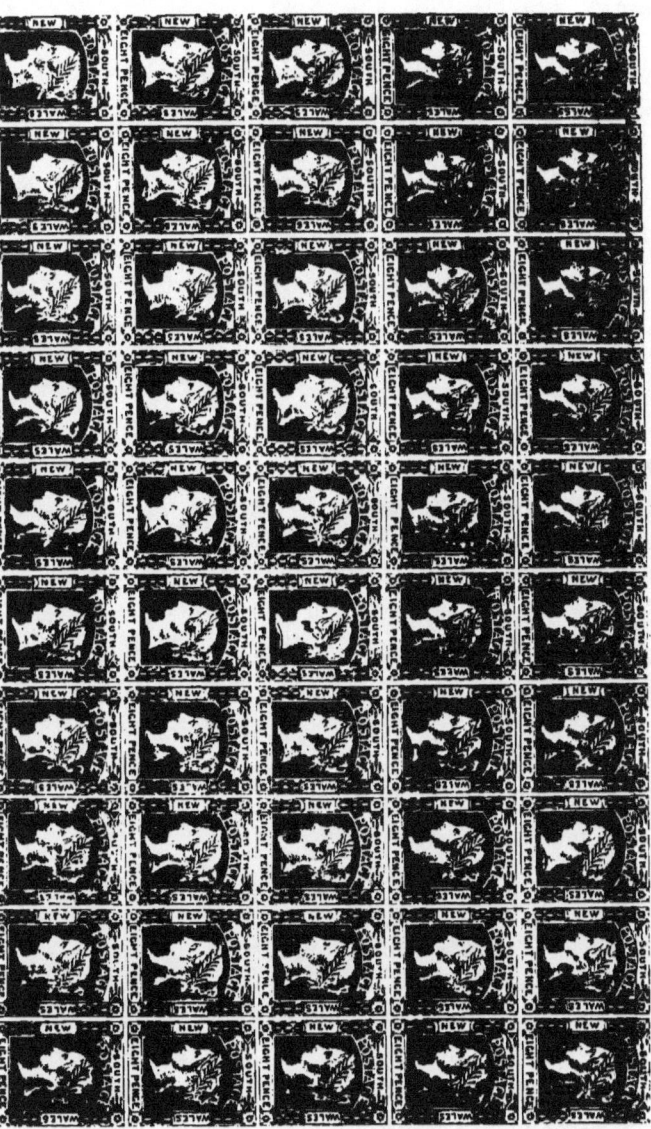

PLATE L.

ON THE EARLIER ISSUES OF NEW SOUTH WALES.

A PAPER PREPARED FOR THE PHILATELIC SOCIETY, LONDON.

By FREDERICK A. PHILBRICK, Q.C., President.

HAVING been entrusted, in conjunction with the Vice-President, to assist in the preparation of a Reference List of these stamps for the Society, and having taken part with him in investigating these issues, and joined in the many discussions which ensued as different points arose and were elucidated, it may perhaps be asked why the Society should be troubled with a second paper on the subject, more especially as the main conclusions which are embodied in the Vice-President's monograph are those arrived at by our mutual consultation and agreement.

And yet, inasmuch as the same matter never strikes two minds precisely alike, and on some points our views are not exactly in accordance, I may be excused for travelling briefly over ground already so well occupied, and adding a few remarks on different points and details which may be of interest to the Society.

Without further preface, then, I will make a few

PRELIMINARY OBSERVATIONS,

by way of introduction to my remarks on the history of these stamps.

The first discovery of Australia, by Captain Cook, in 1770, and the subsequent expedition, headed by H.M.S. *Sirius*, Captain Arthur Phillip, R.N., arriving in Botany Bay, in January, 1788, which laid the foundation of the chief town of New South Wales, are matters of general history; but so far as the present subject is concerned, it may suffice to state that in the first settlement, Port Jackson, now Sydney, a colonial Post-office, for the reception and distribution of ship and other letters, was established in a small wooden building near the Queen's Wharf. Some of the older colonists are still living who can remember this primitive post office, and Mr. Paivon, who acted as Postmaster.

In 1828 the growing importance of the colony and its increasing correspondence led to a colonial Post-office being organized on a more regular and extensive scale. Mr. James A. Raymond was appointed Postmaster-General, and the requirements of the community were met by the adoption, as far as possible, of the British Post-office system as a model.

The New South Wales colonists seem to have been an enterprising and progressive race, and the Postmaster-General was evidently a keen-sighted man of business, fully alive to what was passing in the mother country.

When the agitation for cheap uniform postage began to give promise of fruit in England, about 1838, Mr. Raymond entered into correspondence with the English Postmaster-General on the subject of the prepayment of letters posted in the colony to their ultimate destination in the United Kingdom, an arrangement which had long been desired by the colonists with a view to facilitate their home correspondence, the method of charging giving rise in practice to many complications and overcharges, besides delay and annoyance at both ends. The system adopted by the English Post-office about this period, in the Reciprocal Treaties with several of the Continental powers which secured this desirable end, was thought applicable, and strong representations were made on the existing inconveniences and the overcharges frequently made when exacting the prepayment in the colony.

The Postmaster-General replied officially, through Colonel Maberly, the Secretary to the Post-office, on 30th May, 1839, that he had not the power to grant the request, nor did he think it could be entertained, as many difficulties surrounded the subject. It may here be remarked that the effort of those interested in establishing the new system in the United Kingdom was to make prepayment to the ultimate destination compulsory in all cases, so that this agitation from the colony came at an opportune moment.

The official correspondence appears to have rested here till after the Penny Inland Postage had got well into work in the United Kingdom, when, in February, 1841, Mr. Raymond again returned to the subject, and wrote adverting to the recent postal changes in England, and expressing a desire for legislation to permit of prepayment of all letters and packets forwarded by post in full both for land and ship carriage, and including delivery to the *addressee*, or if the authorities should not see their way to accord these privileges, then that they would permit the British stamps to be exported to Sydney and there sold, so as to ensure free delivery in Great Britain.

This proposal, after being referred to the Treasury, met with disfavour; indeed, the Treasury are reported to have objected to the use of postage stamps upon letters forwarded to England from the colonies or other parts abroad. Fortunately these views no longer prevail, and we see the Chairman of the Board of Inland Revenue, at the Jubilee gathering of the department in 1887, mentioning with complacency the magnitude and extent both of the inland, colonial, and foreign postage of Great Britain, and dwelling with pride on the immense sums represented by the adhesive stamps distributed through the Post-offices both here and abroad.

It was not until the year 1849 that the difficulties and official reluctance were overcome, and the desired system of prepayment by stamps brought within measurable distance. A Select Committee was appointed by the Legislative Council of New South Wales, and in conformity to the report of that committee, an Act was passed in that year to establish a uniform rate of postage, and to consolidate and amend the law for the conveyance and postage of letters. The date fixed for the commencement of this new system was 1st January, 1850. The rates fixed for letters of half ounce weight, including delivery, were as follows:

        Within the town where posted   .   .   . One Penny.
        Within the colony   .   .   .   . Two Pence.
        To Great Britain .   .   .   . Three Pence,

and increasing proportionately, according to weight; and, as will be seen when the stamps issued 1st January, 1850, come to be treated of, the passing of this Act led to the first creation of stamps for the colony. But long prior to this event the Postmaster-General had anticipated the public requirements by the creation and issue of a special stamp for the town of Sydney to frank delivery of letters within the postal limits of the town. We have therefore a purely local official issue which preceded the service of stamps for the colony, an occurrence almost unprecedented in philatelic history, but bearing some analogy to the One Penny and Two Pence temporary envelopes issued in England for the use of the Houses of Lords and Commons in anticipation of the general issue of May, 1840. It will be remarked, however, that the energy and perseverance of Mr. Raymond were in advance of the English officials, who with diffident steps actually managed to devise an issue restricted to certain favoured classes of the community, nor then till *after* the general post rates had been reduced and the new system formally sanctioned by Act of the Legislature, whereas the Postmaster-General of New South Wales prevailed on the colonial Governor, Sir George Gipps, to authorise an envelope for general use in the town of Sydney long before any postage stamps were authorised for public use in the colony or indeed elsewhere. This issue I will now describe.

Sydney Embossed Stamp of 1838.

The official notification was dated 1st November, 1838, and appeared in the *Government Gazette* of the 3rd November following. As varying dates have been assigned, it may be well to set the question at final rest by reprinting the announcement:

"GENERAL POST OFFICE, SYDNEY,
"1st November, 1838.

"Whereas it has been considered that by transmitting letters, invitations, notices, bills, &c., under stamped or Post-office covers, the delivery thereof would be much expedited, by avoiding the delay consequent on the letter carriers awaiting payment, His Excellency the Governor, with this view, and in order to effect a reduction of postage on such communications intended for delivery within the limits of the town of Sydney, has been pleased to sanction their transmission under envelopes, which may be obtained at the General Post-office on payment of one shilling and threepence per dozen, including all charges for paper and delivery. This arrangement is not intended to suspend or interfere with the present Twopenny post delivery, which will proceed in all respects as heretofore. JAMES RAYMOND, *Postmaster-General.*"

This decisively settles all dispute as to date of issue, and shows the exact nature of the information contained in a brief notice I wrote in the *Stamp Collector's Magazine*, vol. xii. p. 5. It is there stated that, in the *Gazette* for 1838, the authority to issue this cover would be found, but no further date or identification was given by me.

The assumption by the writer of the notice on p. 6 *ante*, that I was "misinformed as to the date," is thus shown to be erroneous, and need not be further referred to, except to class it in the already large list of unwarranted inferences which the most acute may be excused for deducing in a subject like the present. The date of 1843 on the specimen I referred to is also shown to be perfectly possible, and it is odd that, when the point I was dealing with was the very question of a figure being an 8 or a 3, it should be supposed by such competent authorities as our respected Vice-President and Secretary that I had blundered and confounded the two. It is satisfactory to have the unchallengeable authority of the official document to fix a date which might *à priori* be deemed so highly improbable as to be almost impossible, and to vindicate for the Post-office of Sydney the honour of first issuing embossed penny postage covers.

The issue being thus authorised, a very ready mode of preparing the required "stamped or Post-office covers". or "envelopes" was adopted. The Post-office seal was utilized, and impressions struck from it by a letter or rather seal press on half sheets of paper foolscap size. No colour being used, the embossing was in white relief only. Design: The Royal Arms, Crest, and Supporters, with motto "*Dieu et mon droit*," under which is "SYDNEY" in capitals, all in a circular ring inscribed in capitals, T. "GENERAL POST-OFFICE." B. "NEW SOUTH WALES." The outer circle measures 29 millimetres in diameter, and the stamp was impressed about the centre of the upper part of the half sheet when folded as an envelope.

The paper used was white wove of ordinary thickness, and blue laid, the sheet measuring $8\frac{1}{2} \times 11\frac{3}{16}$ inches. Examples are found laid both vertically and horizontally. Inasmuch as some fastening—sealing-wax or gum—had necessarily to be used, the contrivance was not particularly handy; and although the price (1s. 3d. per dozen) was cheaper than the Two Pence fee paid on delivery of letters in the town, the public did not greatly appreciate Mr. Raymond's efforts.

To stimulate the adoption of these covers a reduction in price was made in 1841 to 1s. per dozen or 8s. per hundred, as appears by the subjoined notice:

NEW SOUTH WALES.

"GENERAL POST OFFICE, SYDNEY,
"4th January, 1841.
"STAMPED COVERS.

"By a notice from this office, dated 1st November, 1838, it was signified that stamped covers might from that time be obtained, at a charge of 1s. 3d. per dozen, in which to envelope letters, which being posted in Sydney would exempt such letters from any further charge to the full limits of the Twopenny post delivery. His Excellency the Governor now, with a view still further to extend this accommodation, has been pleased to sanction a reduction of the charge to 1s. per dozen, or 8s. per 100; and stamps or covers may in future be obtained at this rate, in any number, upon application at this office.

"JAMES RAYMOND, *Postmaster-General.*"

But still the circulation remained restricted, and these covers were never popular.

The example bearing postmark of 11th October, 1843, which was in my collection, was part of an envelope, so that in addition to the covers above referred to, the seal must have been impressed on envelopes, though probably this was but rarely done.

Major Evans recently reported to the *Philatelic Record* that a correspondent of his in Sydney possesses an envelope, 5¼ × 2½ inches, with the above stamp embossed. Unfortunately my copy was cut, so that it was not possible to ascertain the size of the envelope. The conjecture was hazarded in the *Record* that the envelope Major Evans refers to was made out of a stamped sheet. This is possible, and collectors ought to be on their guard against any such. But in the case of my own specimen the envelope had evidently been made *before* it was put under the die, as the impression went through the two thicknesses of paper as the envelope was folded, and the lines of the *vergeures*, for it was on laid paper, were on the slant (*à biais*), as usual with envelopes on laid paper.

There is little more to add to the preceding to complete this notice, save to advert to the fact that the forgers have recently produced copies in which the word *Sydney* is properly spelt, and the stamp so well imitated that very great circumspection is needed, and reference should be made to an undoubted original copy, if accessible, before pronouncing in favour of any specimen.

The Colonial Engraved Stamps.

No collector of any experience will deny that special interest has always attached to these. The Vice-President has enumerated some of the most eminent philatelists who have made them the object of particular investigation. To these names ought to be added that of M. Georges Herpin, of Paris, one of the pioneers of the science, who possessed in a remarkable degree that intuitive perception which was so prominently developed in the late Mr. E. L. Pemberton; of M. Hanciau, of Brussels, who has also rendered great assistance, both in connection with *Le Timbre-Poste* and by his critical acumen; and of the late M. Pauwels, of Torquay. But first and foremost the name of Pemberton stands undisputed. To his unrivalled sagacity and almost unerring instinct the science is indebted for the first real progress made in the investigation.

The stamps of New South Wales, especially the Sydney views, possessed great attractions for his enquiring and analytical bent of mind; and when, after many years collecting, I had succeeded in getting together a fair number of specimens, we jointly examined, noted, and arranged them according to the best of our then information. Just about that period (1868-9) Mr. Pemberton had undertaken the task of preparing a reference list, in collaboration with Mr. Erskine, of Somerset House, who was a patient and indefatigable collector, devoting his attention exclusively to the Australian Colonies and New Zealand.

At that time of day the importance of establishing and reconstructing the plates, and the relative positions of the stamps thereon, had not made itself apparent. The more advanced collectors were chiefly occupied with questions of watermark and perforations, and I well remember the feelings of surprise with which I first saw, in a Belgian collection, a successful attempt to assemble and place a complete sheet of the forty stamps of the Philippines 10 c. (1854-5). Nor was I then prescient enough to divine the valuable aid which was hereafter to be afforded to philatelic investigations by what was then thought mere ostentatious collecting of a valuable stamp in large numbers. Neither did Mr. Pemberton fully appreciate the truer view until near the close of his career; but had he been longer spared, no one would more zealously or keenly have prosecuted the line of investigation thus opened.

The remarkable results it has achieved in the construction of the entire plates, and the service thus rendered to the history of the science, cannot well be over-estimated; nor is it any reflection on the value of this method of procedure that after the sheet of the One Penny (Sydney views) had been built up and constructed by a tedious process, and many ineffectual trials, that an entire proof-sheet, *with the edges intact*, supplying the full information so painstakingly sought for, should be found, and afford a confirmation, if such were needed, of the accuracy of the conclusions arrived at.

But to revert for a moment to earlier history. Soon after the formation of this Society, Mr. Pemberton obtained from our first President, Sir Daniel Cooper, Bart., a print of the Blue Book containing the proceedings of the Postal Committee, which sat at Sydney in 1849. From this resulted, as has been already mentioned, the discovery of the embossed cover for the town of Sydney; and from it Mr. Pemberton extracted all the passages he thought would assist in preparing an article or monograph on these stamps.

Sir Daniel Cooper gave this book, with such notes and information as he had got, to Mr. Joannis, the then Secretary, that a *précis* might be made to form the basis of a paper to be read before the Society. Unfortunately the gentleman to whom the Secretary confided that duty died before it was completed; and when the President saw the MS., he found it was too meagre for présentation, and therefore determined to let it stand over for future revision.

Soon after this Mr. Ferrary became the possessor of Sir Daniel Cooper's collection, and such notes and information as then were in his possession were, in 1878, given by Sir Daniel to Dr. Legrand, who doubtless found them of service when writing his excellent articles.

After Mr. Pemberton's death careful search was made among his papers for any notes or MS., but without success, and the subject remained nearly in *statu quo* till, in more recent times, the attention of MM. Caillebotte was drawn to it in collecting the varieties on the plates; and the Society, in compiling its Reference Lists, charged the Vice-President and myself with the duty, if possible, of prosecuting these investigations to some definite conclusion.

Sir Daniel Cooper wrote me, that Mr. Pemberton had from him a "large book of mine," containing Reports of the Legislative Council of New South Wales, with "evidence and report of the Select Committee on Postage Stamps, which gave all the particulars about the first set of views of Sydney." This book cannot now be traced; but if it only contained what its description states, our labours would have been facilitated in a marked degree, and most likely many points now open to conjecture finally resolved. In default of these materials, Sir Daniel Cooper has most obligingly furnished me with such information as he had at command.

One naturally desired to consult the file of the *Government Gazette* for the colony, at the office of the Agent-General of the New South Wales Government. The series there commences in 1863. At the Colonial Office there are no copies; while those who resort to the library at the British Museum will find the file of the *Gazette*, from (say) 1848–56, the period within which all useful information is likely to occur, fragmentary and imperfect.

Before referring to such details as have been obtained from the *Gazette*, I may mention an event in my early collecting days which made a strong impression on my mind. But one or two unused copies of Sydney views were known to exist in English collections—the ordinary specimens were, as we but too well know, heavily defaced in the post—when a friend casually informed me that a small dealer in the City had a strip of eight unused Sydney Penny stamps, and was asking the (then) enormous price of 20s. each, or £8 for the strip. On hurrying to the shop, I found but two were left—an unsevered pair from the top row, margins and gum intact—and these I fortunately secured. They were fine copies of the coarsely-engraved type on thick bluish paper. No enquiry I could make led to any information as to the whereabouts of the other six; but the vendor (Mrs. Goodwin) spoke of them all as one "strip;" and when, some few years afterwards, I questioned her as to the precise number in the row, she was positive they were all in one horizontal row (we now know this was not correct). Subsequently, in discussing this with Mr. Pemberton, he found a note of a strip of four, vertically joined, with indications of another above the top one. This gave us five vertically (which we now know is correct). In this way we fell into the error of supposing there were eight and not five stamps to the row; forty and not twenty-five to the sheet.

To return from this digression, it will be convenient here to tabulate the dates and summarize such details as have been collated from the *Government Gazette*, and notes taken, in 1870, of correspondence preserved in the Colonial Secretary's office, Sydney.

12th October,	1849.	Act of Council, directing stamps to be ready on 1st Jan., 1850.
25th December, 1849.		*Gazette* Notice. 1d., 2d., and 3d. stamps would be ready for issue on 1st January, and fixing postal rates.
11th March,	1851.	Authority given to J. C. C. Boyd and A. H. Manning to destroy damaged postage stamps.
2nd April,	1851.	Governor's approval of repair of plates of the Two Penny stamps.
24th July,	1851.	*Gazette* Notice, that new plate for the 2d., with head of Queen, had been engraved, and would be issued to the public immediately.
31st July,	1851.	Governor's approval of 2s. 6d. per 1000 to printer for printing stamps, he finding colours, oil, gum, &c.
18th December, 1851.		Governor returning steel plate of 1d. (head) approved for printing, and ordering inspection of stamps, and old plate to be defaced (view).
23rd December, 1851.		*Gazette* Notice. 1d. stamps (heads) will be immediately issued.
24th January, 1852.		That sheet of 1d. stamps bearing Governor-General's approval was in Colonial Secretary's office.
13th February, 1852.		Board appointed to destroy damaged stamps.
22nd February, 1852.		John Carmichael to Inspector, should he commence engraving 6d. stamp.
1st March,	1852.	Same, repeating request.
13th March,	1852.	Governor approved of a 6d. stamp, and thought it had better be printed in a distinct colour.
16th March,	1852.	Authority to Carmichael to engrave 6d. stamp on copper plate, at cost of £20.
30th April,	1852.	Proclamation-Plate of 6d. had been provided, of same design as 1d. and 2d. "now in use," and would be issued immediately.
8th May,	1852.	6d. plate returned to Inspector, with Governor-General's approval.
8th November, 1852.		Memorandum as to a cancelling-stamp received from Carruthers, suggesting it be tried on damaged stamps.
1st December, 1852.		Colonial Secretary returns to Inspector of Stamps plate of 3d. (head), approved by Governor-General, but stating it was inferior in execution to previous plates of same artist (Carmichael); order to destroy old plate (view).
7th December, 1852.		*Gazette* Notice, that plate of 3d. (Queen's head) had been prepared, and would be issued immediately.
11th December, 1852.		Relating to quality of paper on which stamps were printed.
16th May,	1853.	Colonial Secretary returns to Inspector plate of 8d., approved by Governor-General.
16th May,	1853.	*Gazette* Notice. 8d. would be issued immediately.
27th July,	1853.	Invoice, materials, &c., for printing postage stamps, Perkins, Bacon, and Co., for £449 7s. 1d.
8th August,	1853.	Governor-General approves employment of H. C. Jervis to engrave a new plate for 2d. stamps on copper, as nearly as possible similar to the steel *plates* now in use, at expense of £40, and also to repair the steel plates for £40.
3rd December, 1853.		Colonial Secretary encloses invoice of postage stamps, plates, paper, press, &c., shipped per *Woolloomolloo*.

Although this list is somewhat lengthy, it relates almost entirely to the laureated heads; the references to the earlier series are very scanty.

Issue of 1st January, 1850.

This well known series of three values—One Penny, Two Pence, and Three Pence—known as that of the Views of Sydney, was supplied to the General Post-office by Robert Clayton, of Sydney, under a contract with that department to furnish press dies and plates, for the sum of £36. The stamps were engraved on copper plate, each stamp separately, in line engraving (*taille-douce*), the first and last by Clayton himself, and the Two Pence by his son-in-law, Mason, the latter by his work showing himself much the more skilful engraver of the two. The blocks of the One Penny and Three Pence each contained twenty-five stamps, in five rows of five stamps each, measuring about 111 mm. by 125 mm. There was nothing else upon the plate but the block of stamps themselves. The plate of the Two Pence contained twenty-four stamps, arranged in two horizontal rows of twelve each, divided from each other by plain vertical lines, and the horizontal rows having a similar line above and below, forming a frame to the whole block; while a like line separated the two rows.

The design being cut in sunken lines into the copper plate, the thick ink of the impression, used in the earlier course of the series particularly, was deposited on the surface of the paper, and formed a thick incrustation, from which it may be rubbed or scratched. In this method of printing the paper is necessarily wetted, and printed on while damp; so that after it becomes dry any inequality in the make of the paper causes an uneven shrinkage, and hence variations in size of the stamps may be found, which might lead to a false inference, unless the true cause be borne in mind.

The size of the One Penny stamps is 20 by not quite 24 mm.; the copper-plate measures 141 × 130 mm.

Design: Besides referring to the paper of the Vice-President (*ante* pp. 11, 12), I wish to call marked attention to the circular inscription proclaiming the device to be the seal of the colony. The stamps were imperforate, and the gum usually thick and of a deep brown colour. After these general observations, I will deal separately with each value.

In Jewitt's *Life of Josiah Wedgwood* it is stated that some clay from Australia was sent home to him, with which he modelled a medallion, emblematic of the new settlement. A cast having been sent out, the design was chosen for the colonial seal.

"It represents a figure of Hope addressing three emblematic figures, Peace, Art, and Labour, on the shore of Sydney Cove, a ship, a few houses, and a church being in the background. Underneath is the word *Etruria*, the well-known name of Wedgwood's pottery in Staffordshire, and the date 1789."

The Anchor of Hope leads to the supposition that a chain cable is intended to be represented, rather than fetters or gyves. The stigma of convicts must be removed from the figures of Peace, Art, and Labour; while the significance of the fields, trees, flocks, and bees, and the propriety of the bale of wool as allegorical of the staple product of the colony, may still bear their usual interpretation.

Those desirous of further details may consult a letter from "Fentonia," which appeared in the *Stamp Collector's Magazine*, vol. vii. p. 191 (December, 1869).

One Penny.

There can be no question that the type, as originally issued, was that from the finely-engraved plate. This seems clearly established by the Vice-President's arguments, to which may be added that the information collected by Mr. Pemberton and his own opinion alike agreed in this result. One striking fact is, that whereas all three values were issued simultaneously, on 1st January, 1850, and therefore the paper may be reasonably supposed to be the same in all the values, no other complete set of all three can be found on one kind of paper. This finely-engraved type consequently belongs to that set which was first issued. To my mind this argument is conclusive. Further, this plate shows no clouds. The lines for them could be added to a copper plate, but could not well be removed from it. In the coarsely-engraved plate clouds appear on all save one of the stamps (No. 15 on the plate), to which the engraver no doubt forgot to make the addition when at work on the retouch.

Retouch of the One Penny.—It equally clearly follows from the above that the coarsely-engraved plate must have been a retouch from the former, once the identity of the two is established. The remarks of the Vice-President (*ante* pp. 14–16) must be taken to represent our joint views on this.

The questions of when and by whom this retouch was done remain for solution. I can offer no trustworthy information. The touch of the burin does not look like Mason's handiwork, nor indeed does it resemble Clayton's; but it bears a strong family likeness to the second plate of the Two Pence. The period when the plate required to be retouched, of course, depended on the wear and tear to which it was subjected. And on this, it must be borne in mind, that though the One Penny was the rate for postage within the limits of a town, yet the then colony of New South Wales comprised not only New South Wales as now existing, but also Victoria, separated from the parent colony 15th July, 1851, and Queensland, separated in December, 1859. This remark has also to be remembered when the necessity for renewal of the plates of the Two Pence is under consideration.

The order given to deface the old plate of the One Penny (view) when the One Penny (laureated head) was prepared, on 18th December, 1851, gives nearly two years for the duration of the former plate in its two states; and the relative plentifulness of specimens of the later state appears to make the date of the Vice-President—August, 1850—probably near the mark for the retouch.

On the retouched plate the engraver omitted to insert lines for the clouds in the fifteenth stamp; in the eighth stamp the hill is left unshaded; and in the seventh stamp, though the hill is shaded, the trees are omitted. These three varieties are the more prominent departures from the general type.

To what has been stated on the various papers employed at different times I entirely subscribe, merely adding that there is a distinction to be drawn between *ribbed* and *laid* paper. The former shows the inequalities on its surface, and on being held to the light is of a uniform thickness; the latter has less pulp where the lines of the wires come, but presents generally a smooth surface to the eye.

I have never seen or heard of the finely-engraved One Penny on *true* laid paper; on the finely-ribbed paper it is exceedingly rare. The coarsely-engraved One Penny is found on *true* laid paper of stoutish texture. In some examples of stamps on this paper fragments of the watermark of Britannia, so common on old-fashioned foolscap, are to be met with, as well as other watermarks, which were in the paper used, no doubt on an emergency, for printing the stamps. Large double-lined Roman capitals are also sometimes seen; these formed portions of some legend. On a square block of four copies of the Two Pence, Plate III. (the Vice-President's first retouch), on stout white laid paper, formerly in the collection of Mr. Burnett, the letters "ERS" are plainly visible, extending through several stamps. All the above and similar marks, letters, and devices, are simply what are known as *marques de la fabrique* of the paper, and have no philatelic significance.

I can quite confirm the statements of the Vice-President as to the rarity of this stamp, first state of plate, on the ribbed paper.

PROOFS AND ESSAYS OF THE ONE PENNY.

There remain to be considered the above.

Proofs.—Most first-rate collections can boast of one or more specimens of the first state of the One Penny, clearly and beautifully printed on a dull buff, or nearly flesh, toned paper. The extreme care used in striking these impressions led me minutely to examine my own copies, and all I was able to see elsewhere, and I have never met with one showing any trace of gum having been originally applied to the reverse. The shade of red is peculiar, one not to be found on any other stamps of this value, used or unused. Those to which I am referring are distinguishable at a glance, and are evidently taken before the plate had suffered the slightest trace of wear. The conclusion I drew therefore was, they were *proof* impressions, and I was fortified by the unhesitating verdict of Mr. Pemberton to the same effect. It is known proofs were struck off, in deep myrtle-green, from the plate of the Three

Pence, which contributes to render the supposition that these are proofs more plausible. No other proofs of the One Penny are known to me.

Essays.—In *The New South Wales Stamp Collector's Magazine*, No. 2. (April, 1880), Mr. Edward Buckley describes an essay in the possession of the New South Wales Postal Department as follows :

"View of Sydney, One Penny, with figures in foreground, which is in dashed lines, as in the ordinary types; bale not inscribed; on the hill two trees, and lower down a figure; hill most minutely shaded; houses touching, no clouds. Inscription, '*Sic fortis Etruria crevit*' (the '*ria*' in Etruria so crowded as to look like '*rm*'), within plain circle inscribed 'SEGILLUM (*sic*) NOV, CAMB, AUST.' In top corners Maltese cross, with radiating stars over the centres; between them the word 'POSTAGE;' tops of the letters 'P,' 'A,' and 'E' in a line, all the same size; 'O' and 'G' smaller, and 'T' decidedly larger. In bottom left-hand corner 'N,' and in the right 'L,' between them the words 'ONE PENNY.' Rough border at sides, between the centre circle and stars at top, or letters at bottom. Plain block ground. Printed on thin wove paper, with the old gum on the part not attached to the sheet; colour, soft vermilion (probably toned with age). NOTE.—The inscription 'ONE PENNY' has been affixed in its place, a part of the stamp having been cut away for its reception; but the colour of the printing is identical."

From this not over lucid description, it appears as if some one (in the Post-office?) had been experimenting in the formation of a new stamp, by cutting up and piecing together parts of others. Not having seen the specimen described, this can, at most, be a conjecture on my part. The bottom lettering—'N,' 'L'—does not correspond, however, with any part of a stamp I am acquainted with, and whence those letters came, or what they mean, is to me incomprehensible.*

In addition to the foregoing, there are certain lithographed stamps, described by Sir Daniel Cooper in the paper he read before the Society 29th May, 1869. They certainly are not from a wood block, nor do they look as if reproduced by a transfer from a wood engraving. They are coarse in execution, and in general design like the stamp issued, save that the spandrels are filled in with a pattern of overlapping scale-work.

The paper is deep-toned yellow wove, and thin; no watermark. The colour of the impression, full soft vermilion; not gummed. The row contained several stamps, all identical, showing that by 1849 the Colonial lithographers knew enough of their business to produce a repetition of the same design, line for line like the original. An opinion, broached when these essays first came to light, that they were hurriedly prepared, to ensure a supply of One Penny stamps being ready by 1st January, 1850, seems likely to be correct; but as a stock from the engraved plate was prepared in time, these lithographs were relegated to the category of stamps intended for but never actually put into use.

Whatever be the fact, neither the public nor collectors have any reason other than for thankfulness that these stamps never served postal purposes.

According to Sir Daniel Cooper, these lithographs appear to be lithographic transfers by Clayton, from which I infer Sir Daniel draws this conclusion from the appearance of the essays themselves. I must own I should have hesitated before so doing.

With respect to the wood-engraved stamps, so circumstantially described by Mr. Calvert, it is difficult to suppose his memory could be so treacherous as to induce him to believe he had engraved eight of Well's block drawings with his own hand, unless he had really done so. These separate engravings must necessarily have varied from each other, thus showing that the essays lastly described cannot be those mentioned by Mr. Calvert. No copy appears to exist in the Colonial Post-office, indeed the existence of one anywhere has yet to be shown. Meanwhile the only information we possess is that afforded through Mr. Calvert's statements communicated to the Vice-President. (*Ante* p. 10.)

* They do not correspond with the initials of any of the engravers employed, so far as we are acquainted with their names. A Mr. Nicholas Nelson was an assistant for many years in the Sydney Post-office; but I have not been able to trace any name there commencing with "L" about this period.

The Two Pence.

The plate first constructed and printed from was a copper plate, consisting of twenty-four stamps, arranged in two rows of twelve, each stamp being framed by a plain line. Robert Clayton, who had obtained the order for the plates of the three values, employed Mason, his son-in-law, to assist him, and entrusted him to engrave the plate for the Two Pence. The stamps from the plate produced by Mason are easily recognisable, the spandrels being filled in with vertical lines, whereas in all other plates of this value the lines in the spandrels are horizontal.

There can be no question that this vertical-lined plate was that first produced, from which the stamps issued 1st January, 1850, were printed.

In execution as well as design it is far the best of the Sydney views; indeed, the vignettes, as seen in clear copies, are highly creditable proofs of the engraver's skill. It is almost ungracious to say they are too fine and elaborate for the rough usage to which this plate was inevitably destined.

The arrangement of the twenty-four types on the plate has been satisfactorily established by the labours of the Vice-President and MM. Caillebotte.

On examining the entire sheet, it will be seen that in Nos. 1 to 5 and 9 to 12 there are no trees, and in No. 19 the lines in the spandrels are wavy upon oblique. These constitute the most salient varieties in the engraving.

The paper first adopted was without watermark, wove, soft in texture, and yellow in tone. To this last quality is chiefly due the bronzy-green so often seen, although want of practice in compounding the pigments may partly be the cause that the original blue has gone off to a sort of sea-green shade. When a fresh, bright copy is found, the blue is clear and distinct. Such specimens are unluckily few and far between.

Owing to the fine work of the engraving, and the demand for this value in service, the plate rapidly degenerated, and was retouched (or repaired) in the early part of 1850, most likely by Clayton or some of his assistants. The period is sufficiently proved by the specimen mentioned by the Vice-President, postmarked 24th February of that year. The best researches we have been able to make give retouched stamps from the lower row only, and we have come to the conclusion that such work as was then done on the plate did not extend to the upper row.

It is on this retouched plate that the various double-ruled lines of the external frame, to explain the presence of which has caused so much embarrassment, occur.

We start with the fact, that to the twenty-four known types every known copy of this value, vertical-lined plate, can be referred, either on the original or the retouched plate. It follows that no other vertical-lined plate was printed from. Whence then these lines?

After the best consideration I can give, and bearing in mind the stress there was for this value, and the wear on the current plate, I have come to the conclusion that when the engraver set about his work, his first idea was to engrave on the plate another row of stamps, above the existing top row; that he began to mark the spaces out in which to engrave them; but before he had completed the lines of these compartments, it occurred to him that the press was not large enough to print from a plate of the size which this addition would cause. It will be remembered that the contract price of £36 included "press, dies, and plates," which is a tolerably sure indication that the press was not of very large dimensions; and it is inconceivable the engraver should have begun to rule the lines if the copper plate itself was not large enough to take, at least, one other row of stamps. It may also equally well be supposed that some flaw or obstacle in the part he had begun to manipulate diverted him from his purpose, and caused the attempt to put more stamps on the plate to be given up; or he may have despaired of producing work sufficiently good to pass side by side with the old stamps without challenging objection. Another not impossible suggestion is, that having commenced to rule the lines, the old plate was found so defective that it was judged better to begin with a new plate altogether.

Amongst these various conjectures, each must take that which best coincides with his ideas, unless he can form a more plausible theory for himself. But whatever be the view adopted, I think the fact will be found to remain, that to an attempted extension of the plate the first set of these lines is due.

As pointed out by the Vice-President in his remarks on Mr. W. T. Wilson's criticism, this by no means explains the whole difficulty; for the plate evidently was put to press in different states of these lines; that is, not only after some had been added to the original plate, but after these additions had themselves been altered or effaced, and others re-drawn in their stead. As pointed out, a line can be sunk on a copper plate by way of addition to an engraving already cut thereon; and by a comparatively simple process a straight line can be filled up, and the plate printed from, without showing traces of the effacement. Clayton and his assistants were perfectly competent to do this; and as the stamp vignettes appear to have remained untouched, and the plate was in excellent condition for printing, as these impressions show, I am driven to the conclusion that the engraver tried several successive alterations of the lines before finally discarding the idea of making an addition of stamps to this plate.

The continuous call for the plate in use, and the necessary short time it could be spared to the engraver at any one occasion, perhaps accounts for its being put to press in the intervals, a supposition which the rarity of these specimens with lines in the intermediate states tends to favour. If these remarks are well founded, these copies evidence a continued tinkering, producing successive alterations, which were all obliterated when it was decided to have an entirely fresh plate.

From careful examination of these impressions, I think all these different sets of lines were drawn on the one original plate. I am aware that on this point the views of the Vice-President (*ante* p. 24) are not quite those I entertain; but notwithstanding the weighty reasons which led him to speak of "re-duplicated" plates, deducing their existence from the various states of the ruling, I am more disposed to believe that the engraver altered and varied, and finally suppressed, the added or re-ruled lines, so that in the latest printings from Plate I. they entirely disappear, rather than that there was a second plate, so *absolutely identical* with the first as to have no point of difference whatever but these ruled lines. No process then known, save the Perkins, could have produced this result. That process was not introduced into the manufacture of these Colonial stamps, and I prefer to think that the marks of the tinkering done to the plate were obliterated by the engraver, rather than to adopt the former hypothesis. As the impressions of the latest use of the plate, not showing these re-ruled lines, are "worn to the last stage," I should not expect to be able to detect on them traces of the filling with which these added lines were effaced; and my conjecture therefore is that the intention of placing more stamps on that plate having been definitely abandoned, the printers filled up and obliterated these lines. The rarity of specimens with these ruled lines at the various stages affords some proof that these states of the plate were very short-lived.

On present information, I therefore can admit but one plate only, put to press in two states, so far as the impression of the *stamps* themselves is concerned, but showing, by the ruled lines, various ineffectual attempts to introduce more stamps on the plate. Having thus propounded my theory, I must, like the Vice-President, leave to the future research of better-informed enquirers the final resolution of this debateable and difficult question.

The duration of Plate I., from its preparation in the autumn of 1849 till the retouch in February, 1850, was barely three months. Impressions from the next plate, No. II., of this value were in use in April; so that the retouched Plate I. could have been in use but six weeks or so. It does not appear probable, looking to the worn-down state which the later impressions show, that the plate was put to press after the new one was in service; and although specimens of the Two Pence from Plate I. are nearly as common as those from Plate II., and both much more so than from any other plates, the comparative rarity of those after the retouch point to a very limited use of the plate in that state.

Plate II.—This plate, with spandrels filled in with horizontal wavy lines, is commonly known to collectors as that with the bale dated, and in this respect, while it follows Plate I., differs from all its successors.

There can be no question whatever that we have here a distinct plate. The vignettes of the separate stamps are so entirely different in feeling and execution from those on Plate I. as to strike even a superficial observer.

Arranging my remarks on the plan adopted by the Vice-President in his paper, I consider—

I. *Date.*—The *Government Gazette* here supplies no information; nor indeed is any to be expected from this source. Proclamations or public notifications, it will be seen, were not made except on the occasion of a change of type; *e.g.* to the laureated head, or of postal rates, &c. The notes taken from the correspondence in the Colonial Secretary's office are equally devoid of anything that can assist us in this investigation. We therefore were driven to rely on such data as an examination of the files of letters and cancelled specimens of the stamps might yield.

As already explained by the Vice-President, we have been peculiarly favoured in having the results of careful examination of all the leading collections of the day, English and Foreign, collated for the purposes of our investigation, besides having the continuous correspondence of the Sydney firm mentioned *ante* p. 29.

In the latter impressions from Plate II., the postmarks dated in April, 1850, are the earliest we have been able to trace. They enable us to affirm, as a fact, that Plate II. had been constructed and put to press by that period, and we infer as probable that this is about the true date. More than this we are not in a position to state. Here, as in so many other branches of our enquiries, the destruction of the records of the Sydney Post-office has greatly impeded our labours, and prevented many matters from being definitely and satisfactorily established.

II. *Design and Engraving.*—These stamps, though inferior in drawing and execution to the preceding plate, are, taking all things into account, tolerably well engraved. There is a vivacity and life in the vignettes which is wanting in their more correct and finished predecessors. The roughness is not altogether unsuggestive of the readiness and self-reliance of the people of Sydney.

Among the twenty-four varieties on the plate, one (No. 13) is distinguished by the absence of the word "CREVIT" in the motto; No. 10 by the pick and shovel being omitted; and the so-called fan ornament is peculiar in Nos. 1 and 16—in the one case anticipating that ornament as used on Plate III., but shaded on the inside; in the other the line of the circle is carried through the fan, and in No. 20 the fan has only six segments. These constitute the prominent varieties on this plate.

As remarked, I consider this an entirely fresh plate, not formed by any process of transfer or other duplication from Plate I.

But I am disposed to think that, to facilitate his task, and maintain identity of the sizes of the stamps, when the engraver of this plate sat about his work, he took off a transfer of the dividing lines and of the external edges of the vignettes from Plate I., and applied it to the surface of the new plate, thus drawing the new vignettes in precisely the same places as those of Plate I., and showing the lines in the same positions. Nothing in common within the vignettes can be traced between Plates I. and II.; while, as stated in detail *ante* p. 20, the positions and lines, even to irregularities, are absolutely identical. I will not here repeat the facts and reasoning of the Vice-President's paper, but content myself with a statement of the conclusion.

In this limited sense a transfer from Plate I. found its way on Plate II.; but I am not prepared to admit, because I do not believe in, any further use having been made of Plate I. in the preparation of that we are now discussing; and it is a use of language therefore likely to lead to misconception to speak of Plate II. as being transferred or taken from Plate I.

The engraver's name is not known. The style and touch are so similar to those of the engraver who, in August, 1850, retouched the plate of the One Penny, that we can hardly err in attributing both to the same individual, who not unlikely was one of Clayton's assistants.

III. *Paper.*—This plate is found (though rarely) printed on the soft yellowish paper in which the issue of 1st January, 1850, appeared. This we consider indicates the earliest impressions, the first dated copies—viz., those of April, 1850—being on this paper. To this succeeded a bluish wove paper of a hard, close texture; and the latest impressions are on a dull, very close, grey paper, indicating from their state that the plate was nearly worn out.

I have a note of having seen one specimen on blue laid paper; but I cannot recall another. It is evidently exceedingly rare, as the catalogues do not mention it. My note unfortunately does not enable me to trace the possessor.

IV. *Printing, Colour, &c.*—The printing was done at the Sydney Post-office for this and for all the other values, the plates being in charge of an official called the "Inspector of Stamps," and being given out by him to the printers for daily use in the press-room. We have been informed that in those cases where, from the needs of the service, the plate could not be spared for long, the engraver attended at the office to do any slight work that was wanted on the plates. This course would have an especial application to the views I have expressed about the ruled lines tried on Plate I. of the Two Pence, if adopted when the experiments with that plate were on hand.

The normal colour of the Two Pence was blue of some sort. It will not escape observation that the One Penny was in red, the Colonial Post-office thus following the Mother Country in adopting these as standard colours for the Penny and Two Penny values.

The gum was, as in the case of the lower value, thick and dark. The plates bore no engraver's name, legend, or plate number. This remark applies to all the values and plates of the Sydney views.

V. *Duration of Plate in Service.*—No stamps of the colony were ever put out of currency; consequently the lateness of a date in the postmark is no indication that the plate was in use at any specific time. We are driven therefore to look to the paper. The grey or dirty white paper, employed in the later period of this plate, is first found by us in use in the consecutive series already mentioned (September, 1850), indicating that this plate was being printed from about that period. Examples of this plate are, in my experience, the most commonly met with of all varieties of the Two Pence. They are found in every stage, from the beautifully clear impressions of early days to the worn, deteriorated copies used in the autumn of 1851. The date, 24th July, 1851, given in the *Gazette* for the issue of the succeeding type of the Two Pence (that with the laureated head of the Queen), shows that the printing of the new type began in that month, after which date it is not likely that any plates of the Two Pence (views) were put to press.

But though this plate was so freely printed, the absence of specimens (other than of the latest) on the ribbed or laid papers, which we know were used in the autumn of 1850, points strongly to a cessation of its use in the latter part of that year.

We consequently should assign a primary currency from March till about September, 1850, or a period of six months, during which this plate seems to have been the only one of this value available for use; though, looking at the numerous copies found in the later and worn state of the die, it is not unlikely that recourse may have been had to the plate subsequently. All this, however, is pure conjecture.

It remains to be added that we have not found any evidence that this plate was ever retouched or altered; consequently it could hardly have been one of the *plates* of this value directed to be repaired in April, 1851.

Plate III.—This plate and its sub-variety are usually known as "Bale without date," and may also be distinguished by the absence of the shading in the fan and of the dots on the corner stars. Pursuing a like course with this plate, I consider—

I. *Date.*—The same absence of information that we had to regret in Plate II. attends us here. The earliest date on a postmarked copy we have been able to register is on Mr. Castle's, 23rd October, 1850, which is printed on the hard grey paper.

II. *Design and Engraving.*—This plate was also, in my opinion, engraved on an entirely distinct plate of copper; but the design was placed thereon by a transfer taken from Plate II. For the reasons set forth on page 21, I do not think this a

retouched or repaired state of Plate II. This point, many years ago, formed the
subject of considerable correspondence between Mr. Pemberton and myself, without
any satisfactory result to either of us, until we met and collated against our
collections a large number of the stamps kindly lent by M. Hanciau. A prolonged
examination then led us to the conclusion above stated, on the faith of which Mr.
Pemberton adhered to Plate III. of his arrangement. It was not without satisfaction
I found the Vice-President had, after carefully working at this plate, come to the
same decision.

In the engraving one stamp (No. 20) has the fan with six, in lieu of the
seven segments, which the other twenty-three varieties show; another (No. 10) has
the bale with double lines of the next plate; while in No. 3 the hill is left
unshaded. These are the principal departures from the general type on this plate.

The style of engraving is not unlike Clayton's handiwork, but may be from
one of his assistants, as the master's hand is always more or less imitated, consciously
or not, by those in his atelier. It is not so heavy as that of Plate II.

III. *Paper.*—This plate is found printed on a hard grey paper, without watermark, the pulp of which appears to have been insufficiently cleansed from the *bleachers*
used by the paper maker; for the bulk of the impressions show tendency to
oxidisation. Indeed, I have seen some where the rust has absolutely eaten *through*
the stamp.

The use of this paper is confirmatory of the date of September, 1850; and that
this plate is found only, so far as I am aware, on this kind of paper, is a factor in
helping to decide not only the date, but duration of plate in service. I concur
generally with the remarks of the Vice-President on the paper (*ante* p. 30), which
may be taken to embody the outcome of our joint researches and conclusions. The
only point in which I do not quite follow him is in doubting whether any paper on
which stamps of this series were printed was affected in colour by the adhesive
matter employed. The gum was a pure gum, if coarse and discoloured; and I
cannot trace any chemical agency affecting colour or paper to its use.

As the stamps were printed on wet paper, if, after inking, the surface of the
plate was not wiped off clean, a smudge or run, often colouring the whole face
of the paper, was produced in the press. A close observation can always pronounce
if this be the cause of an apparent variety in the colour of the paper, or if a
coloured or tinted paper was originally put under the plate; for in the former case
the colouring is surface only, and frequently uneven or patchy; in the latter the
paper is evenly coloured through its whole substance.

By analogy one would expect to find Plate III. on the hard bluish paper, used
about this same period for printing the One Penny retouched plate. It does not
appear to be recorded in any of the catalogues or lists, nor have we seen any
specimen that warrants us in inserting it here. Perhaps, now attention is drawn to
the point, an example may be discovered.

IV. *Printing, Colour, &c.*—There is nothing special under these heads to be
stated of this plate, except that, besides the grey shades of blue usually found, and
the full deep blue, a distinct, well-marked ultramarine is occasionally, though rarely,
to be met with.

V. *Duration of Plate in Service.*—For reasons sufficiently appearing when the
plate next in succession is treated of, I am led to believe this plate was in currency
until the early part of April, 1851, when, in common with its successor, it was
directed to be repaired.

Plate IV.—This plate, almost identical with Plate III., is generally known to
collectors by the cording on the bale being *double-lined*, and there being a circle
inserted inside the stars in the angles. I say this plate, because, as will presently
appear, I think it was a distinct plate, and not a second state or retouch of
Plate III. Considering then—

I. *Date.*—The earliest example we found was one belonging to Mr. Rodd, very
distinctly postmarked 20th January, 1851, indicating that this plate was in service

early in that year. Whether its use continued concurrently with other plates will be discussed hereafter.

II. *Design and Engraving.*—This plate presents a closer similarity to Plate III. than exists between any other two plates of this issue. One may say they are alike, but that in this the bale is double-lined, and in the stars in the angles a circle is placed. There are a few other *minutiæ*, indescribable, but showing slight differences. From it general style we can safely infer this plate was by the same hand as Plate III.

The fan with six segments makes its appearance on No. 20; No. 22 is without clouds; and No. 4 has the hill unshaded.

The transfer thus made was very exact, and the engraver faithful in cutting all the lines of his pattern, without pausing to correct errors or supply omissions.

Was it a distinct plate, or a retouch on Plate III.? On this Mr. Pemberton expressed no opinion, as in his day the variations from what we call Plate III. were taken to be only varieties on that plate. The Vice-President and MM. Caillebotte think it a retouch. Mr. Wilson is of opinion it was a separate plate, taken, of course, by transfer. To this latter view, and with great deference to the authorities *contra*, I incline to adhere, though I think the point not one of very great importance.

It is obvious that if this were a retouch of Plate III., some other plate besides that must have been in existence on April 2nd, 1851, when the Governor ordered the plates (plural) of the Two Pence to be repaired. Could this other plate have been Plate II.? It could not have been the variety "Pearl in fan," the last plate, which was not (there is every reason to believe) engraved till later.

We therefore have Plate II., the only other that could possibly answer the description, unless Plate IV. were a separate plate. I do not attach much (if any) weight to the argument derived from the stamps showing no difference *after* the repairs. If this reason carries any conclusion, it shows Plate II. could not be the "other;" for no one has ever pretended to find a trace of retouch on that plate. Clearly the direct inference from the order of 2nd April, 1851, is, that there were then two plates in use, wanting repair. To no two could this apply with anything like propriety if Plate IV. had not been made as a separate plate. The idea of a retouched Plate III. is negatived by the word "Plates" being in the plural.

But I am inclined to admit that this reasoning, however valid, is based on the word in the order being "Plates" in the plural. If singular, all the above is unsupported, and in my judgment this is too slender a foundation on which to present a conclusion differing from MM. Caillebotte and the Vice-President.

We must enquire a little closer; and going to the real source of knowledge, a critical examination of the stamps themselves, the earliest specimens we know of what I have ventured to call Plate IV. show great clearness and fineness in the lines of the engraver's burin. If the plate had been touched up, the engraver could cut a fresh clean edge; but this *must widen the line*, and the general effect would be to show a coarser engraving after the operation. Now this is emphatically not the case with the so-called retouch of Plate III. As any one who carefully examines it, in contrast with its so-called retouch, can judge for himself, I shall not further labour this point.

Are there then "traces" of the old engraving of Plate III. to be detected on this supposed retouch? I frankly own I can see nothing of so clear or distinct a nature as to warrant the same conclusion that one draws without hesitation from the retouched state of the One Penny. Where, I may ask, is anything analogous to the lines of the houses in the first state, faintly showing through the houses, as altered in the second edition of the plate? In the absence of such clearly-defined marks, it would be unsafe to found on a few obscure patches or marks, which might be due to imperfect "cleaning-off" of the plate in the press, or some other accidental cause. If the "imperceptible sense" is of any use, it indicates to me a clear and freshly-engraved transfer. We will next examine—

III. *Paper.*—Here we get the hard grey paper, introduced in September, 1850; the hard bluish; and lastly, the laid or ribbed, which is the last on which this value appeared. This "wealth" of papers points not only to a lengthened continuance of the plate, but also to a similar period with the plate next described.

IV. *Printing, Colour, &c.*—The colours adopted show an admixture of pink or lake with the blue pigments, in what we deem the later printed specimens. Starting at first in a true shade of blue, the final printing was in a purplish tint, which in full light is of a remarkable tone, almost violet, reminding one of certain rare examples of the 1 real fuerte, Philippines (1854-55). Specimens of this shade of the Two Pence are extremely scarce.

V. *Duration of Plate in Service.*—If, as is conjectured, this was one of the plates referred to in the order to repair of 2nd April, 1851, we get a period of not more than three months for its currency before it wanted repair. This want was common to it and another plate, that which I venture to think was Plate III., its predecessor. What were the repairs required, and whether occasioned by wear and tear of current use, or by some accident, the minute does not tell us. It will be remarked that this minute is exceptional, none referring to the various new plates being found. One thing seems certain, no plate that would have been in use at this time shows traces of any retouch done to the stamps *after* 2nd April, 1851, and therefore I am disposed to think that such repairs as were directed did not, if effected, extend to any work involving an alteration on the plates themselves. Whether what I call Plate IV. be a transfer or a retouched state of Plate III. is immaterial to the question, as, whichever be the right view, this plate, new or retouched, was in existence in January, 1851; nor is any later "state" of either plate alleged. The inference is irresistible therefore, either that the order remained unexecuted, or that its performance did not affect that part of the plate which printed the stamps.

Plate V.—This, the well-known fan with pearl, is and has always been deemed the last type of the Two Pence (Sydney views). Its history is free from many of the difficulties that surround the others. Conforming to the plan hitherto adopted, I will take—

I. *Date.*—When engraved is not absolutely known. It certainly was after 2nd April, 1851. The first specimen we have seen with a date was 10th May, 1851, a beautifully clear and early example from the plate.

II. *Design and Engraving.*—A cursory inspection shows this plate is constructed from a transfer from Plate III., following, as it does, that plate with extreme closeness, down to the very varieties of type in the engraving. The salient difference, which at once distinguishes it from all others, is the small circle or pearl in the centre of the fan of the inner circular border bearing the legend. The engraver appears, after he inserted this pearl, to have drawn the straight lines dividing the segments, so as to appear to radiate from it. The style is clean, the lines clear and distinct, and the whole effect light, indicating a new plate, and not one repaired or retouched. The remarks made on Plate IV. being a separate transfer from, and not a retouch of, Plate III., apply to this plate even more forcibly. In forming a judgment, I do not attach any weight to the process of reduplication being known in the colony, because, as we have seen, that which was known was a multiplication of lithographs by a process that any lithographer was equal to. To produce a *fac-simile* from an engraved plate on a fresh sheet of copper is not difficult. As good an impression as can be obtained is taken on thin transparent paper. It is then stretched on the new plate, previously waxed or varnished to receive it. Nothing more is required than to cut the lines exactly as they appear. Manifestly a duplicate of the mother plate is thereby obtained. If the workman be careful, his very fidelity reproduces the old design—errors, varieties, and peculiarities, down to the least ink-mark. And this is what happened in these transfers. Plate III., no doubt substantially a transfer from Plate II., itself became, in turn, the parent plate of Nos. IV. and V.

The original theory of the Vice-President, that Plate V. is a retouched state of Plate III., is, I am glad to see, now modified. We both agree that this plate (No. V.) is a separate transfer. In this not merely Mr. Pemberton, but Dr. Legrand coincide; and whatever question may still be deemed open on what I designate Plate IV., I think we may now take the distinct existence of Plate V. as an ascertained fact.

I cannot with any degree of certainty affirm that there is any difference in style between Plate III. and its two transfers; indeed, all three seem to indicate one engraver's hand.

On this plate is also found the variety fan with six segments (No. 20); and that with the labourer's pick and shovel wanting (No. 17); those catalogued with hill and ground unshaded, with hill only unshaded, and with no clouds, do not exist.

III. *Paper.*—Plate V. is found on the hard grey paper already described, on the hard bluish, and on the vertically laid paper, on which, as we take it, the last printings of this Two Pence took place.

IV. *Printing, Colour, &c.*—A dull grey blue, varying in intensity, is the only colour known to me. The printing presents no feature for remark.

V. *Duration of Plate.*—We learn that the new type of the Two Pence, with laureated head of the Queen, was issued at the end of July, 1851; so that this plate had an existence, for printing purposes, of (say) three months; *i.e.* May, June, and July, about an average period for a plate of this value.

PROOFS AND ESSAYS OF THE TWOPENCE.

I. *Proofs.*—No proofs of this value are known, nor can I trace any reference to such in any of the philatelic publications I have consulted, and I believe my search has been fairly exhaustive.

II. *Essays.*—In my collection was an essay of this value, which Mr. Pemberton obtained directly from the colony. It generally resembled the ordinary type, and bore a close affinity in design to Plate II., having horizontal-lined spandrels, dated bale, and other like characteristics. It differed in being better and more carefully drawn and engraved; but was not so fine or elaborate as Plate I. The lower angles, instead of ornaments, respectively bore the letters (Roman capitals) "E," "W." The work was, in Mr. Pemberton's opinion, from a different hand to any of the stamps, and in this opinion I agree. The impression was struck in bright blue on thick card.

On pages 10, 11, *ante*, the names of Wells and Wall are given as engravers connected with this issue. One enquires if the letters "E. W." were the initials of either man, who thus identified his work? But beyond asking the question I must stop, and leave the answer, if it ever be answered, to some one better informed on the subject.

It is many years since I saw the collection of Count Primoli; but the essay of this value which he possessed was similar to the above, unless my recollection is at fault.

I am not acquainted with any other essays of this value, nor did I ever know of more than my own and Count Primoli's specimens. From *The New South Wales Stamp Collector's Magazine*, already mentioned, it inferentially appears that no essays of the Two Pence are in the possession of the New South Wales Postal Department.

THE THREE PENCE.

This value, of which but one plate was engraved, presents much less debateable ground for controversy.

I. *Date.*—1st January, 1850.

II. *Design and Engraving.*—The former calls for no special remarks. The view enunciated by the Vice-President (*ante* p. 31), that the so-called varieties without clouds proceed from defective plate or printing, is one which I fully share. No distinction of plates, based on whether the pointed ovals of the borders cut each other more or less, can be made. These should be regarded as mere varieties on the plate. In this matter the views of Mr. Pemberton are entirely erroneous.

The plate itself was modelled on that of the One Penny, which in formation it exactly followed, containing twenty-five stamps, in five rows of five each. The engraver was Robert Clayton, and, as in the original plate of the One Penny, there are no varieties to record.

III. *Paper.*—This stamp is first found on the yellow-toned paper of the first One Penny and Two Pence, and afterwards on the hard bluish and the hard grey, as also on ribbed or laid papers, both white and blue. As the plate was never changed till the Three Pence (laureated head) was issued, in December, 1852, this value would naturally be printed on whatever paper was in use when it was put to press.

IV. *Printing, Colour, &c.*—Although there was not great demand for this value, yet the printing strikes one as often careless and poorly done, partly due perhaps to the washy and indecisive tints of green employed, though sometimes a fairly good clear colour was made. The variations are great—from a pale yellow-green, almost illegible, through a full sap-green to a bright emerald. Sometimes the paper is so yellow it is impossible to distinguish the design, and the heavy defacing-marks in use practically spoil a large proportion of used specimens in collectors' eyes. Unused examples, I need hardly remark, occur but seldom.

Most of the early catalogues chronicled this value as printed both in *pink* or *flesh colour* and in *brown*, as well as green. The former was originally inserted by Mount Brown, on the authority of information from the colony, which he subsequently discovered to be erroneous, and he therefore omitted to enumerate it in his later editions. No information of recent years refers to it, and we may consider that its existence as a stamp is entirely mythical. No proof has ever been heard of or seen in this colour, so that we may equally reject it as such. Red was from the first appropriated to the lowest value, so that, *à priori*, a trial in pink colour for higher denominations would be most unlikely.

The so-called *brown*, several specimens of which have been in my possession at various times, was a green stamp when printed, and changed by atmospheric or other agency to a brown colour, as careful scrutiny of the examples never fails to reveal.

I therefore expunge both the flesh and brown from the list of stamps, nor can I admit either to the category of proofs.

V. *Duration of Plate in Service.*—This plate was never retouched, and continued in use, when required, till superseded by its successor, of the new type, in December, 1852.

PROOFS AND ESSAYS OF THE THREE PENCE.

I. *Proofs.*—A proof of this plate was taken in dark myrtle-green on stout yellowish card. Copies were in several English and foreign collections before 1865, and several were obtained by Sir Daniel Cooper on his visit to the colony in 1868–9, and exhibited *en bloc* before the Society on the 29th May in the latter year.

Proofs were also struck in black on similar card; but these are of exceptional rarity.

II. *Essays.*—In the Post-office at Sydney the following essay is described: "View of Sydney, centre same as that described in No. 1 [the essay of the One Penny, *ante* p. 49], except the 'RIA' can be plainly read, and bale is inscribed 'M S.' In the top corners Maltese crosses, with radiating stars, and the word 'Postage' inscribed between them; whilst underneath the circle, from side to side, is the value 'THREE PENCE' in blue letters on white ground. Colour, deep indigo, except centre and inscribed circle, which is of a rich carmine-vermilion. Printed on thicker paper than No. 1, with old gum showing where the specimen has not attached to the sheet."

It is evident some one has made this so-called essay by a scissors and paste operation, taking a type of the Two Pence, probably Plate II., and applying the central part of the One Penny, most likely from the retouched plate.

This is all the information I possess as to essays of this value, and I will now conclude what I have to say by a few remarks, applicable to the issue generally.

GENERAL OBSERVATIONS.

I propose here to notice a few stray facts, and to give some miscellaneous details not stated previously, and which hardly ranged themselves conveniently under the foregoing heads.

Governors of New South Wales.—Those whose names may be useful to remember as connected with our subject are the first Governor—

Capt. Arthur Phillip, R.N., from 26th January, 1788, to 10th December, 1792.
Sir George Gipps, from 24th February, 1838, to 11th July, 1846.
Sir Charles A. Fitz-Roy, from 3rd August, 1846, to 17th January, 1855.

Engraving on Wood of the First Trials.—This history, as related by Mr. Calvert, is, I think, new to most people. It certainly is to me. The catastrophe to the Sydney Post-office probably involved all remains of these trials in the ruin it created. If more light can be cast on the matter, it will probably be through some of the old Post-office *employés*, or other interested person in the colony, who may see this paper and communicate to the Society. On this, and indeed any point connected with our subject, the Society will gladly receive any communications. That printer's metal—a compound of lead and tin, hardened by the admixture of a little antimony—was ever engraved on for one of these plates I do not believe. A plate of printer's metal could not receive work of such fineness as the coarsest Sydney view.

The size and shape of the One Penny and Three Pence plates show they could be printed twice on one side of a page of ordinary foolscap paper laid upright under the press. The plate of the Two Pence is too long to be so printed, so the sheet of paper was necessarily turned and printed on longways; *i.e.* with the lines of the vergeures vertical. This affords some confirmation that the plates of the Two Pence differed in size and shape from those of the other values, the latter always showing the lines horizontal, while in the Two Pence they are vertical. I have never met with the One Penny lines vertical, nor can I give a reference to the Two Pence, supposed to be on the horizontally laid paper (*ante* p. 30), and, for the reason given, its existence seems to me more than dubious.

The comparative service of the plates themselves is instructive. One, and but one, the Three Pence, lasted till December, 1852, two years and eleven months, without retouch. Another, the One Penny, lasted just two years, having been once retouched in the interval. While of the third value, I make five plates, one of which was retouched, and the Vice-President four, with two retouched, extending over a period of nineteen or twenty months, thus averaging a little over three months' use for each of the six. Clearly the wear and tear of these was much greater than that of the other plates; but when one remembers that Two Pence was the single home rate of postage, and that the whole continent, except South and West Australia, made use of these stamps, the large call for this value is not surprising.

Were any plates of this value in use concurrently? One guide in this is the paper; but I do not feel on very sure ground with this alone to judge by, because a glance at the Reference List and comparison of dates tells us that no plate, or "state," is distinguished by a special paper. Our conclusions therefore can but be approximate. They become stronger, however, when, joined to identity in paper, similarity in colour is found. It seems not unlikely, applying these tests, that Plates III. and IV. were printed from, in dull blue, on the hard grey paper, about the same time.

The tints are strikingly alike, and every collector knows how in any long series the dominant colour varies in such a manner as to enable a practised eye to give the date of any shade with great accuracy. For my purpose, all that need be said is, this concurrent use of plates *was* possible and *seems* probable.

The reconstruction of the entire plates, nine in all, has been a necessary preliminary to our work for the Society. Few can speak with better reason of the difficulties this entailed than I; for while I assisted to a small extent, the bulk of the labour fell to the Vice-President. He has, in no overstrained terms, described our prolonged investigations, which often seemed near a fruitful result, almost as often to show that we must begin *de novo* before we could solve even the limited problem of the building up of one entire plate.

Whatever we may have failed to settle, I think this much has been accomplished, that the plates are now correctly and fully made up, with the varieties truly allocated to their proper positions; and that succeeding investigators will commence with firm ground to tread upon thus far.

How greatly their labours will be thus facilitated none but those who have attempted the solution of these questions from such materials as were available when we commenced can form any adequate conception, and the London Philatelic Society may, I think, be content that, under its auspices, all the chief difficulties which have attended these stamps are now nearly, if not entirely, resolved.

ISSUE I.—VIEWS OF SYDNEY.
REFERENCE LIST.

ONE PENNY. *Plate I. Finely engraved. Illustration Plate A.* January 1st, 1850—
  (a) *On soft yellowish paper.* Red, brownish-red, lake-red, pale vermilion-red; shades of each.
  (b) *On bluish paper.* Pale red; shades.
  (c) *On closely-ribbed paper, white or bluish.* Red.

Plate I., retouched. Coarsely engraved. Illustration Plate A. August, 1850?—
  (a) *On hard white or slightly yellowish paper.* Red, brownish-red; shades.
  (b) *On hard bluish paper,* varying in substance. Red, brownish-red, lake, brownish-lake; shades.
  (c) *On white or yellowish widely-ribbed paper.* Same shades.
  (d) *On same paper, but slightly blued.* Same shades.
  (e) *On blue laid paper.* Carmine.
Prominent variety. No. 15. Without clouds.

TWO PENCE. *Plate I. Vertical-lined spandrels. Illustration Plate B.* January 1st, 1850—
  (a) *On soft yellowish paper. Sometimes tinged with blue.* Pearl-grey, dull blue, indigo-blue; pale blue; shades.
Prominent variety. No. 19. Lines of spandrels, wavy on oblique.

Plate I., retouched. Illustration Plate B. February, 1850—
  On similar paper. Dull blue, indigo-blue, pale blue; shades.

Plate II. Bale dated. Illustration Plate C. April, 1850—
  (a) *On soft yellowish paper.* Ultramarine, blue (pale to dark), dark and indigo-blue; shades.
  (b) *On hard bluish paper.* Blue, dull blue; shades.
  (c) *On hard grey or dirty white paper.* Dull blue. (All impressions on this paper are extremely worn.)
Prominent varieties. No. 13. "CREVIT" wanting. No. 20. Fan with six segments.

Plate III. Bale undated. Illustration Plate C. September, 1850—
  (a) *On hard grey paper.* Grey, greyish-blue, dark blue (with a tendency to oxidisation).
Prominent varieties. No. 3. Hill unshaded. No. 20. Fan with six segments.

Plate III., first retouch. Illustration Plate D. (*Mr. Philbrick's Plate IV.*) January or February, 1851—
  (a) *On hard bluish paper.* Full blue, dark blue shades, violet-blue (scarce shade).
  (b) *On hard grey paper.* Dull blue.
  (c) *On paper ribbed or laid vertically.* Same shades.
Prominent varieties. No. 4. Hill unshaded. No. 20. Fan with six segments. No. 22. Without clouds.

Plate III., second retouch. Fan with pearl. Illustration Plate D. (*Mr. Philbrick's Plate V.*) May (?), 1850—.
  (a) *On hard grey paper.* Dull grey-blue; slight shades.
  (b) *On vertically-laid paper.* Same shades.
Prominent variety. No. 20. Fan with six segments.

THREE PENCE. *Illustration Plate E.* January 1st, 1850—
  (a) *On soft yellowish paper.* Yellow-green shades.
  (b) *On hard bluish paper.* Yellow-green, green, emerald-green; shades.
  (c) *On paper laid horizontally.* Yellow-green, emerald-green; shades.

Although the variations in the perforations are small, the sets are perfectly distinct.

1878-82.

5d., dark yellow-green; wmk., "N.S.W." and Crown; perf. 10.
8d., yellow shades   ,,   ,,   ,, (about 1879); imperf.
8d. ,, ,,   ,, ,, ,, perf. 13.
8d. ,, ,,   ,, ,, ,, perf. 10.
8d. ,, ,,   ,, ,, ,, perf. 10 × 12½.

ERRORS OF WATERMARK.
1854-56.

6d., greyish-brown, umber; wmk., large numeral 8; imperf.
1s., brick-red   ,,   ,, 8; imperf. and perf. 12.

1866.

6d., mauve-violet   wmk., large numeral 5; perf. 13.
6d., lilac   ,,   ,, 12 ,,

ERRORS OF IMPRESSION, OR COLOUR TRIALS.
1854-56.

5d., dark blue   wmk., large numeral 5; imperf.
8d., red (in the colour of the 1s.) ,,   ,, 8 ,,

Remarks.—There are probably more shades of the Six Penny value than of any other stamp ever issued. All the values are found with inverted and reversed watermarks, which means nothing except that the sheets of paper have been printed on upside down. There is a curious border in the margin of the sheet, varying with each value, of a reticulated wavy-line design, somewhat after the style of the patterns used to separate bankers' cheques from the counterfoil, with an ornament at each of the four angles. There are fifty stamps to the sheet, in five horizontal rows of ten. The engravers first produced a matrix, or mother die, which, after being hardened, was used to manufacture the plate used in printing, according to the Perkins' process, as employed for the plates of the first One Penny of Great Britain. Plates of the Six Pence and One Shilling were made and printed from at first in England; but those of the Five Pence and Eight Pence were engraved in January, 1855, and when constructed were at once sent out to the colony, with a supply of the watermarked paper, and also colour—green for the Five Pence, and chrome-yellow for the Eight Pence. Neither of these values were printed for issue by Messrs. Perkins, Bacon, & Co. The stamps above described under "Errors of Impression," &c., are doubtless due in the former case to experiments in colour; but the red Eight Pence seems a genuine error in printing by mistake in the ink adopted for the One Shilling value.

Proofs of all the values in black, on plate-paper, are known; these were taken, in England, from the mother dies. Recently proof-sheets of the Five Pence and Eight Pence, in dark blue, on thickish paper, not watermarked, have been discovered in Australia. The colour is a hard dull shade of blue. A proof of the One Shilling, in bright blue, was taken in England probably from the matrix. The specimen known is obliterated "CANCELLED." In 1861-2 Messrs. Perkins, Bacon, & Co. printed, on thick porous card-paper, from the plate of the Six Pence, a series of trials in all the colours they then had in use, as specimens to submit to the authorities at Somerset House. These last proofs may be distinguished by the corner of the impression being effaced: wax having been applied for that purpose. A list of these proofs may be found in Mount Brown's catalogue, third edition.

Issue IV. 1856–82.

Three values. Engraved (? by Wm. Humphreys) and printed by Messrs. Perkins, Bacon, and Co., of London. Coloured impression, on white wove watermarked paper; white gum. Design: Diademed profile of Queen Victoria to left on engine-turned background, with reticulations on each side, between the side borders and the back and front of the head. Above the head is the word "POSTAGE," in a curve, in white Roman capitals. The bottom labels in the Penny and Two Pence values are of solid colour, and inscribed with the value in words in white Roman capitals. In the Three Pence the bottom label is white, and inscribed with the value in words in coloured block letters. In all three values the top and side borders are reticulated and inscribed in white Roman capitals. There are ornamental blocks in each corner, the upper ones differing from those below. Shape, upright rectangular. (*Illustration* 24.)

T. "SOUTH POSTAGE." B. "ONE PENNY," "TWO PENCE," "THREE PENCE." L. "NEW." R. "WALES."

(A.) *Imperf.* 1856.

1d., vermilion-orange, brick (shades); wmk., large double-lined numeral 1.
2d., blue   „   „   „   „   2.
3d., dark-, yellow-, and blue-green   „   „   „   3.
2d., blue   „   single-lined numeral 2 (Evans.)

Proofs of the One Penny, on very blue wove paper, without watermark, were struck in vermilion.

(B.) *Perf.* 12, 12½, 13. 1860.

1d., vermilion, orange-red (shades)   wmk., large double-lined numeral 1.
2d., blue   „   „   „   „   2.
3d., dark-, yellow-, and emerald-green (shades) „ „ „ „ 3.

No specimen of the Two Pence has been met with perf. 12½, but it doubtless exists.

1863.   1d., dark and pale red, probably printed in the colony; wmk., single-lined numeral 1; perf. 12½.
1872–82. 3d., yellow-green (shades); wmk., "N.S.W." and Crown; perf. 13.
1883.   3d.   „   „   „   „   „   „   „ 10.

ERRORS OF WATERMARK.

1856. 2d., blue   wmk., large double-lined numeral 5; imperf.
1872. 3d., green (shades) „   „   „   „   6; perf. 12½, 13.

Remarks.—Some of the later editions of this type have, no doubt, judging from the blotched impressions, been printed in the colony. A number of proofs in various colours were printed on thick yellowish card paper by the engravers, for the same purpose as those of the previous issue. Proofs of all, in black on plate paper, are known. The Two Pence were printed sixty to the sheet in ten horizontal rows of six stamps. There are marginal inscriptions on the sheet as follows: *Top*, "NEW SOUTH WALES." *Bottom*, "POSTAGE TWO PENCE." *Right side*, reading upwards, and with the base of the lettering towards the pane. "PRICE, 2d. per label; 1s. per row of six; 10s. per sheet of sixty." *Left side*, "In affixing the stamp be careful not to remove the cement." White plate number in oval on plain ground, and coloured control number in single-lined oblong frame with rounded corners, in the upper right and lower left corner respectively.

Issue V. 1860-1882.

One value. Engraved in *taille-douce*, and printed by Messrs. Perkins, Bacon, and Co., of London. Coloured impression, on white wove watermarked paper; white gum. Design: Profile bust of Queen Victoria to left, with gothic crown and coronation jewels within a double-lined circle of horizontal lines. The sceptre lies rather awkwardly over her right shoulder, the handle showing in front of the bust, and the upper part behind the neck. Above the handle of the sceptre is a conventional rose with foliage. Curved inscriptions above and below portrait, following the outline of the circle. The upper is in smaller and the lower in larger gothic characters; and the two inscriptions are divided by *cinq-foil* ornaments. Beneath the "E" of NEW and the "E" of WALES are pierced mullets. The engraving of the stamp is so contrived as to give it an appearance of relief like a coin. Shape, circular; diameter, 25 mm. (*Illustration 23.*)

T. "NEW SOUTH WALES."   B. "FIVE SHILLINGS."

1860.	5s., greyish-lilac	wmk., 5s.;	imperf.
1860–82.	5s., lilac, reddish-lilac, mauve	„	mach.-perf. 12, 12½, and 13.
1882.	5s., reddish-lilac	„	perf. 10.

Issue VI. 1862–82.

One value. Engraved and surface-printed by De la Rue and Co. Coloured impression on white paper; white gum. Design: Diademed profile of Queen Victoria to left on ground of horizontal lines. Above, curved, and at bottom and sides, straight white labels inscribed in coloured Roman capitals. There are triangular ornaments above the ends of the upper label, and a wavy white line on coloured ground between the outside of the other three labels and the border of the stamp, which is formed of two plain coloured lines. Shape, upright rectangular. (*Illustration 25.*)

T. "NEW SOUTH WALES."   B. "TWO PENCE."   L. "POSTAGE."   R. "TWO PENCE."

March, 1862.
2d., blue (shades) on surfaced paper; no wmk.; perf. 14.

The following were printed in the Colony:

March, 1863.
2d., blue (shades) on unsurfaced paper; no wmk.; perf. 12½.
2d., „   „   „   „ 13.

1862–63.
2d., blue (shades) on unsurfaced paper, wmk., large double-lined numeral 2 ; perf. 12.
2d.,   „   „   „   „   „   „ 12½
2d.,   „   „   „   „   „   „ 13.

1863.
2d., blue (shades) on unsurfaced paper, wmk., single-lined numeral 2 ; perf. 12½.

1871–82.
2d., blue (shades) on unsurfaced paper, wmk., "N.S.W." and Crown; perf. 12½.
2d.,   „   „   „   „   „   imperf.
2d.,   „   „   „   „   „   perf. 10.

ERRORS OF WATERMARK.

1867. 2d., blue (shades) on white wove paper; wmk., large numeral 8 ; perf. 12½.
  2d.,   „   „   „   „   5   „
1868. 2d.,   „   „   „   „   thin numeral 1   „

Remarks.—There are considerable differences in the shading of the face on some copies of these stamps, probably arising from differences arising in the multiplication of the plate which was sent to the colonies. The colonial impressions were printed by Thomas Richards, Sydney.

Issue VII. 1864-82.

One value. Engraved and surface-printed by De la Rue and Co. Coloured impression on white paper; white gum. Design: Diademed profile of Queen Victoria to left on ground of horizontal lines, within a double-lined oval of solid colour inscribed in small white block letters, the two inscriptions being separated by a rosace on either side. The spandrels are filled in with foliate ornament, and the design is completed by an outer frame of two plain coloured lines. Shape, upright rectangular. (*Illustration* 26.)

T. "NEW SOUTH WALES." B. "ONE PENNY."

1864. 1d., red (shades) on white surfaced paper; no wmk. ; perf. 14.
      1d.,   ,,   ,,   ,,   wmk., thin numeral 1 ; ,, 14.
      1d.,   ,,   unsurfaced ,,   ,,   ,,   ,, 12½.
      1d.,   ,,   ,,   ,,   no wmk.,   ,, 12½.
1871. 1d.,   ,,   ,,   ,,   wmk.,"N.S.W."and Crown; ,, 12½.
1883. 1d.,   ,,   ,,   ,,   ,,   ,,   ,, 10.
 ,,   1d.,   ,,   ,,   ,,   ,,   ,,   ,, 10 × 12½.
Dec. 1886. 1d.,   ,, on bluish-white ,,   ,,   ,,   ,,   ,, 11 × 12.

ERRORS OF WATERMARK.

1867. 1d., red to pale red on white unsurfaced paper; wmk., thin numeral 2 ; perf. 12½.

Remarks.—The two varieties of the Penny, perf. 14, were printed by Messrs. De la Rue. The later printings, and probably all those with the perforation 12½, were done in the colony. The paper with watermark "N.S.W." without Crown is employed for the fiscal stamps of this colony, but during a temporary exhaustion of the supply of the ordinary paper used for this value some sheets of the fiscal paper were substituted. Three thousand sheets are said to have been used, and these were issued to the Post-office at Sydney between the 13th and 17th December, 1886. The letters "N.S.W." measure 27 × 7 mm., and the watermark extends over *two* stamps. The four corner stamps of the sheet are without watermark, and the other eight stamps at either side are watermarked with portions of the words "NEW SOUTH WALES."

Engravers' proofs of the One Penny, also of the Two Pence, of the previous issue, in black, on enamelled card, both before and after hardening, are known.

Issue VIII. 1867.

One value. Engraved by De la Rue and Co., and printed by Thomas Richards. Coloured impression on white wove watermarked paper; white gum. Design: Diademed profile of Queen Victoria to left on ground of horizontal lines, enframed in a double-lined circle, enclosing pearls. Curved labels of solid colour above and below circle, inscribed in white block letters. The corners and spandrels are filled in with conventional ornament. Shape, upright rectangular. (*Illustration* 28.)

T. "NEW SOUTH WALES." B. "POSTAGE TEN PENCE."

10d., lilac (shades) ; wmk., small single-lined italic numerals 10 ; mach.-perf. 12½.

In 1871 this stamp was printed in burnt-sienna, and "NINEPENCE" in black Roman capitals was surcharged over the original value. (*Illustration* 30.)

1871. 9d., red-brown ; wmk., "N.S.W." and Crown ; perf. 12½.

Issue IX. 1867-82.

One value. Engraved by De la Rue and Co.; surface-printed by T. Richards, of Sydney. Coloured impression on white wove watermarked paper; white gum. Design: Diademed profile of Queen Victoria to left in lozenge of horizontal lines. White labels following the outline of the lozenge, inscribed in coloured Roman capitals. The four angles are filled in with white arabesques on coloured ground, and a plain coloured line forms the outer border of the stamp. Shape, upright rectangular. (*Illustration* 27.)

T. "NEW SOUTH WALES." B. "POSTAGE FOUR PENCE."

1867.
4d., red-brown, deep to pale; wmk., small single-lined numeral 4; mach.-perf. 13.
1878-82.
4d., red-brown, deep to pale; wmk., "N.S.W." and Crown; mach.-perf. 13.
1882.
4d., red-brown, deep to pale; wmk., "N.S.W." and Crown; mach.-perf. 10.

Issue X. 1872-82.

One value. Engraved by Messrs. De la Rue and Co., and surface-printed by T. Richards, of Sydney. Coloured impression on white wove watermarked paper; white gum. Design: Diademed profile of Queen Victoria to left on ground of horizontal lines, within a white bordered oval of solid colour, inscribed in thin white block letters, the two inscriptions being separated by a small ornament on either side. The oval is enframed by a hexagonal line of colour, pointed at the top and bottom, and touching the four outer lines of the stamp. The interstices between the oval and hexagon are filled in with arabesques, and the spandrels with reticulations. A plain coloured outer line completes the design. Shape, upright rectangular. (*Illustration* 29.)

1872-82.
6d., reddish to pale lilac; wmk., "N.S.W." and Crown; mach.-perf. 13.
6d.   „   „   „   „   imperf.
1883.
6d., reddish to pale lilac; wmk., "N.S.W." and Crown; perf. 10.
6d.   „   „   „   „   perf. 10 × 12½.

Remarks.—Proofs in black as before.

Issue XI. 1876-82.

One value. Engraved by De la Rue and Co., and surface-printed by T. Richards, of Sydney. Coloured impression, on white wove watermarked paper; white gum. Design: Diademed profile of Queen Victoria to left on ground of horizontal lines, within a frame which is arched at the top and bottom, and straight at the sides. The inner portion of the frame is of solid colour, and is inscribed in small white block letters, with a full stop after each part of the inscription. The spandrels are filled in with arabesques, and the design is completed by a plain outer line of colour. Shape, upright rectangular. (*Illustration* 31.)

T. "NEW SOUTH WALES." B. "ONE SHILLING." L. "POSTAGE," reading upwards.
R. "POSTAGE," reading downwards.

1876. 1s., black;   wmk., "N.S.W." and Crown; perf. 12½.
  „   1s.   „   on brown paper „   „   „   „
1882. 1s.   „   on white paper „   „   „   perf. 10.

Remarks.—The variety on brown paper is probably due to the gum, which is sometimes of a dark brown colour.

Proofs on enamelled card as before, in mauve, are known.

NEW SOUTH WALES.

Issue XII. 4th February, 1886.

Three values, consisting of the *Stamp Duty* stamps, of Five Shillings, Ten Shillings, and One Pound, issue 1868, surcharged in black, with the word "POSTAGE" in Roman capitals beneath the Queen's head, and a thin straight line erasing the words "STAMP DUTY." All three values are watermarked "N.S.W." vertically, and are perforated 12 × 10. (*Illustration* 36.)

      5s., green, violet centre and frame.
      10s., carmine   "   "
      £1   "   "   "

STAMPS EMPLOYED FOR REGISTRATION.
Issue 1853–62.

One value. Engraved on metal, and printed in the colony. The sheet consists of fifty stamps, each separately engraved. There are consequently fifty varieties of type. Design: Laureated profile of Queen Victoria to left on ground of vertical and wavy lines within an upright oval band, inscribed in block letters "NEW SOUTH WALES" at top, and "REGISTERED" at bottom, the two inscriptions being separated by engine-turned ornamentation at each side. Bicoloured impression (red or orange for the centre, and blue for the oval band) upon stoutish white wove paper. The value, which is not expressed, is Six Pence. Those first issued were imperforate; but in 1860, and afterwards, the stamp appeared perforated 12 and 13; and in 1862 the paper was watermarked with a large numeral 6. The colours first employed were red and blue, the red being afterwards changed to orange, which was again, later on, changed back to red. Owing to the difficulty of obtaining unsevered pairs and blocks of these stamps, it has hitherto been found impossible to replace the varieties of type in the original order. The illustration of the plate represents the fifty varieties, but with the exception of some six or eight specimens, the positions of which have been ascertained, the arrangement is quite arbitrary. (*Illustrations*, 33 *and Plate M*.)

    1853. (6d.) red and blue (shades of each); imperforate.
             (6d.) orange "   "   "
    1860. (6d.) red   "   "   "   perf. 12 and 13.
             (6d.) orange "   "   "   "   (13 ?)
    1862. (6d.) red   "   "   "   wmk., large 6; perf. 13.

STAMPS FOR OFFICIAL CORRESPONDENCE.

In January, 1880, the current adhesives were surcharged for official use with "O.S." in large block letters, signifying "On Service," or "Official Service." The surcharge is found in red and black. At least three distinct sets may be found of this surcharge, the differences lying in the spacing of the letters "O. S." (*Illustration* 32.)

The following is a list of the varieties:

                I. *Surcharged in black.*
      (A) Watermark, large numerals; perf. 12½.
          5s., violet. (Type of 1860.)

      (B) Watermark, Crown, and "N.S.W."
  (1) *Perf.* 12½. 1d., pale red.   (Type of 1871.)
                 2d., blue.   ("   ")
                 3d., yellow-green. ("   1875.)
                 4d., reddish-brown. ("   1867.)
                 6d., lilac.   ("   1882.)
                 8d., orange-yellow. ("   1877.)

NEW SOUTH WALES.

(2) *Perf.* 10. 1d., pale red.   (Type of 1871.)
              2d., blue.   („   „   )
              4d., reddish-brown. („   1867.)
              6d., lilac.   („   1882.)

II. Surcharged in red.

(A) Watermark, large numerals; perf. 12½.
    5d., green. (Type of 1860.)

(B) Watermark, small numerals, perf. 12½.
    10d., lilac. (Type of 1867.)

(C) Watermark, Crown, and "N.S.W."

(1) *Perf.* 12½. 3d., yellow-green.   (Type of 1875.)
               8d., orange-yellow.   („   1877.)
               9d., on 10d., pale red. („   1871.)
               1s., black.   („   1876.)
(2) *Perf.* 10.   1s., black.   („   „   )

ENVELOPES.
Issue I. January 1st, 1871.

One value. Engraved by Messrs. De la Rue and Co., and type-printed in the colony in colour, on medium white laid paper. Design: Same as the adhesive of April 1st, 1864. The stamp is impressed in the right upper corner. Long gum. Size $5\frac{6}{10} \times 3\frac{1}{10}$ inches, or 142 × 78 mm. There are numerous varieties of the *tresse* impressed on the upper flap. In all probability these are not official, but were done to private order. (*Illustration* 26.)

(A) *Upper flap rounded.*
    1d., dull red (shades).
Variety. Without *tresse.* 1d., dull red.

(B) *Upper flap pointed.*
    1d., dull red.
Variety. Without *tresse.* 1d., dull red (shades).

NOTE.—In the collection of the Vice-President there is an envelope which is unchronicled, and in reference to which no information is available. It is made of white paper, laid obliquely, and bears in the right upper corner a stamp of the same type as that used for the first wrappers. Size $5\frac{3}{10} \times 3$ inches, or 134 × 75 mm. (*Illustration* 34.)

1d., vermilion.

It is uncertain whether this envelope was actually issued.

Issue II. End of 1881.

One value. Engraved by Messrs. De la Rue and Co., and type-printed in the colony, in colour, on medium white laid paper. Design: Same as the adhesive of March, 1862. The stamp is impressed in the right upper corner. Long gum. Upper flap rounded and impressed with *tresse.* Size $5\frac{6}{10} \times 3\frac{1}{10}$ inches, or 142 × 78 mm. (*Illustration* 25.)

2d., blue.
Variety. Without *tresse.* 2d., blue.

NOTE.—In 1865 or 6 a set of three envelope essays was produced. They bore the head of Queen Victoria to the left, without any legend or value expressed, and were printed on plain white wove paper, the die being impressed in the right upper corner in red, green, and mauve.

REGISTRATION ENVELOPES.

Issue I. January, 1880.

One value. These envelopes are made of stout white wove linen-lined paper. The face and back of the envelopes are each divided into four equal compartments by two lines, which cross at right angles, and are continued from the face to the back of the envelopes. On the face, in the upper part, is an inscription in two lines, "This letter must be given to an Officer of the Post Office to be Registered, and a Receipt obtained for it," in thin block capitals. The vertical crossing line falls between the words "Officer of" and "Receipt obtained," in the two lines of inscription. In the left upper compartment, below the lines of direction, is the word "REGISTERED," in thick block capitals, enclosed in an oblong single-lined frame. In the right upper compartment occur the words, "The Stamp to Pay the Postage must be Placed Here," in thin block capitals, within a single-lined rectangular frame. The whole is printed in vermilion. Rounded flap; yellowish gum. On the flap there is a stamp, engraved and type-printed in rose-red by Messrs. De la Rue and Co.; coloured impression. Design: Diademed profile of Queen Victoria to left on a background of horizontal lines, within a white oval band, containing two inscriptions in coloured block capitals. The two inscriptions are separated by dots. Shape, upright oval. T. "REGISTERED NEW SOUTH WALES." B. "FOUR PENCE." Beneath the flap, on the back of the envelope, are the words, "MCCORQUODALE & Co., PATENTEES," in coloured block capitals; serrated seams. (*Illustration 35.*)

(A) Size F, 5¾ × 3¾ inches, or 130 × 81 mm.
(B) Size G, 6 × 3⅞ inches, or 153 × 98 mm.

4d., rose and vermilion, and rose-red.

Variety.—Size G, no stamp on flap.

OFFICIAL ENVELOPES.

Issue I. 1883.

Two values. These are the same envelopes as those of the ordinary issues of 1871 and 1881, but are surcharged "O.S." in black, in the same way as the adhesives. (*Illustration 32.*)

1d., dull red.
2d., blue.

Issue II. December, 1885.

One value. Engraved and type-printed in colour, on medium white paper, laid obliquely; pointed flap, without design. Size 5¾ × 3$\frac{1}{10}$ inches, or 138 × 78 mm. The stamp is in the right upper corner. The design is the same as that of the 1d. adhesive, issue April, 1864, except that the foliate ornaments in the spandrels are replaced by the letters "O.S.," in block letters. One letter is placed in each spandrel, so that the letters "O.S." are repeated.

1d., vermilion.
1d., brick-red.

WRAPPERS.

Issue I. April 1st, 1864.

One value. On white wove or white laid paper, measuring 300 × 120 mm., or 11¾ × 4¾ inches. The watermark consists of the letters "N.S.W." in fancy capitals with ornaments at each end, and a narrow border, formed of a small chain running between two straight lines, above and below. The sheet contains eight wrappers, and the watermark extends across four of these, so that it is therefore repeated in each sheet. The stamp is embossed about three inches from the upper end of each wrapper, and was produced by Messrs. De la Rue and Co. from a steel die. Design: Diademed profile of Queen Victoria to left in white relief, surrounded with four stars on ground of solid colour, within an upright oval band, with ornamented outer rim, inscribed at top "POSTAGE ONE PENNY," and at bottom "NEW SOUTH WALES;" two star-like ornaments separate the two inscriptions. (*Illustration 34.*)

(A) *On stout white wove paper.*
1d., red (shades).

(B) *On thin yellowish-white wove paper.*
1d., red (shades).

(C) *On white laid paper.*
1d., red (shades).

Issue II. 1865.

One value. On precisely similar laid paper as the previous issue, the watermark and dimensions of the band being also the same. The stamp, *type of* One Penny *adhesive issue, April,* 1864, occupies a like position. (*Illustration 26.*)

1d., pale red.

Issue III. 1869.

One value. The same as the last, but with watermark "ONE PENNY" in Roman capitals on each band in addition to the watermark on the sheet. White laid paper. (*Illustration 26.*)

1d., pale red.

Issue IV. 1872.

One value. Similar to the last, but the watermark "ONE PENNY" is changed to a Kangaroo, Emu, and the letters "A.P." (Australian Postage?) (*Illustration 26.*)

1d., red.

Issue V. 1872 (?)

One value. The same. Watermark, a Kangaroo and an Emu. (*Illustration 26.*)

1d., red.

Remarks.—These two last bands are only known surcharged "SPECIMEN."

Issue VI. 1872 (?)

One value. The same as issue 1869, but the watermark "N.S.W." &c. on the sheet is suppressed. (*Illustration 26.*)

1d., red (shades).

POST CARDS.
Issue I. December, 1875.

One value. Designed and printed by Messrs. De la Rue and Co. upon stoutish white wove paper. Size $4\frac{7}{10} \times 3\frac{1}{4}$ inches. At the top, in the centre of the card, in a straight line, in large block letters, is the word "POST CARD;" and underneath this the arms of Great Britain. Below these, in a straight line, in italics, are the words, "*The Address only to be written on this Side;*" and lower down, to the left, the word "*To,*" also in italics. The stamp is in the right upper corner, and is of the same type as the 1d. adhesive issue, April, 1864. The whole is enclosed within a fancy Oxford frame, broken at intervals by crescent-shaped ornaments. Size of frame $4\frac{2}{8} \times 3\frac{1}{10}$ inches. (*Illustration* 41.)

1d., pale rose (shades).

Variety.—A specimen is known with the word "*To*" in script type; and the horizontal portions of the frame at the top and bottom are terminated by the crescent-shaped ornaments described above. A proof in black has also been seen.

Issue II. February, 1876.

One value. Similar to the preceding, but printed upon medium white card of smaller dimensions. Size $4\frac{7}{10} \times 2\frac{1}{8}$ inches. "*The Address only,*" &c. is in smaller type, and the frame measures $4\frac{1}{8} \times 2\frac{3}{4}$ inches.

1d., rose (shades).

Issue III. 1877.

One value. Similar to the last, but printed upon thicker card. The centre portions of the frame at the top and bottom (divided off by the crescent-shaped ornaments) are slightly larger, making the frame measure $4\frac{9}{20} \times 2\frac{13}{16}$ inches.

1d., rose (shades).

REPLY PAID CARD.
Issue I. January 5th, 1883.

One value. Printed upon stout yellowish-white card. Size $4\frac{9}{10} \times 3\frac{3}{4}$ inches. The stamp is the same, and the inscription and arms are similarly disposed, as on the single cards; but the type employed is slightly different. Three dotted lines for the address, two long and one short. At the bottom of the first half, in a straight line, are the words, in brackets, "*The Receiver should cut or tear off this half and send the reply on the other half;*" and the second half bears the word "REPLY" in Roman capitals, directly beneath the Royal Arms. The cards are folded along the top, and the inscriptions, &c., are printed upon the first and third pages; the cards have no frame.
1d. + 1d., rose (shades.)

OFFICIAL CARD.

One value, consisting of the One Penny card, issue III., with the stamp surcharged across the top "o.s." (On Service), in black block letters.

1d., rose.

FISCAL STAMPS USED POSTALLY.

In 1883 some of the fiscal stamps of the colony were presumably used for postage. There is little reason to doubt that here, as in other cases, a number of them, if not all, were merely postmarked for sale to collectors.

NEW ZEALAND.

Issue I. 1852 (?).

Three values. Engraved on steel by Humphreys, and printed by Messrs. Perkins, Bacon, and Co., of London. Coloured impression on stout wove blue paper; white gum; no watermark. Design: three-quarter face bust portrait of Queen Victoria, crowned, with garter, ribbon, and royal robes, in low-necked dress, on engine-turned background within a double-lined circle, which nearly touches the sides of the stamp. Above and following the upper curve of the circle are the words "NEW ZEALAND" in the hue of the paper upon colour. Beneath the circle upon a small straight label, in small letters, is the word "POSTAGE" in colour. This label rests upon another straight one, forming the bottom of the stamp, which is changeable with the value, and inscribed with the value in full in the hue of the paper upon colour, and has a small double-lined square at each end containing a conventional ornament. The spandrels are filled in with ornamentation resembling an *œil de perdrix* groundwork, and are so strongly shaded in the upper corners as to give them the appearance of being rounded off. The inscriptions on the One Penny and Two Pence are in Roman capitals, and on the Shilling in block letters. Shape, longish upright rectangular; imperforate. (*Illustration* 37.)

T. "NEW ZEALAND." B. "POSTAGE ONE PENNY," "TWO PENCE," "ONE SHILLING."

    1d., vermilion.
    2d., blue and slaty-blue (very distinct shades).
    1s., green (a yellowish shade).

Remarks.—One mother die did duty for all the values, the designation of which in the bottom label was altered in each case. Unused copies of this issue are rare, and the Shilling is practically unattainable in this condition.

Issue II. 1855-59.

Four values. Precisely similar in design to the preceding, and from the same dies. The Six Pence, like the Shilling, has the value in block letters. Coloured impression upon white paper; white gum; no watermark. The paper is soft, unsurfaced, and varies greatly in substance. Sets may be made from very thick to very thin. (*Illustration* 37.)

    1d., orange-vermilion, pale to dark ⎫
    2d., blue, bright and dull   ⎬ imperforate.
    6d., reddish-brown, light and dark ⎭
    1s., pale green, blue-green.

Series on hard white paper, slightly surfaced; no watermark; imperforate.

    1d., orange-red (shades).
    2d., deep, bright and pale blue.
    6d., orange-bistre, pale and dark fawn.
    1s., pale green, blue-green.

Varieties.—Some of the values of this issue are to be found with unofficial perforations. The following are known to the Society:

A are on the soft, unsurfaced paper.
B are on the hard, slightly-surfaced paper.

	Rouletted, about 7.	Rough pin-hole perforations, about 10.	Serrated fine perforations, about 16.
1d.		A B	B
2d.	B	A	B
6d.	A B	A	B
1s.	B	A	A B

Remarks.—By the *Gazette* notice the Six Pence was issued 8th August, 1859. The Two Pence has been seen on a letter postmarked August, 1855, showing the issue of the series extended over at least four years.

Issue III. 1862-3.

Four values. Identical in design with the preceding issues. Coloured impression upon very thin greyish paper (the pelure of catalogues); white gum; no watermark. (*Illustration* 37.)

1d., orange to carmine shades of vermilion
2d., pale lavender, ultramarine
6d., grey to blackish-brown, red-brown
1s., dark green, green.
} imperforate.

Varieties.—The Penny, orange-vermilion, Six Pence, dark brown, and Shilling, of this issue exist unofficially rouletted about 7, and all the four values machine-perforated 13.

To this period, late in 1863, must be referred the Two Pence and Six Pence on thick white paper; no watermark; machine-perforated 13.

2d., blue, deep blue
6d., red-brown
} perf. 13.

Issue IV. 1862-3.

Five values. Unchanged in design. The new one, Three Pence, has the value in block letters. Coloured impression upon white paper varying in substance; yellowish gum; watermark, a large six-rayed star. In the margin of the sheet are five parallel lines, forming a border to the whole. The paper varies much in thickness, and is sometimes as thin as the so-called pelure paper of Issue III. (*Illustration* 37.)

1d., orange-red, vermilion, deep crimson
2d., blue, deep, light, and chalky, and ultramarine
3d., bright violet, violet, violet-brown, lilac
6d., red-, black-, and dull brown
1s., dark yellow- and blue-green (shades)
} imperforate.

Varieties.—The Two Pence and Shilling are found on paper showing a distinctly blue appearance, probably due to chemical action. All five values and shades of each exist unofficially rouletted 5½ to 8. Other values are found with a fine pin perforation measuring about 16; viz., the Penny, Two Pence, Three Pence, and Six Pence; and the Six Pence and Shilling with an oblique perforation.

NEW ZEALAND.

Issue V. 1864.

Four values, of the same design as the preceding, seemed to have been issued in 1864. They are printed in colour upon white paper varying in substance, and are watermarked with the block letters " N.Z." instead of with a star. (*Illustration* 37.)

    1d., vermilion (a carmine shade)
    2d., pale blue
    6d., red-brown
    1s., green (shades)
    } imperf., rouletted 5½ to 8, and machine-perf. 13.

Remarks.—The Shilling is also known with oblique serrated perforations. The paper with the watermark "N.Z." was manufactured specially for the fiscal stamps of the colony, and during a temporary lack of that appropriated to postage stamps, was made use of for this issue.

The Six Pence, rouletted, is a very scarce stamp. An undoubted specimen is in the possession of a member of the Society.

Issue VI. 1863-66.

Six values. Identical in design with the preceding. The new one, Four Pence, issued in 1865, has the value printed in block letters. Coloured impression upon white paper varying in substance; white gum; watermark, six-rayed star. (*Illustration* 37.)

    1d., vermilion, orange
    2d., deep, pale, and chalky-blue
    3d., bright, pale, and brown-violet, purple
    4d., dull rose-red
    4d., canary-yellow, orange (1866), ochre-yellow
    6d., red-, black-, and dull brown
    1s., dark and yellow-green (shades)
    } officially machine-perf. 13.

Varieties.—A set of this issue may also be made up on very thin, almost pelure, paper. The Four Pence, orange, is found upon a hard paper, unwatermarked.

Issue VII. 1872.

Three values, of preceding types, but changed as regards colour. Coloured impression on white paper, varying in substance; white gum; watermark, six-rayed star. (*Illustration* 37.)

1. *Imperf.*
2. *Perf.* 10.
3. *Perf.* 10 × 13.
4. *Perf.* 13.

    2d., orange.
    1d., deep and pale bistre.
    1d.   „   „
    2d., vermilion, orange.
    6d., pale and full blue.
    1d.
    2d. } Same colours and shades.
    6d.

Varieties.—The Penny exists without watermark, perf. 13, and is said by M. Moens to have been issued in January, 1872. The Two Pence of this issue is also to be found: first, without watermark; second, watermarked "N.Z.;" and third, with a lozenge-patterned watermark, the alternate lozenges of which are shaded with vertical lines; all perf. 13. The Six Pence exists imperforate horizontally.

Issue VIII. 1873.

One value. For newspapers; lithographed in the colony. Coloured impression upon white wove paper, varying in substance; white gum. Design: Diademed profile of Queen Victoria to left within double-lined white oval. Straight white label at top, inscribed with coloured block letters. Curved white scroll below, similarly inscribed, with pearls beneath the scroll. Sides and spandrels filled in with arabesque ornaments, and the value, in coloured numerals, on each side of the oval. Shape, small upright rectangular. (*Illustration* 38.)

T. "NEW ZEALAND." B. "NEWSPAPER POSTAGE." R. AND L. "½d."

½d., rose (shades) { wmk.,"N.Z." } perf. 10, 12, and also compound 10 × 12.
{ „ Star } „ 12, 10.
{ no wmk. } „ 10 × 12.

Variety.—Imperf., horizontally; perf. 12, vertically.

Issue IX. 1873.

Six values. Engraved by Messrs. De la Rue and Co., and type-printed in colour upon medium white wove paper, slightly surfaced; white gum; watermark, "N. Z." in small block capitals, above a small five-rayed truncated star. The design is different for each value, except for the diademed profile of Queen Victoria to left, which is the same in all. (*Illustrations* 39, 40, 42, 43, 44, 45.)

ONE PENNY. Portrait, on ground of horizontal lines, within an oval band of solid colour; inscribed "NEW ZEALAND" in the upper, and "POSTAGE" in the lower curve, in white Roman capitals, the two inscriptions being separated by foliate ornaments. Straight white double-lined label at bottom, inscribed "ONE PENNY," in coloured Roman capitals. The spandrels are filled in with conventional ornaments, and the whole stamp is enclosed in a double-lined frame.

TWO PENCE. Portrait, on ground of horizontal lines, enclosed in circular band of colour with white pearls. Straight white labels at top and bottom, the first inscribed "NEW ZEALAND POSTAGE," and the second "TWO PENCE," in coloured block letters. Spandrels filled in with conventional ornaments, differing slightly from those in the previous value.

THREE PENCE. Portrait, on ground of horizontal lines, within double-lined circle. Curved coloured labels above and below circle, lettered, in white block letters, "NEW ZEALAND POSTAGE" and "THREE PENCE." Spandrels and sides filled in with conventional ornaments; border of plain double lines.

FOUR PENCE. Portrait, on ground of horizontal lines, within rectangular double-lined frame. Straight double-lined white label above, inscribed "NEW ZEALAND POSTAGE" in coloured block letters; the same below, inscribed "FOUR PENCE," with a block at either end containing a conventional ornament. The side labels are filled in with scrollwork. Same border as in preceding values.

SIX PENCE. Portrait, on ground of horizontal lines, within an oval of solid colour, which overlaps a hexagon frame of quadruple lines. The oval is inscribed, in white block letters, "NEW ZEALAND POSTAGE" and "SIX PENCE," the two inscriptions being separated by small ornaments. The spandrels are filled in with network, and the outer frame is the same as in the other values.

ONE SHILLING. Portrait, on ground of horizontal lines, enframed in double oval of solid colour, inscribed "NEW ZEALAND POSTAGE" in the upper, and "ONE SHILLING" in the lower curve, in white Roman capitals, the two inscriptions being separated by small ornaments. Corners filled in with arabesque ornaments; outer frame the same as in preceding values. Shape, upright rectangular; machine-perforated 13 and 12, and compound 13 × 10 and 11½.

(A) Fine clean impression on *glacé* paper.
(B) Coarser impression on rougher paper.

    1d., lilac   (shades.)
    2d., rose to pale lake („)
    3d., brown   („)
    4d., burnt-sienna   („)
    6d., Prussian-blue („)
    1s., green .   („)

Varieties.—Most of these values are to be found on paper which has been blued by the action of the gum, or some other cause. In 1877 two of the values—the Penny and Two Pence—were issued on paper watermarked with the old large six-rayed star, but the "NZ" and small star watermark was soon reverted to.

Remarks.—There appear to be two series, readily distinguishable by the superior care and greater neatness of the impression, which is on *glacé* or surfaced paper, in the one case, and the duller, more confused printing, on rougher paper, of the other. It is believed the former were printed in London by Messrs. De la Rue and Co., and the latter were printed in the colony. It is only the latter series that is found on the blued paper.

Issue X. 1878.

Two values. Engraved by Messrs. De la Rue and Co., and type-printed in colour on slightly surfaced white paper; white gum; watermarked "NZ" and star. Design: Diademed profile of Queen Victoria to left, on ground of horizontal lines, engraved in pearl circle. Straight white labels at top and bottom, inscribed in coloured block letters—"NEW ZEALAND POSTAGE" above, and "TWO" or "FIVE SHILLINGS" below. The spandrels are white, and in the Two Shilling value have the numeral 2 in the two upper, and a fern leaf in the two lower ones. In the Five Shilling value the numeral 5 is repeated in each of the four spandrels. Outer border of plain double lines. Shape, upright rectangular; perforation 11½. (*Illustrations* 46, 47.)

    2s., dull carmine.
    5s., grey-black.

Issue XI. April, 1882.

Seven values. Engraved by Messrs. De la Rue and Co., and type-printed in colour upon medium white wove paper, slightly surfaced; white gum; watermark "NZ" in small block capitals, above a small five-rayed truncated star. The design is different for each value, except for the diademed head of Queen Victoria to left, which is the same in all. (*Illustrations* 48, 49, 50, 51, 52, 53, 54.)

ONE PENNY. Portrait on ground of horizontal lines, within a double-lined oval band of solid colour, inscribed "NEW ZEALAND POSTAGE AND REVENUE" in the upper, and "ONE PENNY" in the lower curve, in white block capitals; the two inscriptions being separated by white dots. The spandrels are of solid colour, filled in with white arabesque ornamentation, and two coloured outer lines complete the design.

NEW ZEALAND.

Two Pence. Portrait on ground of horizontal lines within a double-lined oval band of solid colour, inscribed "NEW ZEALAND POSTAGE AND REVENUE" in the upper, and "TWO PENCE" in the lower curve. The upper inscription is printed in white block, and the lower in white Roman, capitals, and they are separated from each other by white dots. This portion of the design is enclosed by a white double-lined hexagonal band, which is cut at the sides by the oval. The spandrels are filled in with reticulations, and the design is completed by two outer lines of colour.

Three Pence. Portrait on ground of horizontal lines, within a double-lined oval band of solid colour inscribed "NEW ZEALAND" in the upper, and "POSTAGE AND REVENUE" in the lower curve, in white Roman capitals; the two inscriptions being separated from each other by white arabesque ornaments. Beneath the oval is a straight white single-lined label, containing the words "THREE PENCE" in coloured block capitals. The spandrels are filled in with white arabesque ornamentation on colour, and a single outer coloured line completes the design.

Four Pence. Portrait to left on ground of horizontal lines, within a narrow-pearled circle of colour. Above and beneath the circle are two straight white bands, containing the words T. "NEW ZEALAND," B. "POSTAGE AND REVENUE" in white block capitals. The spandrels are filled in with arabesque ornamentation, and with four circular coloured blocks, each containing the value, 4d., in white. An outer line of colour completes the design.

Six Pence. Portrait to left on ground of horizontal lines, within a single-lined upright rectangular frame. Above the frame is a white label containing the words "NEW ZEALAND" in coloured block capitals. The two top corners are filled in with white single-lined blocks in the same line with the white label, and containing star-shaped ornaments. Beneath the rectangular frame, and running across the whole width of the stamp, is a white label containing the words "POSTAGE AND REVENUE" in coloured block capitals. Straight perpendicular bands at the sides, filled in with arabesque ornamentation, and with two straight coloured labels rounded at the ends, and containing the words L. "SIXPENCE" reading upwards, and R. "SIXPENCE" reading downwards in white block capitals.

Eight Pence. Similar in every respect to the two pence except that the spandrels are filled in with arabesque ornamentation instead of reticulated lines.

One Shilling. Portrait to left on ground of horizontal lines within a double-lined circle. Above and beneath the circle, and following it in shape, are two curved bands of solid colour, straight at the ends, and containing the words T. "NEW ZEALAND POSTAGE AND REVENUE," and B. "ONE SHILLING" in white block capitals. The spandrels are filled in with white arabesque ornamentation on colour, and a single outer line of colour completes the design.

Shape, upright rectangular.   Machine-perf. 11½.

1d., rose
2d., lilac-mauve
3d., canary-yellow
4d., green   } slight shades.
6d., brown
8d., dark blue
1s., brownish-lake

NEW ZEALAND.

PROOFS.

The following are known, printed in black ink, on China or plate paper:
1st *type.*—Of the matrix with the bottom label for value left blank.
      1s. (other values no doubt exist).

1873 *Issue.*—On *glacé* paper (the paper of the issue); gummed, perforated, and surcharged "SPECIMEN" in black (De la Rue and Co.).

  1d., red-brown.   4d., carmine-rose.
  2d., ultramarine-blue.   6d., fawn-brown.
  3d., mauve.   1s., full green.

NEWSPAPER WRAPPERS.

Issue I. April 1st, 1878.

One value. On stoutish white unwatermarked paper. Size $12\frac{1}{2} \times 4$ inches, or 315×97 mm.; brown gum. Stamp of the same design as the Halfpenny Newspaper Stamp. Above, in an oblong label, the four angles of which are broken by ornaments, is printed in four lines—"This wrapper may only be used for Newspapers, and must not enclose any letter or communication of the nature of a letter (whether separate or otherwise). If this rule be infringed, letter rates will be charged." (*Illustration* 38.)
  $\frac{1}{2}$d., carmine.

NOTE.—The gummed flap is found with the corners cut square, and with the corners cut off.

Issue II. 1881.

Same as the preceding, but printed on thinner *toned* paper, watermarked with a crown between two large five-pointed stars, and with the inscription, "ONE HALFPENNY, NEW ZEALAND," in two lines, in large block capitals, the initial letters being larger than the others. Size 11×4 inches, or 275×95 mm. (*Illustration* 38.)
  $\frac{1}{2}$d., carmine.

Remarks.—Specimens are known with the watermark reversed. The size of this wrapper and that of the preceding issues varies from 5 to 10 mm. The varieties are probably accidental, and not worth separate classification.

OFFICIAL WRAPPERS.

M. Moens catalogues two wrappers for official use, presumably issued in 1885, bearing the arms of Great Britain and an inscription, "ON PUBLIC SERVICE"—"NEW ZEALAND GAZETTE"—"EXEMPT FROM POSTAGE." No value is expressed. Two varieties are mentioned, on white and blue paper.

POST CARDS.

Issue I. November, 1876.

One value. Printed upon medium light buff card. Size $5 \times 3\frac{1}{10}$ inches. At the top of the card there are three lines of inscription—first, "POST CARD" in Roman capitals, the two words being separated by the Royal Arms; second, "NEW ZEALAND" in small block letters, directly beneath the Arms; third, "THE ADDRESS ONLY TO BE WRITTEN ON THIS SIDE," in larger block letters. The stamp—type of adhesive, issue IX., 1873—is in the upper right corner. The design of the card is completed by a border composed of trefoil ornaments, within thin inner and thick outer lines; size $4\frac{9}{10} \times 2\frac{13}{18}$ inches. (*Illustration* 55.)
  1d., pale to deep brown.

NEW ZEALAND.

Issue II. 1881.

One value. Precisely similar to the last issue, except that the two lines of the border of the card are considerably thicker.

1d., pale to deep brown.

Issue III. 1886.

One value. The same as the last issue, but with a different ornamental border of slightly larger dimensions. Size $4\frac{9}{10} \times 2\frac{3}{4}$ inches. (*Illustration* 58.)

1d., brown (shades).

REPLY PAID CARD.
Issue I. 1886.

One value. Printed upon medium light buff card. Size when open, $4\frac{1}{8} \times 6\frac{1}{8}$ inches. The arms, stamps, and inscriptions are the same as those on the single cards, with the exception that the words "NEW," "ZEALAND," "THE," "ADDRESS," "ONLY," "WRITTEN," and "SIDE," have the initial letter in larger type than the rest of the word, and these two lines of the inscription are differently spaced. Under "NEW ZEALAND," on the first half, are the words "WITH REPLY CARD," in block letters, within brackets; and under "THE ADDRESS ONLY," &c., on the second half, "REPLY CARD," in Roman capitals. The borders of the cards are composed of intertwined cords, with square block at the four corners containing cross-like ornaments. Size, $4\frac{9}{10} \times 2\frac{3}{4}$ inches. The cards are folded between the two halves, rouletted $7\frac{1}{2}$, and the inscriptions, &c., are printed upon the first and fourth pages. (*Illustration* 59.)

1d. + 1d., brown (shades).

FISCAL STAMPS USED FOR POSTAGE.

From 1881 the fiscal stamps of this colony have been available for postage. In some cases there is no doubt of the *bonâ fide* use; but in the majority there is equally little doubt that unused specimens of the various issues were hunted up and used for the benefit of collectors. To give a detailed list of the varieties thus used would be attaching undue importance to stamps which do not possess any special significance.

QUEENSLAND.

Issue I. Early in 1861.

Four values. Engraved on steel (by Humphreys), and printed in *taille-douce* by Perkins, Bacon, and Co., of London, on stoutish white wove paper; white gum; watermark, large six-rayed star. Design: Full-faced diademed portrait of Queen Victoria, in low-necked dress, with conspicuous necklace and ear-rings, on ground of vertical and horizontal lines, enframed in a white oval border, inscribed with name of colony above, and value below in coloured block letters. Arabesques on either side separate the two inscriptions. The spandrels are filled in with reticulations, and two plain outer lines complete the design. (*Illustration* 56.)

T. "QUEENSLAND." B. "ONE PENNY," "TWO PENCE," "SIX PENCE," "ONE SHILLING."

    1d., carmine; imperforate.
    2d., deep blue   „
    6d., dark green   „
    1s., grey-lilac   „

Judging from the scarcity of most of these stamps, especially the Two Pence and Shilling, it was probably not long before they were superseded by a perforated series of the same values, with a Three Pence added of similar design.

    1d., carmine
    2d., blue, deep blue
    3d., dark brown   (A) Roughly punctured 15.
    6d., green, deep green   (B) Clean cut machine-perf. 14, 15.
    1s., greyish-lilac, brownish-lilac

Remarks.—A specimen of the Penny, imperforated, with postmark of Bath, England, 23rd August, 1861, was shown. A copy of the Six Pence is known upon thin *pelure* paper; watermarked.

There are two sizes of the star watermarks on the perforated stamps, and complete sets are found of each variety. It seems probable that both varieties of watermark exist on the same sheet.

Issue II. 1864.

Five values. In every way similar to the preceding, but printed on stout, soft, yellowish, unwatermarked wove paper. (*Illustration* 56.)

    1d., brown-orange, orange-vermilion
    2d., pale to deep blue   (shades)
    3d., brown   („)   roughly perf. 13.
    6d., green, and yellow-green („)
    1s., brownish-grey   („)

Varieties.—The Two Pence, blue, and the Six Pence, yellow-green, imperforate. The Two Pence, blue, exists on blued paper.

Issue III. 1866.

Two values. Identical in design with the preceding, but *lithographed* on stout, soft, yellowish unwatermarked paper. (*Illustration* 56.)

    4d., dull violet (shades) }
    4d., slate-grey („)   roughly perf. 13.
    5s., rose   („) }

Varieties.—There are at least three varieties of the Four Pence, arising from the size and shape of the letters comprising the word "FOUR," and its distance from "PENCE;" similar varieties occur in the Five Shillings.

Issue IV. 1866.

Three values. Of preceding design, printed in *taille-douce* on medium white paper; watermarked with the star of the first issue, and perforated with a square punch-like perforation gauging 13. (*Illustration* 56.)

    1d., orange-vermilion.
    2d., blue (shades).
    6d., yellow-green (shades).

Issue V. 1867.

Two values. Of preceding design, printed in *taille-douce* on medium white wove paper; watermarked in the sheet with "*Queensland Postage Stamps*" in large script capital letters. White and brown gum. (*Illustration* 56.)

    1d., orange-vermilion ; roughly perf. 13.
    2d., blue (shades)   „

Issue VI. 1868.

Two values. Of preceding design, printed in *taille-douce* on medium white wove paper; watermarked in the sheet with "QUEENSLAND" in large single-lined Roman capitals, and with a small six-rayed truncated star to each stamp. White and brown gum. (*Illustration* 56.)

    1d., orange-vermilion ; roughly perf. 13.
    2d., blue (shades)   „

Remarks.—Many of the stamps show the star watermark only, and no stamp can show more than a portion of one of the letters forming the word "QUEENSLAND."

Issue VII. 1869.

Three values. Of preceding design, printed in *taille-douce*, on white wove paper, varying in substance, and watermarked with a crown over the letter "Q." (*Illustration* 56.)

    1d., orange-vermilion   (shades) ; perf. 13, clean and rough perf.
    2d., blue   („)   „   and 12   „
    6d., yellow-green and green („)   „   „   „

Varieties.—The One Penny and Two Pence exist imperforate.

Issue VIII. 1872–75.

Three values. Of preceding design, printed in *taille-douce*, on white wove paper, varying in substance, and watermarked with "QUEENSLAND" and truncated star, as in the issue of 1868. (*Illustration* 56.)

    3d., brown (shades) }
    3d., greenish-brown (shades)
    6d., deep green   perf. 13.
    6d., yellow-green
    1s., reddish-brown (shades)
    1s., bright mauve }

QUEENSLAND. 87

Issue IX. June, 1875.

Four values. Of preceding designs, printed in *taille-douce*, on white wove paper, varying in substance, and watermarked with Crown over "Q," as in the issue of 1869. (*Illustration* 56.)

	1d., rose-red	(shades)
1876.	3d., brown	(„)
	6d., green, yellow-green, emerald-green	(„)
	1s., mauve, bright mauve	(„)

perf. 13.

Varieties.—The Six Pence, printed in emerald-green, and the One Shilling, in bright mauve, may be found unwatermarked.

Issue X. 1875-81-83.

Six values. Of preceding designs, *lithographed* on thinnish white paper; watermark, Crown over "Q." (*Illustrations* 56, 60.)

4d., yellow, canary-yellow	
2s., deep to pale blue	(shades)
2s. 6d., vermilion	(„)
5s., orange-brown, pale to deep	(„)
10s., brown	(„)
20s., rose-pink	(„)

perf. 12.

Remarks.—The higher values of this issue were no doubt primarily intended to serve as fiscals, but all have done postal service.

Issue XI. 1879-80.

Five values. Lithographed in the colony, on medium white paper; watermarked Crown over "Q;" white gum. Design: Apart from the portrait of Her Majesty, which is a diademed profile to left on ground of horizontal lines, the design of this series is a copy of the original one. The name of colony and value in full are found in the same positions, but in white block capitals on a coloured oval, and the inscriptions are separated by arabesques. The spandrels are filled in with network, and two plain outer lines complete the design. (*Illustration* 61.)

T. "QUEENSLAND." B. "ONE PENNY," "TWO PENCE," "FOUR PENCE," "SIX PENCE," "ONE SHILLING."

July, 1879.	1d., brown-orange, deep vermilion, rose-red (shades)	
	2d., pale, chalky-, and ultramarine-blue	(„)
Dec., 1879.	4d., orange-yellow	(„)
March, 1880.	6d., green, yellow-green	(„)
Nov., 1880.	1s., violet-mauve	(„)

roughly perf. 12.

Error.—A One Penny, yellow, found its way into one or more of the sheets of Four Pence. The mistake seems to have been soon corrected.

Varieties.—The One Penny exists imperforate. The "U" of Queensland, owing to defective printing, is more like an "O" on certain of the One Penny stamps. In some of the One Shilling stamps the "I" is so long as to break into the upper part of the oval. Many minor varieties can be found in the lettering of all the values.

Issue XII. April, 1880.

One provisional value, formed by surcharging the last issued One Penny, "HALFPENNY," vertically down the centre of the stamp, reading upwards. (*Illustration* 62.) ½d., brownish-orange (shades); black surcharge; perf. 12.

Variety.—Of course, the defective "u" and the other varieties are to be found on this as on the unsurcharged value.

Remarks.—This stamp was prepared for the purpose of making up a rate of 1½d., which was at that time charged on newspapers between Queensland and the United Kingdom, and before a special stamp of that value could be procured the rate was changed.

1880.

Of the preceding type the One Penny and Two Pence, *unwatermarked*, with a purple band of *burelé* pattern on the back, were used. This paper appears to have been formerly employed for fiscal stamps.

Issue XIII. May, 1882.

Five values. Engraved and printed in *taille-douce* on white wove paper; watermarked Crown over "q;" white gum. Design: Portrait of Queen Victoria, as in the first issues, on ground of horizontal lines within pearled oval border. White curved band with straight ends, above portrait, lettered with name of colony in coloured block type. A similar coloured band beneath portrait with value in full in white block letters. Coloured circles in each corner with numeral of value. The remainder of the stamp is filled in with background of horizontal lines and arabesques, and an ornamental border completes the design. Shape, large upright rectangular. (*Illustrations* 64, 65.)

T. "QUEENSLAND." B. "TWO SHILLINGS," "TWO SHILLINGS AND SIX PENCE," "FIVE SHILLINGS," "TEN SHILLINGS," "ONE POUND."

    2s., ultramarine
    2s. 6d., scarlet-vermilion
    5s., carmine   perf. 12.
    10s., dark brown
  1883. £1, deep green

Remarks.—From the omission of the words "*Stamp Duty*" it is evident that these stamps were intended to fulfil a double service, and they seem to be used both postally and fiscally.

Issue XIV. 1883.

Five values. Lithographed and printed in the colony on medium white wove paper; watermarked Crown over "q;" white gum. Design: These stamps are very similar in design to the issue of 1879–80. The execution is somewhat bolder and better; the spandrels are filled in with horizontal lines, and ornamented with arabesques, and there is a pearled outer border. Shape, upright rectangular. (*Illustration* 63.)

T. "QUEENSLAND." B. "ONE PENNY," "TWO PENCE," "FOUR PENCE," "SIX PENCE," "ONE SHILLING."

    1d., vermilion, red, pale, and dark ; perf. 12.
    2d., ultramarine-, chalky-blue ; perf. 12.
    4d., yellow   "
    6d., green   "
    1s., mauve   "
  Error. 1d., yellow, printed in the colour of the 4d.

Varieties.—In some of the One Penny stamps the first "E" of Queensland is an "F," in others it resembles an "s." In some of the Six Penny stamps the "c" of Pence is a distinct "o," and other varieties in the lettering are to be found.

QUEENSLAND.

STAMPS FOR REGISTERED LETTERS.

One value. Engraved and printed in *taille-douce* by Perkins, Bacon, and Co. Identical in design with the other stamps of the first issue, but having the word "*Registered*" in block type beneath the portrait instead of value; watermarked large six-rayed star. (*Illustration* 57.)

Nov., 1861. (6d.), dull ochre, olive-yellow (shades); perf. 14, 15.
1865. (6d.), yellow, bright yellow („); square perf. 13.

Variety.—The (6d.), bright yellow, is known imperforate.

REGISTRATION ENVELOPES.
Issue I. 1880.

One value (probably Four Pence). In paper, size, inscriptions, gum, &c., the envelope is very similar to that already described for New South Wales, and to the English Registered envelope of 1878, size G. The inscriptions, however, on the face are in rather thicker block letters, printed closer together; and the rectangle for the stamp is larger, measuring 25 × 23mm. There is no stamp on the flap, beneath which are the words "Mc. Corquodale and Co., *Contractors.*" Size 6 × 3½ inches, or 152 × 97mm.

Without value (4d.?) vermilion.

Remarks.—M. Moens catalogues an envelope similar to the above, but measuring 97 × 52mm. This is probably a misprint for 152mm. No such size is known to the Society among the Registered envelopes of either Great Britain or the colonies, and the specimen described above is doubtless what M. Moens refers to.

POST CARDS.
Issue I. End, 1880.

One value. Lithographed upon thick white, and light buff card, varying in substance. Size 5⅞ × 3⅜ inches. At the top of the card in the centre there is a fancy oblong label with *moiré* groundwork, bearing two lines of inscription, first "POST CARD" in plain Roman capitals; second, "QUEENSLAND AUSTRALIA," in coloured block letters. Below the label, and between two straight lines is "THE ADDRESS ONLY TO BE WRITTEN ON THIS SIDE." On the right side of the label is the stamp, which consists of the oval portion of the first issued adhesives, with an extra outer line of colour; and on the left are the Royal Arms, Crown, Supporters, and Motto. Lower down to left is the word "*To*" in script type, followed by four dotted lines for the address. The design of the card is completed by a fancy ornamental border composed of intertwined cords, size $5\frac{3}{10} \times 3\frac{3}{10}$ inches. (*Illustration* 66.)

        1d., carmine, rose (shades), on thick white card.
        1d.   „   „   on thick light buff card.
        1d.   „   „   on thinner   „   surfaced card.
1884.   1d., lake   „   „   „

FISCAL STAMPS USED POSTALLY.

During the years 1880–1883 several values of the fiscal stamps were used to defray postage. They are all inscribed "Stamp Duty," and range in value from One Penny to One Pound.

A list of the varieties will not be necessary, but it should be added that these stamps appear to have been more legitimately used for postage than in certain other cases mentioned in this work.

SAMOA ISLANDS.

Issue 1877–81.

Seven values. Lithographed in colour upon white paper of medium substance by Messrs. S. T. Lee & Co., of Pitt Street, Sydney, and by them supplied to Messrs. Griffiths & Co., Sydney, agents for Samoa; the stone being altered for each value. White gum; no watermark, machine-perforated 13. Design: in the centre a circle of solid colour, with white frame containing irregular coloured dots. In the upper and lower parts of the circle white arabesque ornaments. A straight label crosses the middle of the stamp, debruising the circle and its ornaments, bearing the inscription in white block letters upon ground of horizontal line, "EXPRESS." Curved white labels, ornamented with arabesques above and below the circle, inscribed with coloured letters. The design is completed by a double outer line of colour. (*Illustration* 67.)

T. "SAMOA." Centre, "EXPRESS." B. "POSTAGE," and value in words.

December, 1877. 1d., ultramarine (shades).
" 3d., vermilion (")
" 6d., mauve (")
May, 1881. 9d., red-brown (")
July (?), 1878. 1s., ochre-yellow (")
" 2s., chocolate-brown (")
" 5s., emerald-green (")

Variety. Rouletted. July, 1877. 6d., mauve.

Remarks.—The above stamps do not constitute a Government issue. They were employed for a Private Post first established in 1877 by Mr. W. E. Agar, for the conveyance of letters from and to Apia and neighbouring islands and New Zealand. In 1879, the undertaking was transferred to Mr. A. Speirs; and on his death, in 1880, Mr. Griffiths, then residing at Apia, took over the concern, which was abandoned in 1882, in consequence of its not paying, when, of course, the stamps became obsolete.

The stamps are seldom found perforated on all four sides, so that probably some of the sheets are imperforate vertically or horizontally.

The Six Pence, *rouletted*, is given on the authority of M. Moens. It is not known to the Society.

REPRINTS.

After the discontinuance of the post in 1882 all the stamps were reprinted, and a new value of Two Pence was added to them. The colours are for the most part brighter, and the stamps are perforated 12 generally on all four sides.

1d., deep blue.
2d., violet-rose.
3d., rose-red.
6d., bright violet.
9d., pale red-brown.
1s., " ochre-yellow.
2s., deep chocolate-brown.
5s., bright emerald-green.

SOUTH AUSTRALIA.

Issue I. 1855-57.

Four values. Engraved on steel by W. Humphreys, and printed by Messrs. Perkins, Bacon, & Co. Coloured impression upon stoutish white wove paper; brownish gum; watermark, a six-rayed star. Design: Diademed profile of Queen Victoria to left, upon engine-turned background, within a circle which nearly touches the sides of the stamp; white curved label above the circle, inscribed "SOUTH AUSTRALIA" in coloured Roman capitals. This label is shaded at the corners in the One Penny and Six Penny values, and unshaded in the Two Pence and One Shilling. Straight coloured labels at top and bottom of stamp, the upper one inscribed "POSTAGE," and the lower one with the value in words, all in white Roman capitals, except in the One Shilling, which has the value only in block letters. In the four corners are square white blocks, containing eight-rayed stars, with hollow centre, the diagonal rays of which are much thicker than the others, upon a background formed of two square outlines, one within the other. The spandrels are filled in with diapered groundwork. Shape, upright rectangular; imperforate. (*Illustration* 68.)

T. "POSTAGE." B. "ONE PENNY," "TWO PENCE," "SIX PENCE," and "ONE SHILLING."

October, 1855. 1d., dark and yellow-green.
January, 1855. 2d., brick- and venetian-red (shades).
October, 1855. 6d., dark, purplish-, and chalky-blue.
July, 1857. 1s., orange, light and dark.

Varieties.—The Two Pence is known watermarked, with a faulty star with truncated points.

Issue II. 1859-62.

Five values, four of which are the same as those of the preceding issue in design, paper, watermark, and gum, but differ somewhat in shade. The new value, Nine Pence, is engraved on steel by C. H. Jeens for Perkins, Bacon, and Co., on similar paper, has the same watermark and white gum. Design: A larger diademed profile of Queen Victoria to left, upon reticulated background, within a double oval, which touches the top, bottom, and sides of the stamp. In the upper part of the oval is "SOUTH AUSTRALIA," and in the lower "NINE PENCE," in coloured block letters upon white. The sides of the oval are ornamented with open bars of coloured lines, and the spandrels with reticulations. All the values in this issue are rouletted 9. (*Illustrations* 68, 69.)

T. "SOUTH AUSTRALIA." B. "NINE PENCE."

1859. 1d., dark green shades.
1862. 2d., vermilion, light (1860) and dark and venetian-red (shades).
October, 1862. 6d., violet- and chalky-blue (shades of each).
December, 1860. 9d., lilac, pale and dark.
1859. 1s., orange- and canary-yellow.

Remarks.—A copy of the Nine Pence (of the dark and early shade) imperforate was in the President's collection, but it ought probably to be classed as a proof.

The One Shilling, orange, is found printed on both sides.

In the later printings of this issue the paper varies very considerably in texture; and whilst the One Shilling value was entirely changed in colour, the others exhibit varieties of shade, which are tabulated below in the order in which, judging from postmarked specimens, they are supposed to have appeared.

      1864. 1d., full to light green, yellow-green.
      1862. 2d., vermilion, dark to light, with variations caused by oxydisation.
 November, 1863. 6d., Prussian-, deep, slaty-, and chalky-blue, ultramarine.
         9d., greyish-lilac.
 July,   1862. 1s., deep reddish to pale brown.

Issue III. July, 1866-67.

One value. This stamp is printed from the die of the Nine Pence, the original value being obliterated by a curved surcharge of "TEN PENCE," in Roman capitals, printed in blue ink. Stoutish white paper; yellow gum; watermark unchanged; rouletted 9. (*Illustration* 70.)

    10d., orange-red (July, 1866), canary-yellow (1867), blue surcharge.

Remarks.—There are in this and subsequent issues of the same value about six varieties of surcharge arising from the greater or less curve of the inscription, and some irregularities in the placing of the letters composing it in the form.

Issue IV. January, 1867.

Two values. Engraved on steel by C. H. Jeens for Perkins, Bacon, and Co. Coloured impression on stout and thin white wove paper; white and brown gum; same watermark. Design: Diademed profile of Queen to left, on engine-turned ground, within a circle consisting of a simple white line, "SOUTH AUSTRALIA" above, and value in words beneath the circle in white Roman capitals; conventional scroll ornaments at the top and sides of stamp, which, owing to the want of an outer-line border, has a somewhat unfinished appearance. Shape, upright rectangular; rouletted 9. (*Illustration* 71.)

    T. "SOUTH AUSTRALIA." B. "FOUR PENCE," "TWO SHILLINGS."
     4d., dull purple, light and dark.
     2s., carmine.

Issue V. September, 1868.

One value. This stamp, type-printed by Messrs. De la Rue and Co., is a copy, upon a somewhat reduced scale, of the immediately preceding design. The background to the portrait is formed of horizontal lines instead of engine-turning. Coloured impression upon white wove paper, varying in substance; white gum; watermark a Crown, with the letters "SA" beneath it. Shape, upright rectangular. (*Illustration* 72.)

    T. "SOUTH AUSTRALIA." B. "TWO PENCE."
     2d., orange, deep to light; rouletted 9.
     2d.   „   „ perf. 11½.

Remarks.—The distance between the letters "SA" of the watermark varies considerably on different stamps. This remark applies to all stamps with this watermark.

Issue VI. 1868-9.

Seven values. Of the preceding types, watermarked with star, machine-perforated 11½, otherwise unchanged. (*Illustrations* 68, 70, 71.)

     1d., green, dark and light.
     2d. (1st type), vermilion.
     4d., dark purple.
     6d., Prussian-, deep, and chalky-blue.
  1869. 10d., orange and yellow, blue surcharge.
     1s., red-brown (shades).
     2s., carmine („)

Varieties.—The One Penny, Four Pence, Six Pence, Ten Pence, and One Shilling are found machine-perforated 11½ horizontally, and rouletted 9 vertically. The Two Shilling is met with without vertical perforation between certain rows of stamps.

The Ten Pence presents several varieties, which, from the difficulty experienced in classifying them otherwise, are chronicled under this issue.

1st. Blue surcharge, watermarked Crown and "SA" instead of star; perf. 11½.
2nd. 9d., without surcharge, star watermark; printed in orange.
   (A) Rouletted 9.
   (B) Perforated 11½, and rouletted 9.

This last and rare variety is due, in all likelihood, to the accidental omission of the surcharge. Copies are to be met with which have passed through the post, the absence of all surcharge not preventing the authorities from regarding them as of the postal value of Ten Pence, rather than of the apparent facial value of Nine Pence.

Issue VII. 1869.

Two values. Of preceding types; watermarked star; rouletted 9. (*Illustrations* 72, 70.)

   2d. (type 2), orange-red.
   10d., yellow, bright and pale; black surcharge.

Varieties.—The Ten Pence is found with the surcharge inverted, and printed above instead of below the head.

Issue VIII. 1870.

Three values. Two varieties of the Two Pence (type 2) were issued in this year: the first is perforated 10 horizontally, and rouletted vertically; and the second is machine-perforated 10 throughout. Both varieties are watermarked with Crown and "SA." A new value was formed by printing a stamp from the Four Penny die, in ultramarine, and obliterating the original value by printing over it, in a straight line, "3 PENCE," in carmine. This stamp is machine-perforated 10; watermark star. The Ten Pence was surcharged in black instead of blue. (*Illustrations* 72, 75, 70.)

     2d. (type 2), orange-red (shades); perf. 10, and rouletted 9.
     2d. („) „ to yellow „ 10.
August, 1870. 3d., ultramarine, carmine surcharge „ 10.
   1869 (?). 10d., orange-yellow, black „ „ 11¼.

In August, 1870, the surcharge on the Three Pence value, just described, was altered, being printed in black instead of carmine, and the machine-perforation was changed to 11½; watermark star, as before.

   3d., ultramarine; black surcharge.

Variety.—Identical in shade and perforation with the above, the Four Penny stamp exists unsurcharged. Whether this stamp represents a Four Penny label printed in the wrong colour, or a Three Pence with the surcharge accidentally omitted, it is not easy to determine.

Issue IX. 1871.

Six values. Of preceding types; watermark star. This emission was originally, we believe, issued with a regular machine-perforation of 10. In course of time, however, it became extremely irregular, and compound perforations of 11½ × 10,

12 × 10, 13 × 10, 11½ × 12½, and probably others, are commonly met with. (*Illustrations* 68, 75, 71.)

    1d., bright and yellow-green.
    3d., ultramarine, Prussian-blue, black surcharge.
    4d., lilac (shades), dark grey.
    6d., deep blue, ultramarine (1886).
    1s., red-brown.
    2s., deep carmine.

Issue X. 1871.

Two values. Consisting of the Two Pence (type 2) and the Four Pence perforated 10, and watermarked with a Crown and "v." These two stamps probably deserve to be classed as errors, having evidently been printed by mistake upon paper intended for stamps of Victoria. (*Illustrations* 72, 71.)

    2d. (type 2), orange-red (shades).
    4d., dull purple and slate.

Issue XI. 1872.

One value. This is the original Nine Penny value revived; printed on rather thinner and inferior paper to that employed for the old Nine Pence; watermark unchanged; machine-perforated 11½. (*Illustration* 69.)

    9d., lilac-grey.
    9d., reddish-lilac, varying to mauve.

Varieties.—This stamp and the Two Pence (type 2) exist with a double perforation. Specimens have been seen rouletted, and in addition perf. 11½ all round. Other specimens of the Nine Pence are known, printed in rose; but the colour has probably been chemically changed.

Issue XII. 1874.

One value. The makeshift Ten Pence surcharged in black, and perf. 10. (*Illustration* 70.)

    10d., bright yellow, black surcharge.

Issue XIII. January, 1875.

One value. Type-printed by Messrs, De la Rue and Co. Coloured impression on white surfaced paper of medium substance; white gum; watermark Crown and "SA." Design : Diademed profile of Queen to left, on ground of horizontal lines, within double-lined oval; curved label above the oval, and straight label below, occupying the whole width of the stamp—the first inscribed "SOUTH AUSTRALIA," and the second with value in words, all in white block letters upon coloured ground. The sides and spandrels of the stamp are filled in with foliate and arabesque ornaments. Shape, upright rectangular; various perforations. (*Illustration* 76.)

    1d. (type 2), green (shades); perf. 10, 11, 12½, and compound.

Issue XIV. September, 1876.

One value. That most useful die of the early Nine Pence is again brought into requisition. A stamp is struck from it of a burnt-sienna colour, and the original value is obliterated by a black surcharge of "8 PENCE." Medium white wove paper; white gum; watermark, star; machine-perf. 13. (*Illustration* 77.)

    8d., burnt-sienna; black surcharge.

Remarks.—Other perforations than 13 are also to be found, 11½ × 12½; indeed, most of the perforations are compound.

SOUTH AUSTRALIA.

Issue XV. 1880.

During this year the Four Pence, whilst remaining unaltered in other respects, underwent a considerable change in colour. (*Illustration* 71.)

4d., reddish-purple.

Issue XVI. January 1st, 1882. Provisional.

One value. This is the Penny green, of 1875, converted provisionally into a Halfpenny stamp by means of a black surcharge, "HALF PENNY" in block letters, and in two lines; a black bar obliterating the original value "ONE PENNY." In other respects the stamps are the same. (*Illustration* 78.)

½d., black and green; perf. 10.

Issue XVII. March, 1883.

One value. Engraved and type-printed by Messrs. De la Rue and Co., in colour, upon medium white wove paper; watermark, Crown and "SA;" white gum. Design: Diademed profile of Queen Victoria to left, on ground of horizontal lines, enclosed in an octagonal frame. Above and below are two labels of solid colour, inscribed in small white block letters. The spandrels are filled in with small triangular colour blocks, each containing a white dot, and the design is completed by a single outer-line of colour; perf. 10. Shape, small upright rectangular. (*Illustration* 79.)

T. "SOUTH AUSTRALIA" (in two lines). B. "HALFPENNY."

½d., reddish-brown.

Issue XVIII. 1884 (?). Provisional (?).

One value. Engraved and type-printed by Messrs. De la Rue and Co. Coloured impression on white wove unwatermarked paper; white gum. Design: Diademed profile of Queen Victoria to left, on solid ground, enclosed by a single white oval line. Below the oval is a straight label of colour, inscribed "HALFPENNY" in white Roman capitals. The spandrels are filled in with arabesques, and the design is completed by a double outer-line of colour. Shape, upright rectangular; machine-perf. 12. (*Illustration* 74.)

½d., mauve.

Remarks.—This stamp is identical with that found upon the wrappers (type II.), described below. It is printed upon the same paper, and it seems probable that, during a temporary exhaustion of the stock of the current Halfpenny, the dies used for the wrappers were set up, and a few sheets of stamps printed from them. The only specimen known to the Society is used upon an ordinary wrapper, the stamp of which is of the same type, the two together making up the postal rate of 1d.

Issue XIX. August, 1885.

One value. Same in every respect to the Halfpenny of 1883, but changed in colour. (*Illustration* 79.)

½d., green.

NOTE.—This stamp is catalogued by M. Moens, but it does not appear to have been issued. An imperforate pair exists in the collection of the Vice-President.

REPRINTS.

In 1885 a reprint of the various South Australian stamps was taken, it is understood, to oblige a collector. All the specimens have "REPRINT" struck on the face, in black Roman capitals, with the exception of the provisional Halfpenny, green, which is surcharged "REPRINT" in red. They may be classified as follows:

(A) *Imperf.*	1d., green, light yellow-green	(Type 1855).	
	2d., rose-red	(„ „).	
	6d., indigo-blue	(„ „).	
(B) *Rouletted.*	1d., olive-green	(„ „).	
	2d., pale and bright vermilion	(„ „).	
	2d., reddish-brown	(„ 1868).	
	6d., pale blue, dark lilac	(„ 1855).	
	9d., dull lilac	(„ 1860).	
	10d., orange, blue surcharge	(„ 1866).	
	10d., canary-yellow, blue surcharge	(„ 1867).	
	1s., canary-yellow	(„ 1857).	
	1s., brown	(„ 1862).	
(C) *Perf. 12.*	3d., blue, red surcharge	(„ 1870).	
	3d., blue, black surcharge	(„ 1870).	
	4d., purple-black, mauve	(„ 1867).	
	4d., dark lilac	(„ 1867).	
	6d., blue	(„ 1855).	
	8d., reddish-brown, black surcharge	(„ 1876).	
	8d., brown, black surcharge	(„ 1876).	
	9d., mauve	(„ 1872).	
	10d., orange-yellow, black surcharge	(„ 1869).	
	1s., brown	(„ 1862).	
	2s., carmine	(„ 1867).	
(D) *Perf. 10.*	½d., orange, black surcharge (Moens)	(„ 1882).	
	½d., green, black surcharge	(„ 1882).	
	¾d., brown	(„ 1883).	
	1d., green	(„ 1875).	
	2d., orange	(„ 1882).	
	8d., brown, black surcharge	(„ 1876).	

OFFICIAL OR DEPARTMENTAL STAMPS.

To describe in detail the immense number of varieties which exist of these stamps would prove a most tedious task, and the result would be of doubtful interest. When we have given a list of the various surcharges and their signification, and have pointed out which of the values so surcharged are least frequently met with, we do not consider ourselves further called upon to trace the surcharges upon all the varieties of stamps which we have enumerated in the reference list of postage stamps proper. Suffice it to say, that the lettering is found printed in various colours upon almost every variety of type, colour, shade, watermark, and perforation.

The use of stamps surcharged with certain capital letters, forming the initials of the Department of Government in which they were used, probably commenced in 1863, as we find the surcharges on the rouletted stamps of that issue, but not on those of the two previous ones. They continued in use until about eight years ago, since when all stamps, we believe, employed to frank official correspondence have been indifferently surcharged "o. s.," which signifies, "On Service," or "Official Service." The surcharge is in block letters, with a stop, as a rule, after each.

SOUTH AUSTRALIA.

LIST OF SURCHARGES.

A.	in black and red	Architect.
A.G.	„ black, red, and blue	Attorney-General.
A.O.	„ „ „	Audit Office.
B.D.	„ red	Barrack Department.
B.G.	„ black	Botanical Gardens.
B.M.	„ red	Board of Magistrates.
C.	„ black, blue, and red	Customs.
C.D.	„ „ and red	Convict Department.
C.L.	„ „ blue, and red	Crown Lands.
C.O.	„ „ and red	Commissariat Office.
C.S.	„ „ red, and blue	Colonial Secretary.
C.Sgn.	„ „ and red (2 types)	Colonial Surgeon.
C.P.	„ red	Commissioner of Police (?).
D.B.	„ black, blue, and red	Destitute Board.
D.R.	„ „	Deed Registry.
E.	„ „ red, and blue	Engineer.
E.B.	„ black and blue	Education Board.
G.P.	„ „ red, and blue	Government Printer.
G.S.	„ red	Government Survey.
G.T.	„ black and red	Goolwa Tramway.
H.	„ „	(?).
H.A.	„ „ and red	House of Assembly.
H.G.	„ „	(?).
I.A.	„ red	Immigration Agent.
I.E.	„ black	(?).
I.S.	„ red and black	Inspector of Sheep.
L.A.	„ black and red	Lunatic Asylum.
L.C.	„ red and black	Legislative Council.
L.L.	„ „	Legislative Library.
L.T.	„ black, blue, and red	Land Tenures.
M.	„ „ and red	Militia (?).
M.B.	„ „ „	Marine Board.
M.R.	„ „ „	Marine Registry (?).
M.R.G.	„ „ and blue	Manager Railway, Gambier Town.
N.T.	„ „	(?).
O.	„ „	Ordnance (?).
O.A.	„ „ red, and blue	Official Assignee.
O.S.	„ „	On Service.
O.S.	surcharge inverted on 1d. (1875)	......
P.	in black	Police.
P.A.	„ „ and red	Protector of Aborigines.
P.O.	„ „ red, and blue	Post Office.
P.O.	2nd type in long thinner capitals	......
P.S.	in black and red	Principal Secretary.
P.W.	„ „ „	Public Works.
R.B.	„ red, blue, and black	Road Board.
R.G.	„ black, red, and blue	Registrar-General.
S.	„ red, blue, and black	Sheriff.
S.C.	„ black, red, and blue	Supreme Court.
S.G.	„ „ „	Solicitor-General.
S.M.	„ „ „	Stipendiary Magistrate.
S.P.	„ „	Superintendent of Prisons (?).
S.T.	„ „ red, and blue	Superintendent of Telegraphs.
T.	„ „ „	Treasury.
T.R.	„ „	(?).
V.	„ red	Volunteers.
V.A.	„ black	Volunteer Artillery.
W.	„ „	Waterworks.

The above surcharges are common on the 1d. (type 1), rouletted and perf.

Scarce except o.s.	"	1d. (type 2).	
Common	"	2d. (types 1 and 2), rouletted and perf.	
Scarce	"	3d., black surcharge.	
Unknown (?)	"	3d., red.	"
Common	"	4d.	
"	"	6d., all shades, rouletted and perf.	
o.s. Only	"	8d.	
Scarce	"	9d., grey-lilac.	
o.s. Only	"	9d., mauve (1872).	
Scarce	"	10d.	
Unknown (?)	"	1s., orange or yellow.	
Common	"	1s., brown, rouletted and perf.	
Not many	"	2s.	

"TOO LATE" STAMPS.

It is doubtful whether stamps bearing this surcharge are worthy of any attention. It is most probable that, as is the case with similar stamps in Trinidad, the words, "Too late" are, at best, a postmark struck with a hand-stamp after the letters have been posted. No "Too late" stamps are sold to the public in Trinidad, and the unused specimens seen in collections have simply been stamped to order. The following South Australian stamps are met with having this surcharge in black:

1d. (types 1 and 2).	6d.
2d. (type 2).	8d.
3d. (black surcharge).	9d., grey-lilac.
4d.	

WRAPPERS.
Issue I. January 11th, 1882. Type I.

One value. Engraved and type-printed by Messrs. De la Rue and Co. Coloured impression on medium white wove paper; unwatermarked. The stamp is in the right upper portion of the wrapper. Design: Diademed profile of Queen Victoria to left, on solid ground, enclosed by a single white oval line. Below the oval is a straight label of solid colour, inscribed "HALFPENNY" in white Roman capitals. The spandrels are filled in with arabesques, and the design is completed by a double outer-line of colour. Shape, upright rectangular.

To the left of the stamp is the inscription "SOUTH AUSTRALIA" and "NEWSPAPER ONLY," in two lines, the two former words being printed in Roman capitals, and the latter in block letters. Between the words "SOUTH" and "AUSTRALIA" are the arms of Great Britain. Two sizes are found. (*Illustration* 73.)

Size A, $11\frac{1}{4} \times 4\frac{3}{10}$ inches, or 290 × 110 mm.
Size B, $17\frac{2}{8} \times 5\frac{3}{4}$ inches, or 443 × 145 mm.

½d., bright mauve, dull mauve (shades).

Remark.—Specimens are met with so badly printed that the details of the arabesques are almost obliterated.

Issue II. 1884. Type II.

One value. Similar to the preceding, but differing in detail of the design. The spandrels of the stamp are more ornamented; the letters of "HALFPENNY" are more spaced and slightly larger; and the lines of shading on the neck of the bust are nearly horizontal, instead of being oblique. The lettering of "SOUTH AUSTRALIA" is considerably larger, and the Royal Arms are smaller. Two sizes, as before. (*Illustration* 74.)

Size A, $11\frac{1}{2} \times 4\frac{3}{10}$ inches, or 290×110 mm.
Size B, $17\frac{3}{4} \times 5\frac{3}{4}$ inches, or 443×145 mm.
½d., mauve (shades).

Remark.—The stamp of this wrapper is identical in type with the Halfpenny adhesive of 1884.

Issue III. 1885. Type II.

One value. The same as the last issue, but printed upon *manilla* paper. Two sizes A and B, as before. (*Illustration* 74.)

½d., mauve (shades).

OFFICIAL WRAPPERS.

Issue I. 1882.

One value. Similar to the ordinary wrapper of the issue of January, 1882, but the stamp is surcharged in black "o.s.," in large block letters. There are two types of the surcharge, in one of which the letters "o.s." are larger and rounded than on the other.

½d., mauve. Sizes A and B (?).

Issue II. 1884.

One value. In every way the same as the ordinary wrapper of this date; but the stamp is surcharged "o.s.," the same as in the preceding issue.

½d., mauve. Sizes A and B (?).

Issue III. 1885.

One value. The same as the last issue, but printed upon *manilla* paper.

½d., mauve. Sizes A and B (?).

POST CARDS.

Issue I. December, 1876.

One value. Printed upon medium light buff card. Size $4\frac{1}{4} \times 2\frac{9}{10}$ inches. At the top of the card there are two lines of inscription—first, "SOUTH AUSTRALIA," in thin Roman capitals, the two words being separated by the Royal Arms; second, "POST CARD," in larger Roman capitals. Lower down to left the word "To." The stamp is in the right upper corner. Design: Diademed head of Queen Victoria to left, in solid oval; solid label below inscribed "ONE PENNY," in Roman capitals; spandrels and sides filled in with arabesques, all within treble-lined frame. The design of the card is completed by a double-lined narrow ornamental border; size $4\frac{1}{10} \times 2\frac{3}{4}$ inches. (*Illustration* 80.)

1d., lilac (shades).

Variety.—The same, printed upon stout white cardboard, probably as proofs, have passed through the post.

REPLY PAID CARDS.

Issue I. March, 1883.

One value. Similar in every way to the single card, except that the first half has the words "WITH REPLY CARD," and the second half the word "REPLY," both in fancy capitals above the Royal Arms. The cards are folded along the top, perforated 6, and the design is impressed upon the first and third pages.

1d. + 1d., rose.

OFFICIAL CARD.

Issue 1883 (?).

One value. Consisting of the single card, with the stamp surcharged "o.s.," in thick black block letters across the centre. There are two types of the surcharge, one having the letters "o.s." larger and more rounded than the other.

1d., lilac (shades).

REPLY PAID OFFICIAL CARD.

Issue 1886.

One value. The ordinary reply paid card of March, 1883, with the stamp on each half surcharged "o.s.," in thick black block letters across the centre. Only one type of the surcharge, that with the larger letters, is known to the Society.

1d. + 1d., rose.

TASMANIA.

Issue I. 1st November, 1853.

Two values. Engraved in *taille-douce* by C. W. Coard, and printed in the colony by A. and C. Best, on white wove paper, varying considerably in substance from stout to nearly *pelure;* brownish gum. Design: Diademed bust profile of Queen Victoria to right, on ground of cross-hatched lines enframed by an oval border in the One Penny, and an almost circular one in the Four Penny value. In each stamp the border is white, and inscribed with name of colony above, and value in full below, in coloured block letters. In the One Penny the oval is placed on an erect oblong frame, cross-hatched and voided, and shaded at the corners. A single outer line completes the design. In the Four Pence the circle is placed upon an octagonal frame of reticulated groundwork, and a plain outer line completes the design. In both values the letters "C. W. C.," the initials of the engraver, are cut on the shoulder part of the bust. (*Illustrations. Plates N, O, P.*)

T. "VAN DIEMEN'S LAND." B. "ONE PENNY," "FOUR PENCE."

1d., blue, light blue.
4d., bright and dull orange-yellow, orange-red.

Variety.—The Four Pence is found in orange-red, on horizontally narrow laid and on vertically wide laid paper.

Remarks.—Of both the Penny and Four Pence there were twenty-four stamps to the sheet, in four horizontal rows of six; and as these were separately engraved by hand, there are twenty-four varieties of each value. The differences are minute, and no errors exist. Specimens of both values are known, with a small triangular hole punched out of them. The object of this is unknown; but it is not improbable that, like the Western Australians, it was to distinguish official correspondence.

An investigation by the Vice-President into the arrangement of the varieties on the sheets, led to the discovery that two separate plates of the Four Pence were prepared. The papers written on the subject for the Society, together with one by Mr. Basset Hull, and a letter from Mr. W. F. Petterd, are here reprinted from *The Philatelic Record.*

THE FOUR PENCE OF THE FIRST ISSUE OF TASMANIA.

A PAPER READ BEFORE THE PHILATELIC SOCIETY, LONDON.

By T. K. TAPLING, M.P., Vice-President.

Within the last three or four years a good deal of attention has been directed to the issues of certain countries, the stamps of which were each separately engraved on the plates, and are consequently found in as many varieties of types as there are stamps on the sheet. The examination of these varieties, and the attempts to reconstitute the plates, have proved a most interesting branch of study, and have led in some cases to discoveries of considerable importance. It occurred to me that an occasional note on one or two matters not generally known could hardly fail to be of interest to the members of the Society, and I will therefore ask you to give your attention for a few moments to the subject of these remarks—"The Four Pence of the First Issue of Tasmania." The stamp in question is a most troublesome one, the differences of type being very minute, and the difficulty of identifying the varieties being largely increased by the colour of the impression. Of this there are two very distinct shades—orange-red and yellow. I am unable to say which came first, but am inclined to think the former. Tradition says there were twenty-four stamps on the sheet, each differing from the others, and printed in six rows of four. I lately began to attempt the reconstitution of the plate—in other words, to try to place the varieties of type in the right order—and with this object I applied to three friends, who were the fortunate possessors of several fine blocks and pairs of these stamps, and who very kindly placed their specimens at my disposal.

On examining the different collections with my own specimens, I was much puzzled to find that there were apparently considerably more than twenty-four varieties of type. After a most careful investigation, and making every allowance for defective printing, I was unable to resist the conclusion, that not only were there more than twenty-four varieties of type, but that in the united collections there were to be found exactly forty-eight. The experience of the first and second issues of New South Wales at once suggested the idea of a retouch of the plate, or possibly of a transfer, but further examination showed that this was not the case. Of course, to prove a retouch, it is necessary to compare the same stamps or varieties; *i.e.* those occupying the same position on the sheets. To do this, it is further necessary to be in a position to prove the arrangement, or a portion of the arrangement, of the varieties on the plate, before we can compare the same stamps. When I began some years ago to get together the varieties of type, the idea occurred to me of making up a sheet in each of the two shades—dull red and yellow. In this I had partially succeeded; and recently, on looking more carefully at the two sheets, I was struck with certain peculiarities which seemed to run through all, or most of the yellow stamps, but which could not be traced on those specimens printed in dull red. I accordingly began to suspect the existence of two distinct plates. Now at the bottom of the sheet there are to be found the words, "Printed by H. & C. Best," and "C. W. Coard, Sc." There is some reason for thinking these words were printed respectively at the left and right lower corners of the sheet, but this is immaterial for our present purpose. Their importance lies in the fact that they enable us with certainty to ascertain the actual position on the plate of certain varieties of type. I looked accordingly among my specimens, and at length found two — one printed in dull red, the other in yellow — and both with sufficient margin to show portions of the words, "Printed by H. & C. Best," immediately below. It was therefore morally certain that these two specimens occupied the same position on the plate, except on one hypothesis, which I will refer to directly. Two minutes' examination was sufficient to prove conclusively that the stamps were not the same type or variety; and further, that neither was a retouch or transfer of the other. Again, the letters and words, "Printed by H. & C. Best," were differently spaced; and, in the case of the yellow stamp, occupied much less space than on the other specimen. These facts seem to point very strongly to two separate plates of the four pence having been prepared. It is just possible, of course, that the sheet was much larger than had been commonly supposed, and consisted, say, of forty-eight varieties. But in this case the words, "Printed by H. & C. Best," must have been repeated on the sheet—a most unlikely thing to have occurred; and it must not be forgotten that, according to the information at the disposal of the Society, and apparently of M. Moens also, twenty-four has always been assigned as the number of specimens on the sheet. Our united collections give just forty-eight varieties; and I think we are justified in concluding that, for some reason or other —probably wear, or injury—two separate plates of the Four Pence were prepared. One other point should be noticed. I mentioned that the stamps were supposed to have been printed in six rows of four. I am able to show that in the case of the second plate they were printed in four rows of six. Whether this was the arrangement of both plates or not, I am unable to say. I have only now to indicate, as far as possible, the differences between the two plates. These, like those between the stamps themselves, are by no means clearly defined. In the absence of dated specimens, or documentary evidence, it is impossible to say which should come first;

and until both plates are completely reconstituted, and the varieties arranged in the right order, I am afraid the tests of distinction will not be found altogether satisfactory.

1. *The Colour of the Impression.*—Roughly speaking, specimens from Plate I. are printed in dull orange-red, those from Plate II. in yellow. Specimens from both exist in *bright* orange-red; but I have never seen a stamp from Plate I. printed in yellow, or one from Plate II. in the particular shade of dull red peculiar to Plate I.

2. *The Impression.*—Although both plates were engraved by Mr. C. W. Coard, Plate I., in my opinion, shows better workmanship than Plate II. The impressions from the former are generally clearer, and the lines somewhat thinner, than in the case of stamps printed from Plate II., especially of those printed in yellow.

3. *Design.*—On Plate I. the Queen's back hair seems to be gathered up in loops, or rather twisted coils, which I am told is the correct expression. On Plate II. it has the appearance of twisted plaits. The stamp is enclosed by a double octagonal line, and just within this, and following the shape of the octagon, you will notice a number of small tooth-shaped ornaments, pointing inwards. On Plate I. these are considerably larger than on Plate II., and vary in number, as far as I have counted them, from seventy-eight to eighty. Those of Plate II. are smaller, and vary in number from eighty to eighty-two.

4. *The Lettering of "Van Diemen's Land" and "Four Pence."*—On Plate I. the letters of these words, as a rule, are more elongated than those on Plate II., the difference being especially noticeable in the two A's of "VAN" and "LAND." On Plate II. these are, so to speak, squat-shaped and flatter. The same remark applies, to a lesser extent, to the four N's. The sheets which I have the pleasure of presenting for your inspection will assist you in verifying these details as far as they go. I am afraid the distinctions are very vague, yet it seems almost impossible to give others. It is principally by patient study and examination of the specimens that it will be found possible to readily recognize the characteristics of the two plates; and I will only add in conclusion Mr. Pemberton's words of advice, "Study the stamps, and an imperceptible sense will come to you."

SECOND PAPER ON

THE FOUR PENCE OF THE FIRST ISSUE OF TASMANIA.

By T. K. TAPLING, M.P., Vice-President, Philatelic Society, London.

The readers of the *Philatelic Record* will recollect a short paper published in the March number for this year, which I wrote for the Philatelic Society, on the subject of the two plates of the "Four Pence of the First Issue of Tasmania." At that time I was working comparatively in the dark, with single specimens, and a few pairs and blocks, and was compelled to leave one or two questions unanswered. Through the courtesy of Major Evans, and of a correspondent in Tasmania, I am again in a position to take up the thread of the story, and to bring a very difficult investigation to a satisfactory conclusion. It is of course well known that both values of the first issue have been reprinted, and some years ago a sheet or two of each passed into the hands of a well-known dealer.

Unfortunately the stamps were separated and dispersed before collectors began to give the same attention to these questions of plates and varieties of type that is devoted to them at the present day. Even single reprinted specimens have now become comparatively scarce. Major Evans has been fortunate enough to obtain an uncut reprinted sheet of each value, and has very kindly forwarded for my inspection the sheet of the Four Pence, which lies before me as I am writing. I am glad to find that, with one exception, every theory I advanced has been completely confirmed, and I will now deal one by one with the points which at that time I was compelled to leave unsettled. They were as follows:

I. The question of priority of the two plates.

II. The constitution of BOTH plates, and the minor question of the position on the sheet of the words "Printed by H. & C. Best" and "C. W. Coard, Sc."

III. The distinctions between the two plates.

I. Major Evans' reprinted sheet is struck from what I then called Plate I. There is obviously every probability that a reprinted sheet would be taken from the plate last in use; but this matter is now definitely settled on the authority of a correspondent in Tasmania, who informs me that the first plate was lost long ago, but that he possesses a photograph of *the reprint from Plate II.*, which he kindly offers to send to me. What I designated Plate I. accordingly becomes Plate II., and Plate II. becomes Plate I. A point which tends to confirm this, but which I scarcely realized the importance of before, is that specimens from Plate I. show far more traces of wear and use of the die than any I have come across from Plate II. This seems to indicate that the new plate was made in consequence of the old one wearing out. I may mention here that the reprinted sheet, which by-the-way is printed in the yellow colour peculiar to Plate I., shows but little sign of wear except in the top row, and a portion of the second.

II. The accompanying photograph of the reprint from Plate II., and the diagram marked "A," showing the *modus operandi* of the reconstruction of Plate I., prove conclusively that the stamps on both sheets were arranged in four rows of six. It will be noticed that the words "Printed by H. & C. Best" and "C. W. Coard, Sc.," are placed at the left and right lower corners respectively on Plate II., and the existence of specimens with large margins in more than one collection proves that they were similarly situated on Plate I.

The photograph of Plate I. is taken from the specimens in my own collection, and speaks for itself; but the diagram needs a little explanation. The sheet is divided into twenty-four compartments, corresponding to the numbers of the stamps, and within them will be observed certain dotted lines. These represent various pairs and blocks of stamps, whose position on the sheet has been ascertained. The large block has been constructed from overlapping pairs and triplets existing in the collections of several friends who were good enough to lend them to me for examination. The positions of the three-corner stamps—Nos. 1, 19, and 24—were ascertained by specimens with large margins, or showing traces of the words "Printed by," &c. &c., referred to previously. Having settled the places of these three varieties, a little examination of the diagram will show that no other arrangement of the sheet is possible. For the sake of completeness, I give here a detailed proof of the arrangement indicated by the diagram. The different pairs and blocks are located in the following collections:

No. 1 is the top left corner stamp.		Mr. Rodd's collection.		
„ 19 „ bottom left „		Mr. Tapling's „		
„ 24 „ „ right „		„ „		

PAIRS AND BLOCKS.

Nos.					
„	1, 7	. . .	are in Mr. Wilson's collection.		
„	2, 8	. . .	„	„	„
„ 7,	8, 9	. . .	„	Mr. Garth's	„
„	3, 9	. . .	„	Mr. Thornhill's	„
„	3, 4	. . .	„	MM. Caillebotte's	„
„ 4,	5, 6	. . .	„	„	„
„	9, 15	. . .	„	Mr. Tapling's	„
„	14, 15	. . .	„	Mr. Rodd's	„
„	13, 14	. . .	„	MM. Caillebotte's	„
„	15, 16	. . .	„	Mr. Tapling's	„
„	15, 21	. . .	„	„	„
„	21, 22	. . .	„	„	„
„	10, 16	. . .	„	Mr. Thornhill's	„
„	16, 17	. . .	„	Mr. Tapling's	„
„ 11,	17, 23	. . .	„	Mr. Rodd's	„
„	11, 12	. . .	„	Mr. Tapling's	„
„	19, 20	. . .	„	„	„

I have not yet come across variety No. 18 in a pair or block; but, as there is only one vacant space left, the position I have assigned to it is the correct one.

The photograph of Plate II. is taken from Major Evans' uncut sheet, and the varieties of type are of course all in the right order.

PLATE I.   DIAGRAM A.

1	2	3	4	5	6
7	8	9	10	11	12
13	14	15	16	17	18
19	20	21	22	23	24

III. I am afraid I can add but little to my remarks on the distinctions between the two plates. The photographs will be found of more assistance than pages of description, if they are studied side by side with the observations I made in my first paper, to which I refer my readers. I will only remark that, having now seen the entire sheet from Plate II., I think the test of the lettering, which is fully described in my former paper, will be found the easiest.

I may take this opportunity of saying a word or two about the Penny of the same issue. Fortunately there is only one plate of this value, consisting of twenty-four varieties of type, arranged in precisely the same way as those of the Four Pence, and with the same lettering at the two lower corners of the sheet. The varieties of type are somewhat easier to identify; but the stamps have become so scarce that it is very difficult to get anything like a quantity together for the purpose of making up a plate. In conclusion, I wish to express my thanks to MM. Caillebotte, Major Evans, and my other friends for the loan of their specimens, which have been of the greatest assistance to me in this investigation. Collectors will now be in a position to judge of the value of some of these researches into questions of plates and varieties of type. To me they seem to add very largely to the scientific character of philately, and I think it is a matter of congratulation that by their means an obscure but most interesting bit of philatelic history has at length been satisfactorily elucidated.

NOTE.—This paper was finished a few days only before I saw Mr. Basset Hull's able contribution on the same subject. I am glad to find my theories on every point of importance fully confirmed, and Mr. Hull will notice that I had by somewhat different means already discovered my error, and arrived at the same conclusion as himself as to the question of priority of the two plates. I congratulate him on the valuable information he has obtained. Some of the same points are dealt with by Mr. Hull and myself; but as this article seems to supplement his so completely, I decided not to alter it in any way, and make no apology for publishing it exactly as it was written.

THE 1853 ISSUE OF THE STAMPS OF VAN DIEMEN'S LAND.

By A. F. BASSET HULL, Hobart.

WE have received the following from Mr. Basset Hull:

"I have read with the deepest interest Mr. Tapling's article on the 'Four Pence of the First Issue of Tasmania,' and now beg to add a few notes and data on these 1853 stamps, which may be of some interest to collectors.

"I have experienced great difficulty in obtaining any official information on the subject. However, I submit several items, the chief of which confirm Mr. Tapling's conclusion as to the existence of two plates of the Four Pence.

"I am, &c.,   A. F. BASSET HULL."

THE first public notice that adhesive stamps were obtainable appears in the *Hobart Town Gazette* (the official organ) of Tuesday, 27th September, 1853, as follows:

"GENERAL POST OFFICE, *6th September, 1853*.

"Notice is hereby given, that the new Post Office Act of 1853 will come into operation on the First day of November next. That on and from that date all Letters and Packets (Newspapers alone excepted) posted at any of the Post Offices of this Colony must be prepaid by means of adhesive stamps.

"That the stamps will be sold at Hobart Town, in large or small quantities as may be required, at the General Post Office, Messrs. Walch and Sons, Elizabeth Street, and Messrs. Huxtable and Co., Murray Street; at Launceston Post Office, and the most respectable booksellers in Launceston; and at the various Post Offices throughout the Island."

On Tuesday, 25th October, 1853, regulations for the guidance of the Post Office Department, under Act of Council 17 Vict. No. 6, were published in the *Gazette*. The only item having reference to stamps was the following:

"PRICE OF STAMPS.—The stamps will be of the following rates; viz.:

"Penny Stamps.—1d. each | Fourpenny Stamps.—4d. each."

In the Post Office Letter-book appears a letter which states that a clerk was engaged exclusively in superintending and checking the striking-off of stamps at the printers. An eye-witness describes the process as being a somewhat arduous one; for the printer kept a lemonade-bottle full of rum at his side, to which he had recourse at frequent intervals. Possibly, however, this was to drown his remorse at having perpetuated so many villanous caricatures of our gracious Queen.

The engraving and printing account of Messrs. H. and C. Best, dated 30th September, 1853, contains the following items:

"To Engraving Plate of 1d. Stamps, 24 Heads at 30s. . £36 0 0
Do.   do.   4d.   do.   do.   . £36 0 0"

And after a number of other items, relative to the engraving of date-stamps, &c., appears the following entry:

"To re-engraving Plate of 4d. Stamps, 24 Heads at 25s. . £30 0 0"

No less than 11,100 sheets (266,400 stamps) were printed from the Four Penny plate before re-engraving became necessary. No doubt the wearing of the plate was the immediate cause of the necessity for providing a new one. It will be noticed that the word *re-engraved* is used in the account, thus putting aside the idea that Plate II. was a re-touch of Plate I.

Mr. Tapling gave the more roughly-engraved plate of the Four Pence the second place. I am, however, convinced that it was the first, and adduce the following evidence in support of my conclusion:

1st. The defaced plate—the only one now in the possession of the Postal Department, and from which the reprints were struck off—is the finely-engraved one.

2nd. The only dated specimen I have is from the finer plate, and is dated August, 1855, two years after the date of the printing account.

3rd. Impressions from Plate I. show signs of wearing which do not appear on impressions from II. Also the letters "c.w.c." appear distinctly on the base of the Queen's neck on all stamps of the 1d. plate (of which only one was engraved), and on all stamps of the rougher 4d. plate, but only in a few instances on the finer one.

The Penny stamp was printed in sheets of twenty-four stamps, in four rows of six. Size of the entire sheet 5 × 3¾ inches, including inscription at foot; the space between each stamp slightly exceeds $\frac{1}{16}$ of an inch. The words "Printed by H. & C. Best" appear in lower left corner, projecting beyond the first, and extending to the lower left angle of the second stamp in the fourth row. "C. W. Coard, Sc.," appears in the lower right corner. The paper was soft yellowish-white and white wove, varying in thickness. The colour varies from pale blue to blue, and the later impressions seem very much worn.

The Four Penny stamp was printed from two plates, both in sheets of twenty-four stamps, in four rows of six. Size of the entire sheet slightly exceeds 5¼ × 3¾ inches; space between each stamp rather more than $\frac{1}{16}$ of an inch. The chief points of difference between the two plates of the Four Pence are as follows:

PLATE I.—Colour—yellow, dull yellow, orange, and bright orange. Letters "c.w.c." distinctly visible on base of Queen's neck. Band bearing legend comparatively narrow; letters short, and closely set together. Loop ornaments within outer double octagonal line small, from eighty to eighty-four in number. At foot the words "Printed by H. & C. Best" shorter than in Plate II., smaller, and clear of stamp immediately above; "B" of "Best" to the left of angle at right of base of stamp above. "C. W. Coard, Sc.," smaller, shorter, and more to the right than II. General appearance meaner than II. Many impressions show wearing of plate.

PLATE II.—Colour—orange, bright orange, orange-red, and dull orange-red. Base of Queen's neck in most instances merely shaded, letters "c.w.c." appearing thereon in only a few instances. Band bearing legend more open; letters generally well shaped, larger, and more spaced than I. Loop ornaments larger, numbering not more than eighty. "Printed by H. and C. Best" large, and almost touching stamp immediately above; "B" of "Best" directly under right angle of base of stamp above. "C. W. Coard, Sc.," larger and clearer. General appearance cleaner-cut and more finely-engraved than I.

The Four Pence is printed on soft yellowish-white and white wove paper, varying in thickness, from both plates. Plate I. also appears on *vergé* paper, in an orange shade.

I have seen several specimens, both of the Penny and Four Pence, with a small triangular piece punched out of the stamp, evidently done before the stamps were used, but no explanation can be given as to whether this has any special significance or not.

THE FOUR PENCE OF THE FIRST ISSUE OF TASMANIA.

To the Editor of "The Philatelic Record."

SIR,—I have taken very great interest in the valuable and instructive papers that have lately appeared in your journal on the above stamps, and they have led me to hunt up all the information I could obtain on the subject, more especially with the idea of obtaining positive data as to the priority of the plates and the date of the change. In this I have lately been greatly facilitated by the acquisition of a large and fine series of the Four Pence value on the original covers and envelopes. To my great surprise I incontestably find that Mr. Tapling's first arrangement of the plate numbers is correct, and that my philatelically-learned friend, Mr. Basset-Hull, is altogether wrong. That which Mr. Tapling in his first paper designated Plate I. is in fact really so; and my large series of specimens show that the alterations subsequently made are not according to the evidence. My earliest cover, with five stamps attached, is dated—

> Camp Town
> 23 . Nov, 53

only a few weeks after the stamps were issued to the public. The strip evidently was taken from the right-hand upper corner of the sheet, and the stamps are of the characteristic shade, and agree in every respect with the details of the photo of the reprinted sheet termed Plate II. by Mr. Hull. My latest dated cover with a stamp of this plate is the 13th April, 1854; my earliest of the other plate is the 20th April, 1854; and the latest, the 27th September, 1855. Not a single example shows any admixture of the stamps; for after April, 1854, I have not a cover with a stamp from what Mr. Hull calls the first plate. To thoroughly satisfy myself upon this point, I forwarded two stamps to Mr. Hull, removed from covers dated the 21st December, 1853, and the 18th July, 1854, respectively, and marked Plate I. and II., according to that gentleman's arrangement. These he has kindly examined, and informs me that the plate numbers assigned are quite correct, according to his theory. Herewith I enclose two examples of the covers for your examination, dated the 17th December, 1853, and the 18th August, 1855; and I feel sure that they will prove that the plate numbers given by Mr. Tapling in his first paper in the March number, 1886, are correct, and that the later arrangement is not so.

It appears strange to me that the engraving and printing account of Messrs. H. and C. Best, dated 30th September, 1853, should contain the two items:

and
"To Engraving Plate of 4d. Stamps, 24 Heads at 30s. . £36 0 0."

"To Re-engraving Plate of 4d. Stamps, 24 Heads at 25s. £30 0 0."

Is it (*Vide* Mr. Hull's paper, August, 1886) not reasonable to suppose that this really refers to a second plate? for a re-engraving of the plate would only occur at a much later date. Anyway, my large series of specimens prove to my mind that the defaced plate now in the postal department at Hobart is in reality the first one used, and that the second and roughly-engraved plate must be either lost or destroyed. I am sure this interesting subject needs no apology for trespassing upon your space, more especially as this examination puts a fresh aspect upon what was supposed to be satisfactorily elucidated.

I am, yours respectfully,

LAUNCESTON, TASMANIA, *February* 11*th*, 1887. W. F. PETTERD.

Issue II. October, 1855.

Three values. Engraved in *taille-douce*, and printed by Perkins, Bacon, and Co., London, in colour, on stoutish white paper, watermarked with large six-rayed star; white gum. Design: Three-quarter diademed portrait of Queen, with necklace and earrings, to left, on ground of vertical and horizontal lines, within an engine-turned oval, lettered with name of colony in white block letters in the upper curve. Across the lower portion of the oval is a straight, narrow, white label, with POSTAGE in small Roman capitals, and immediately below this is a straight coloured label, having a square ornamented block at either end, with the value in words in white Roman capitals. The spandrels are filled in with engine-turned ornament, and a plain single outer line completes the design. (*Illustration* 81.)

T. "VAN DIEMENS LAND." B. "ONE PENNY," "TWO PENCE," "FOUR PENCE."

1d., dull carmine, verging on brick-red.
2d., deep green.
4d., blue (shades).

Issue III. 1856-57.

Three values. The same in every other respect as the preceding issue, but without watermark. (*Illustration* 81.)

    1d., brown-red.
    2d., emerald-green (shades).
    4d., blue (shades).

Varieties.—The One Penny is found on thin greyish paper, almost pelure, and on thicker rough paper. The Two Pence and Four Pence are only found on the latter paper.

Issue IV. January, 1858.

Three values. The same in every other respect as Issues II. and III., but watermarked with double-lined numeral of value. (*Illustration* 81.)

    1d., red, orange, brick, carmine.
    2d., dark and light green, olive- and yellow-green, bottle-green.
    4d., blue (shades).

Many shades of all values of this issue are to be met with.

The following varieties of perforation exist; whether they are official or not is unknown.

    (A) *Rouletted* 8.
    1d., red. | 2d., dark green.

    (B) *Rouletted* 11½.
    1d., red.

    (C) *Serrated perforation* 20.
    1d., red | 2d., yellow-green | 4d., blue.

    (D) *Perforated with oblique parallel cuts.*
    1d., red | 2d., green. | 4d., blue.

The oblique perforation was performed with an instrument which made oblique cuts, and left, when the stamps were severed, a ragged, irregular edge.

Issue V. 1860.

Two values. Engraved in *taille-douce*, by Humphrey, and printed by Perkins, Bacon, and Co., London, on thick and thin white paper, watermarked with double-lined numerals of value 6 and 12. Design: Portrait of Queen, as in last issue, on background of vertical and horizontal lines, within fancy, reticulated, octagonal frame, for the Six Pence; inscribed with name of colony above, and value in words below, in white block letters. The frame of the One Shilling is an elongated octagonal, with engine-tracery, and bears similar inscriptions to the Six Pence in coloured block letters. (*Illustrations* 82, 83, 81.)

    T. "TASMANIA." B. "SIXPENCE," "ONE SHILLING."
    6d., violet, mauve, lilac, grey, slate-blue, and many intermediate shades.
    1s., vermilion-red, bright and dull.
    Rouletted 8. 6d., grey.

Remarks.—The One Shilling, vermilion, rouletted, is also catalogued by M. Moens, but no specimen is known to the Society. Proofs of both values in black on plate paper, and also on yellowish card, are known.

Issue VI. 1864-70.

Five values, differing only from those of the last two issues, inasmuch as they are machine-perforated. The smaller was undoubtedly the earlier perforation. (*Illustrations* 81, 82, 83.)

    1d., carmine (shades), brick, orange-vermilion
    2d., yellow-green, bottle-green
    4d., blue (light and dark)   } perf. 13, 12, 11½, 10.
    6d., same shades as in Issue V.
    1s.   „   „

Varieties.—The One Penny exists in dull carmine, with watermark 2, and in brick-red, without watermark; both perf. 12.

Issue VII. 1870.

Four values. Engraved by Messrs. De la Rue and Co., and type-printed in the Colony, in colour, on white wove watermarked paper; white gum. Design: Diademed profile of Queen Victoria to left, on ground of horizontal lines, within a beaded oval. Scrolled framework, with curved inscriptions in white block letters, above and below. Shape, upright rectangular; machine-perf. 11½. (*Illustration* 84.)

T. "TASMANIA." B. "ONE PENNY," "TWO PENCE," "FOUR PENCE," "TEN PENCE."

    1d., carmine (shades); watermark, small slanting *10*.
    2d., green   „   „   large   „   *2*.
    4d., blue   „   „   small   „   *4*.
    10d., black   „   „   „   „   *10*.

Variety. March, 1871. 1d., red; watermark, small numeral *4*.

Issue VIII. 1871-2.

Six values. Same type, engraving, paper, perforation, &c., as last; watermark, "*TAS.*" (*Illustration* 84.)

    1d., carmine (shades), vermilion, rose.
    2d., green, very dark to pale.
    3d., dark purple-brown, maroon, brown, chocolate, brown-pink.
    4d., blue (?), chronicled by M. Moens, but not known to the Society.
    9d., blue and bright blue.
    5s., mauve and bright mauve.

Varieties.   1d., red; imperforate.
             2d., blue; error for green.
             9d., blue; imperforate.

Issue IX. 1876.

One value. Same type, paper, watermark, and perforation as the Four Pence of 1870, but changed in colour. (*Illustration* 84.)

    4d., yellow-ochre (shades).

Issue X. 1880.

After 1879, some of the values appear to have been printed by Messrs. De la Rue and Co. These may be distinguished by the superiority of the impression and by the glazed paper. Same types, watermark, &c., as before. (*Illustration* 84.)

(A) *Perf.* 11½
    3d., purple-brown; on glazed paper.

(B) *Perf.* 14.
1d., bright rose; on glazed paper. | 3d., purple-brown; on glazed paper.
2d., green   „   „ | 8d., violet-brown   „   „

TASMANIA.

REPRINTS (End of 1879).

On plain paper; machine-perforation 11½; white gum.

1d., blue	(Type 1853).	24 varieties of type.
4d., orange-yellow	(„ „).	24 varieties of type.
1d., dull red	(„ 1855).	
2d., green	(„ „).	
4d., blue	(„ „).	
6d., violet	(„ 1858).	
1s., vermilion	(„ „).	
1d., rose	(current type).	
2d., deep green	(„ „).	
3d., violet-brown	(„ „).	
4d., deep blue	(„ „).	
4d., ochre-yellow	(„ „).	
8d., violet	(„ „).	
9d., blue	(„ „).	
10d., black	(„ „).	
5s., deep violet	(„ „).	

OFFICIAL OR DEPARTMENTAL STAMPS.
Issue I. 1883.

Hand-stamped, coloured impression, on white or blue envelopes. Design: Arms of Great Britain in a single-lined circle. Below the arms is the word "TASMANIA," in block letters, in a straight line. Following the shape of the circle, and printed in block capitals, are the inscriptions—T. The name of the Department, and D. "FRANK STAMP." It will be sufficient to indicate the names of the departments, or of the officials, employing these stamps, which are found in various colours—the Attorney-General, Chief Secretary, Education Department, Government Statistics, Governor of Tasmania, Minister of Lands, Postmaster-General, R.E. Duties Department, Tasmanian Railway, Treasury, Secretary of Mines, North District. Some of these are given on the authority of M. Moens.

ENVELOPES.
Issue I. April 3rd, 1883.

One value. Engraved and printed by Messrs. De la Rue and Co. Coloured impression, on white laid unwatermarked paper; pointed flap; long gum, slightly yellowish. Design: Diademed profile of Queen Victoria to left, embossed in white on a solid ground, and enclosed by an upright reticulated oval band, inscribed in coloured block letters, "TASMANIA POSTAGE" above and "TWO PENCE" below, the inscriptions being separated from each other by coloured dots. Surrounding this is a white embossed beaded oval line. The design is completed by an outer line of colour, dented similarly to a serrated perforation. The stamp is impressed in the right upper corner. Size, 5½ x 3 in., or 140 x 80 mm. (*Illustration* 85.)

2d., yellow-green.

REGISTRATION ENVELOPES.
Issue I. April 3rd, 1883.

One value. These envelopes are made of stout white wove linen-lined paper. The face and back of the envelope are each divided into four equal compartments by two lines, which cross at right angles, and are continued from the face to the back of the envelopes. On the face, in the upper part, is an inscription in two lines—"This Letter must be given to an Officer of the Post Office to be Registered, and a Receipt obtained for it"—in small block capitals. Above this inscription, in large block capitals, are the words "REGISTERED LETTER," divided from each other by the perpendicular crossing line which falls between them. In the left upper corner is a large block capital "R," and in the right the inscription, in block letters, "The Stamp to Pay the Postage must be Placed here," enclosed in a single-lined rectangular frame. The flap is rounded, with white gum. On it is impressed a stamp engraved by Messrs. De La Rue and Co.; coloured impression. Design: Embossed diademed profile of Queen Victoria to left, on solid ground, within a circular reticulated embossed band, inscribed T. "Tasmania Registration." B. "Four Pence," in coloured block letters. Within the circular band, and enframing the bust, is a kind of twelve-sided figure, touching the band at each of the twelve angles. There is a white dot in each interstice. The design is completed by two outer circular lines, one embossed, the other coloured, the latter being *notched* by the former. Shape, circular. Beneath the flap, on the back of the envelope, are the words, "McCorquodale and Co., Contractors," in coloured block letters. The whole of the design, inscriptions, &c., are printed in blue. (*Illustration* 86.)

Size A. 5¼ × 3¼ inches, or 132 × 82 mm.
B. 5⅞ × 3⅞ inches, or 150 × 100 mm.

4d., pale blue.

Issue II. 1885.

Similar as to design, inscriptions, sizes, &c., as the last; but the letter "R" on the face is enframed by a single-lined oval. (*Illustration* 86.)

4d., pale blue.

POST CARDS.
Issue I. January 1st, 1882.

One value. Lithographed in the colony, upon medium light buff card. Size, 4⅞ × 3 1/10 inches. At the top there are three lines of inscription: 1st. "POST CARD," in Roman capitals, the two words being separated by the Royal arms. 2nd. "TASMANIA," in small block letters, directly beneath the arms. 3rd. "THE ADDRESS ONLY TO BE WRITTEN ON THIS SIDE," in larger block letters. Lower down, the word "*To*," in script type, followed by three dotted lines for the address. The stamp—type of adhesive issue VII., 1870—is in the right upper corner. The design of the card is completed by an ornamental border, consisting of a fancy chain pattern, with trefoil ornaments at the four corners, enclosed within thin inner and thick outer lines. Size, 4 7/10 × 2⅜ inches. (*Illustration* 87.)

1d., rose.

Remarks.—Before the introduction of post cards by the Government, a Mr. Walch, in October, 1880, had some privately printed, for the use of himself and his friends, of which the following is a description: At the top of the card, in six lines, is the inscription—1st. "WALCH'S" 2nd. "TASMANIAN POST CARD," all in block letters. 3rd, 4th, and 5th. "All persons who approve of the introduction of a PENNY POSTAL CARD—for delivery in any part of the Colony, are solicited to encourage the move—ment by the use of this card." 6th. "THE ADDRESS ONLY TO BE WRITTEN ON THIS SIDE," in Roman capitals. Between the second and third lines there is a wavy line, composed of dots. To left the word "*To*." A space is ruled off in the right upper corner for an adhesive stamp, and is divided in the centre by a thin line. The upper half bears "INLAND POSTAGE, 2D.," and the lower "TOWN POSTAGE, 1D.," each in three lines, in slanting Roman capitals. The design of the card is completed by an ornamental border. Size, $4\frac{3}{8} \times 2\frac{9}{10}$ inches.

Without value, rose on white.
„ „ brown, reverse side white.

Issue II. February, 1882.

One value. Designed and printed by Messrs. De la Rue and Co., upon thick white card. Size, $4\frac{9}{10} \times 2\frac{9}{10}$ inches. At the top of the card there are three lines of inscription—1st. "POST CARD," in fancy capitals, with the Royal arms between the words. 2nd. "TASMANIA," in Roman capitals. 3rd. "THE ADDRESS ONLY TO BE WRITTEN ON THIS SIDE." The stamp—type of adhesive issue VII., 1870—is in the right upper corner, and the card is without border. (*Illustration* 88.)

1d., rose-carmine.

Issue III. July 18th, 1884.

One value. Printed in the colony. The design is precisely similar to the last issue, except that the impression is coarser and not so well printed. (*Illustration* 88.)

1d., carmine.

Issue IV. July, 1885.

One value. In every way the same as Issue III., but for the change of colour. (*Illustration* 88.)

1d., maroon.

OFFICIAL CARDS.

There are a number of varieties of cards in use for the different Government Departments. They are all franked by one of the official stamps already described, which is struck, generally in blue, in the right upper corner of the card. The Society thinks it is useless to give any detailed list of the varieties, as they are of so little interest, and any list that might be made could not fail to be very imperfect.

FISCAL STAMPS USED POSTALLY.

All the fiscal stamps of 1863 and 1880 appear to have been used postally in 1882. Following the rule adopted in other cases, no list is given by the Society of these varieties, which do not possess any special significance.

VICTORIA.

THE two colonies of New South Wales and Victoria were originally under one Government, and this arrangement continued until July 15th, 1851, when, for reasons which it is not necessary to consider here, they became practically independent of each other. Until the date of separation, the stamps of the first issue of New South Wales were also used in Victoria, and postmarked with the obliteration "v and parallel lines," somewhat resembling a butterfly in shape. No specimen of the Three Pence so postmarked is known to the Society; but there is little reason to doubt that all three values of the "Sydneys" were used in Victoria. No more complicated series exists than the stamps of Victoria themselves, and considerable difficulty was experienced in the compilation and arrangement of the following list. After much discussion and consideration, it was arranged to take the stamps in order of design or type, tracing out under these headings, in the order of issue as far as possible, all the varieties of perforation, watermark, &c. This plan in some cases has the disadvantage of separating from each other stamps issued at the same time, though of different design. On the other hand, it has the merit of shortening and simplifying the catalogue, and of rendering all references to it much easier.

It is not easy to say how far this principle of cataloguing by the designs, and not by the issues, could be extended to the stamps of other countries; but obviously it is only in exceptional cases, like the present, that its adoption would be found necessary.

Type I.

Three values. Lithographed and printed by Campbell and Fergusson, of Melbourne; fifty (?) stamps to the sheet. Coloured impression upon white wove paper, varying in substance; whitish gum. Design: Half-length portrait of Queen Victoria, in low-necked dress, with diadem and coif. In her right hand is a sceptre, and in the left a mound or orb. The head is a three-quarter portrait turned to the right. The background is formed of wavy lines, which, in the One Penny value, have a *moiré* appearance. Solid coloured labels above and below the portrait are inscribed with the name of the colony in the upper and the value in words in the lower, the first in small white Roman and the second in small white block type. In the corners of the upper labels are small ornaments of a star-like character, and in those of the bottom ones the letters "E" and "W" in the One Penny, "T" and "H" in the Two Pence, and "E" in the left corner of the Three Pence, the right corner being occupied by an indistinct ornament, apparently resembling a Maltese cross. The sides of the stamp are bordered by undulating lines. Shape, upright rectangular. (*Illustrations* 89, 90, 91, 92.) The Two Pence exists in three states, indicating as many transfers:

(A) With fine background and fine side borders.
(B) With coarse background and fine side borders.
(C) With coarse background and coarse side borders.

T. "VICTORIA." B. "ONE PENNY," "TWO PENCE," "THREE PENCE."

1st July, 1850.	1d., reddish-brown, vermilion, rose, rose-red; shades of each.
1861 (?).	1d., rose-red; *rouletted*, wide dents 8 and small dents 18.
15th July, 1851.	2d. (A), dull lilac, reddish-lilac, pale grey.
	2d. (B), dull lilac, lilac-brown, grey-lilac; cinnamon shades.
	2d. (c) ,, ,, ,, ,,
1st July, 1850.	3d., dull blue, indigo, deep to pale blue; shades.
March, 1861.	3d., dull blue; shades. Rouletted, wide dents 8.
July, 1861.	3d., pale and dull blue, dark blue; machine-perf. 12.

Variety.—The Two Pence (c) exists without the value in the bottom label.

Remarks.—Varieties of the Two Pence lettered "VICTOPIA," "T.B.," and "T.R." are chronicled. These appear to be due merely to defective printing. At least two transfers were taken of the One Penny and Three Pence, as is proved by the great difference in space between the two horizontal rows. Considerable differences exist in the impression of the three values. It is probable that the roulettes of the One Penny and Three Pence were done privately; but the machine-perforation 12 appears to have been official. Some doubt exists as to the exact date of the rouletted specimens. The varieties of the Two Pence are not found on the same sheet, but are printed from distinct plates.

Type II.

(A) *One value.* Engraved on copper and printed in the colony. Coloured impression on yellowish spongy paper, varying considerably in substance; whitish gum. Design: Full-length portrait of Queen Victoria in regal robes and crown, with orb and sceptre, seated in coronation chair, with footstool, which is placed on the uppermost of two steps. The background is formed of engine-turned lines, and is enframed by a kind of Gothic portal, consisting of pillars, supporting at the sides a flat-pointed arch, with floreate ornaments in the spandrels. Under the lowest step of the throne is a white label, inscribed with the value in words in small coloured Roman capitals, and having a square block at either corner, with letters varying for each stamp on the plate. Fifty stamps, each separately engraved, to the sheet, in five vertical rows of ten. Shape, long, upright rectangular; imperforate. (*Illustration. Plate Q.*)

B. "TWO PENCE."
1852. 2d., brown, reddish-brown.

Remarks.—This stamp presents one of the few instances in which the lettering in the angles, adopted in the stamps of Great Britain as a safeguard against fraud, has been imitated. This issue is distinguished by the clearness of the engraving and the red-brown shade of the impression, which render it impossible to be mistaken for any of the later printed stamps.

A	E	B	F	C	G	D	H	E	I	F	K	G	L	H	M	I	N	K	O
L	P	M	Q	N	R	O	S	P	T	Q	U	R	V	S	N	T	X	U	Y
V	Z	W	A	X	B	Y	C	X	D	A	F	B	G	C	H	D	I	E	K
F	L	G	M	H	N	I	O	K	P	L	Q	M	R	N	S	O	T	P	U
Q	V	R	W	S	X	T	Y	U	X	W	Z	X	A	Y	B	Z	C	W	M

The lettering beginning with the stamp at the left top corner of the sheet was "A E," and continued through the alphabet, "B F," &c., omitting the letter "J" altogether, repeating in the twenty-fifth stamp "X" for the "Z," which should naturally come there. The twenty-sixth stamp began with "A F," and so on again. In the forty-sixth stamp "V" is replaced by "W," and the letters in Nos. 47, 48, 49, and 50 run "X A," "Y B," "Z C," "W M," which last are supposed to be the initials of the engraver.

The sequence of the right corner letters, beginning with "E" (and omitting "J"), is complete, and the alphabet recommences on stamp No. 22—"W A." On No. 26 the letter is "F," the "E" being omitted to avoid identity with the first series. The forty-fifth stamp is lettered "U X," the forty-sixth "W Z," and from forty-seven to the last as noted above. An error in the lettering will be noticed in Issue B.

(B) *One value.* Lithographic transfers of the stamp just described, resembling it as closely as lithography can follow engraving on copper. Coloured impression on yellowish and white paper, varying much in substance; imperforate. Fifty stamps to the sheet, each varying in type, and arranged in the same way as those from the copper plate. (*Illustration. Plate R.*)

Jan. 1st, 1854 (?). 2d., grey, grey-black, red-lilac, mauve (many shades).

Variety.—An error in one transfer gives the lettering "D I" and "W A" in stamps Nos. 29 and 30, instead of "D I" and "E K."

Remarks.—The date of the first transfer is uncertain, but a pair in a very early state of impression has been seen on a letter dated "Melbourne, Jan. 25th, 1854." There would appear to be four editions of these lithographs. At least, two separate plates, or rather stones, were prepared, which may be distinguished from each other by the difference of the impression, and to a certain extent by the colour of the stamps. Specimens printed from the first stone have the lines of the background behind the throne very fairly clear, and the other details of the design are distinct and readily recognizable, though, of course, the execution is far inferior to that of the copperplate. The impression from the second stone is so bad that the background often presents the appearance of a mass of solid colour, while the other details of the design are blurred and indistinct. The specimens from the first stone are usually, but not invariably, printed in a much colder shade of lilac or grey-lilac than those from the second. Of each stone two stages of impression or wear may be distinguished. To the second should be assigned those specimens with a white background behind the throne, the absence of the shading being due to wear of the stone.

There is some reason for thinking that more than these two transfers took place, though there are no means of indicating any difference between the fresh transfers and those already referred to. Two specimens, lettered respectively "Y B" and "Z C" exist, showing the steps of the throne broken; and on one specimen the "W" of "TWO" has been transformed into a "V," making an error "TVO PENCE." Apparently some kind of slip took place in the process of transfer. These peculiarities are not found on stamps printed from the two stones mentioned above, and the inference therefore may be drawn that there was a third transfer. The two specimens are in the collection of a member of the Society.

Type III.

Two values. Engraved on metal and type-printed; engraver and printer unknown. Design: Diademed profile of Queen Victoria to left, on ground of fine horizontal lines in the Six Penny, and of solid colour in the Two Shilling value.

VICTORIA.

Straight coloured label above, with name of colony in white Roman capitals, and white label below, with value in words in coloured Roman capitals. Curved coloured labels at sides, inscribed with white letters of similar type. The remainder of the stamp is filled in with scroll-like ornaments, and the whole is enframed by two plain outer lines. In the upper scroll-work the Six Pence is inscribed in minute white block letters—"six" on the left and "pence" on the right side; and the Two Shillings has "one" on the left and "florin" on the right side in minute white double-lined block letters. Shape, upright rectangular. (*Illustration* 93.)

T. "VICTORIA." B. "SIX PENCE." "TWO SHILLINGS." L. "POSTAGE" (reading upwards). R. "STAMP" (reading downwards).

1854.
6d., deep to pale orange, on stoutish white wove paper; no watermark; imperforate.

1857.
6d., deep to pale orange, on stoutish white wove paper; no wmk.; rouletted, wide dents 7.
6d.   „   „   „   „   „   serrated, punch 19.
6d.   „   „   „   „   „   serpentine, punch 10½.
6d.   „   „   „   „   „   compound large and small punch.

1861.
6d., deep to pale orange, on stoutish white wove paper; no wmk.; machine-perf. 12 (?).

1862.
6d., blk. to grey, on thinnish white wove ppr.; wmk. value in words; machine-perf. 12.

1858.
2s., sea-green (shades), on stoutish white wove paper; no watermark; imperforate.
2s.,   „   „   „   „   „   roul., wide dents 7½.

1861.
2s., sea-green (shades), on stoutish white wove paper; no watermark; machine-perf. 12.

1864–81.
2s., blue (shades), on yellow-green wove paper; watermark 2; machine-perf. 12 and 12½.

Varieties.—The Two Shillings is known printed upon *blue* paper, corresponding exactly with that employed for the One Shilling value, issued in October, 1876, but watermarked with the thin numeral "2," instead of with "v." over Crown, which is the watermark of the One Shilling. Some of the later printings of the Two Shillings show the indentation of the die to such an extent as to present almost an appearance of relief to portions of the impression; while some copies of the later editions of this value seem to have been printed upon paper which has accidentally escaped the watermark, no trace of it being, at any rate, discoverable on individual stamps. These varieties, however, are at most accidental, and do not merit being catalogued in any other category.

Remarks.—There are very considerable variations of type of each of these two stamps. It appears probable that they arose from an imperfect process of reduplication from the original matrix. The differences, though numerous, are very small, and the stamps have not the appearance of being separately engraved. The size of the sheet is not known, but most likely there were as many varieties of type as there were stamps to the sheet, or at any rate to the row. Specimens of the 6d., black, are found with dark brown gum, which completely discolours the paper. The roulette and punch perforations were probably not official.

Type IV.

One value. Lithographed (probably) in the colony by transfer from a copper-plate line engraving. Coloured impression on stoutish white wove unwatermarked paper, white gum. Design: Small profile of Queen Victoria with fillet to left, upon ground of vertical and horizontal lines, crossed, within a white circular border, inscribed in coloured block letters; the whole upon a coloured octagon of vertical lines, crossed by wavy horizontal lines disposed in threes. Border, a single coloured outer line. Shape, octagonal. (*Illustration* 94.)

T. "VICTORIA." B. "ONE SHILLING." (The two inscriptions are separated by a small cross.)

    1854. 1s., blue, deep to pale; imperforate.
    1857. 1s., blue, deep to pale; rouletted, wide dents 7½.
    1861. 1s., blue, deep to pale; machine-perforated 12.
          1s., ,, ,, ,, ,, rouletted horizontally.

The same remark as that made previously applies to these roulettes also.

Type V.

Two values. The same die, serving for both, was engraved on metal, and surface-printed by Perkins, Bacon, and Co., of London. Coloured impression on medium white wove unwatermarked paper, white gum. Design: The design of these two stamps is essentially the same, and consists of a diademed profile of Queen Victoria to left, on ground of solid colour, with the name of the colony in white Roman capitals in the uppermost part of the stamp. "POSTAGE," reading upwards, on the left, and "STAMP," reading downwards, on the right side of the stamp, in small white block letters. There is a white curved label, shaded with coloured vertical lines, above the head, and a straight one, ruled with horizontal coloured lines, below it. The side borders are formed of white reticulated lines, resembling in pattern, but rather wider apart than in, the first One Penny of Great Britain. In the lower spandrels are the words "ONE SHILLING," in minute hair-line block letters. The stamps are without frame, and the upper corners are voided. In the "TOO LATE" value the labels are overprinted with green block letters. In the "REGISTERED" stamp the over-printing is in blue block letters above, and in Roman capitals below; and the whole stamp is enframed by a heavy blue line, broken at the upper voided angles. Shape, upright rectangular. (*Illustrations* 95, 96.)

"TOO LATE" stamp. T. "VICTORIA TOO LATE." B. "SIX PENCE." L. "POSTAGE." R. "STAMP."
"REGISTERED" stamp. T. "VICTORIA REGISTERED." B. "ONE SHILLING." L. "POSTAGE." R. "STAMP."

July 1st, 1855.
6d. (for late letters), grey-lilac (shades), green and white inscriptions; imperforate.

December 1st, 1854.
1s. (for registration), rose (shades), blue border, blue and white inscriptions; imperforate.

1861 (?).
1s. (for registration), rose (shades), blue border, blue and white inscriptions; rouletted.

Remarks.—The surcharge Six Pence on the stamp bearing One Shilling on its face is somewhat noteworthy. Copies or proofs of the lilac stamp without the over-printing are known. A specimen of the Registration stamp exists in the collection of one of the members of the Society, with the word "REGISTERED" erased with pen and ink, and apparently used for ordinary postage. Minute varieties of type exist of these two stamps, but the same remarks will apply to them, and to the roulette perforations, that were made in reference to the two stamps just described, under the heading of Type III.

Type VI.

Two values. Engraved on steel in line engraving, and printed by Perkins, Bacon, and Co., of London. Coloured impression on medium white paper, yellowish gum; watermark, a large six-rayed star. Design: Full length portrait of Queen Victoria, as in Type II., with coronation robes, diadem, orb, and sceptre, on engine-turned background; reticulated side borders. Curved white label above throne, inscribed with coloured Roman capitals. There is only one step to the throne, which bears the word "POSTAGE" in small coloured Roman capitals. Plain coloured label at bottom of stamp, with value in white Roman capitals. In the four corners of the stamp are square blocks with white circular ornaments. Shape, long, upright rectangular. (*Illustration* 97.)

T. "VICTORIA." B. "POSTAGE "POSTAGE
                   ONE PENNY." SIX PENCE."

July, 1856. 1d., yellow-green (shades); imperforate.
April, 1861. 6d., blue, very deep to light; rouletted.

Varieties.—Specimens of the One Penny, *rouletted*, and of the Six Pence, *imperforate*, as well as of both values with serpentine perforations, also the Six Pence, perforated 12, are noted in some catalogues. Some of these were shown to the Society, but no further information respecting them was available. Proofs, in black, on India paper, exist.

Type VII.

Three values. The original die was engraved on steel by Perkins, Bacon, and Co., of London, and sent out to the colony, where it was electrotyped by Mr. Calvert for surface-printing, and the impressions were produced by Mr. F. W. Robinson. The paper with the star watermark was also imported from England. Coloured impression on various white papers, white and dark brown gum. Design: Diademed profile of Queen Victoria to left, on oval of solid colour, enframed by an outer white oval which almost touches the top, bottom, and sides of the stamp, and is inscribed with name of colony in coloured shaded block letters in the upper, and with value in coloured Roman capitals in the lower curve, floral ornaments separating the two inscriptions. The spandrels are reticulated, and in each of the four corners is a small vignette. In the left upper corner are a cow and a sheep; in the right, a three-masted ship in full sail. In the left lower corner are a painter's palette, brushes, set-square, and compasses; and in the right, a cradle, used by miners for washing gold, and other mining implements. The stamp is enframed by a single coloured outer line. Shape, upright rectangular. (*Illustration* 98.)

T. "VICTORIA." B. "ONE PENNY," "TWO PENCE," "FOUR PENCE."

I. July, 1857. White wove paper, varying in substance; wmk. large six-rayed star.
    (a) *Imperf.*   1d., yellow-green shades.
                   4d., vermilion, brick-red, rose-red (shades).
1861 (?). (b) *Rouletted* 8. 1d., yellow-green.
                        4d., brick-red, rose-red (shades).
    (c) *M. Perf.* 12. 1d., yellow-green.
      Variety.   1d., green; perf. 12 horizontally, rouletted vertically (Moens).

II. 1860 (?). White wove paper, varying in substance; unwatermarked.
    (a) *Imperf.*   1d., green, emerald-green (shades).
                  2d., dull lilac.
                  4d., red, vermilion (shades).
    (b) *Rouletted* 8. 1d., yellow-green, emerald-green (shades).
                  2d., dull lilac (shades).
                  4d., vermilion, rose-red (shades).
    (c) *M.-Perf.* 12. 1d., yellow-green, emerald-green (shades).
                  2d., lilac.
                  4d., rose, rose-red (shades).

III. 1861 (?). White paper, laid (1) vertically, (2) horizontally; unwatermarked.
    (a) *Imperf.*   2d. (?).
                  4d., rose-red, laid horizontally.
    (b) *Rouletted* 8. 2d., dull brownish- and deep grey-lilac (shades), laid horizontally and vertically.
                  4d., rose, rose-red (shades), laid vertically and horizontally.
    (c) *M.-Perf.* 12. 1d., yellow-green, emerald-green (shades), laid horizontally.
                  4d., rose, rose-red (shades), laid horizontally.

IV. 1862. White wove paper; watermark, value in words.
    (a) *Perf.* 12. 1d., yellow-green, emerald-green (shades).
                 2d., lilac, reddish- and grey-lilac, dull lilac (shades).
    Errors.   2d., lilac, watermarked "THREE PENCE."
                  2d., lilac, watermarked "THRSE PENCE."

V. 1863. White wove paper; watermark, thin numeral 2.
    (a) *Perf.* 12. 2d., lilac, pale to deep reddish, and grey-lilac (shades).

Varieties.—In some of the later printings of the Two Pence, notably in those issued in 1863, the shading of the letters composing the word "VICTORIA" has, either owing to defective transfer or to wear and tear, disappeared, and the word seems to be printed in plain block letters.

Proofs in black upon India paper of these stamps are to be met with.

Type VIII.

Three values. Type-printed (probably) in the colony. Coloured impression on various papers, white and dark brown gum. Design: Diademed profile of Queen Victoria to left, on oval of solid colour, with beaded and plain outer frames, the latter inscribed in the upper and lower curves with small white Roman capitals. On either side, extending from the outer edge of the stamp to that of the central oval, is a small oval of solid colour, with double-lined white border, containing the Arabic numeral of value. The corners of the stamp are rounded, and filled in with arabesques. Shape, fancy irregular upright. (*Illustration* 99.)

T. "VICTORIA POSTAGE." B. "THREE PENCE," "FOUR PENCE," OR "SIX PENCE."
R. AND L. "3," "4," OR "6."

I. 1861. Stout white paper, laid horizontally; no watermark.
    Perf. 12.   3d., deep ultramarine.

II. 1862. Medium white wove paper; watermark, value in words in two rows of block type enframed by a single line
    Perf. 12.   3d., blue to chalky-blue.
                4d., rose, deep to pale.
                6d., orange, orange-yellow (shades).
                6d., black to grey.
    Error.   4d., rose; watermarked, "FIVE SHILLINGS" diagonally within a single-lined frame.

VICTORIA.

III. 1863. Thinnish white wove paper; watermark, single-lined numeral 4.
    (a) *Imperf.*   4d., rose.
    (b) *Rouletted* 8.   4d., rose.
    (c) *Perf.* 12.   4d., rose, pale to deep.
    (d) *Perf.* 12½.   4d., rose.
    Variety.   4d., rose; perf. 12½ on slightly blued paper.

IV. 1863. Thin white surfaced paper; no watermark.
    Perf. 12.   4d., rose.

V. 1866. Medium white wove paper; watermark, value in words, as above.
    Perf. 12.   3d., brown-lake (shades).
    Error.   4d., perf. 12. Printed in brown-lake, the colour of the 3d.

Remarks.—It is not easy to account for the existence of the Four Pence printed on paper watermarked Five Shillings. The Society does not know of any Australian fiscal stamps with a similar watermark, on the paper of which the Four Pence might have been printed in error. It seems hardly probable that paper was prepared with this watermark for the purpose of printing the Five Shilling postage stamps, which did not make their appearance until 1868, and then only upon paper watermarked with "v" over Crown.

The error Four Pence, brown-lake, is excessively rare. The only copy known is in the collection of the Vice-President.

Type IX.

One value. Type-printed in the colony. Coloured impression on white wove paper varying in substance, white and brownish gum. Design: This stamp is a modification of Type VIII. The beaded oval is suppressed and replaced by a white one of larger dimensions, inscribed with larger and coloured letters. The double-lined ovals at the sides are also larger, are white, and have coloured numerals of value. It seems likely that the die for this stamp was in two parts, the centre or head of Type VIII. being used together with the modified frame of this issue. In some specimens the central oval is filled up with colour, whilst in others, more especially in the later printings, there is a white border, varying in width, between the background of the portrait and the inner edge of the oval. These differences may arise from the two portions of the die not fitting properly, or from the centre and frame of the stamp being printed separately, as in bi-coloured stamps. (*Illustration* 101.)

March, 1862.
6d., black to grey on white wove paper; wmk., value in words; machine-perf. 12.

1863.
6d., black to grey on white wove paper; wmk., single-lined numeral 6; mach.-perf. 12.
6d.,   "   "   "   "   " none; machine-perf. 12½.

Remarks.—That the last described variety exists is clear, for numerous specimens are known; but that it is an error, produced by inadvertence, seems more than likely.

Type X.

One value. Type-printed in colony; coloured impression on white wove paper, varying in substance; white and dark brown gum. The design is a modification of that of Type VII. The portrait is larger; the inscriptions in the outer oval are in plain coloured block letters, are more spaced, and are divided by a *quatrefoil* ornament on either side. The last letter in the word "VICTORIA" is not an "A," but a reversed "v." The small vignettes in the four corners are suppressed, and the

VICTORIA.

spandrels are more distinctly reticulated. In the central oval, behind the curl, and just opposite to the *quatrefoil* ornament, on the right side of the inscribed oval, is a white circle, arising probably from a flaw in the die, but present in every stamp. (*Illustration* 100.)

1862.

1d., yellow-green, shades; white wove paper; wmk. value in words; machine-perf. 12
1d., green   ,,   ,,   ,,   ,, thick double-lined numeral 1; machine-perf. 12.
1d., pale green, shades; white wove paper; wmk. none; machine-perf. 12.

1863.

1d., green, shades; white wove paper; wmk. thin single-lined numeral 1; machine-perf. 12 and 12½.

Type XI.

(A) *Four values.* Typographed and produced in the colony by Mr. Richards, of Sydney. Coloured impression on white and toned papers, varying greatly in substance from stout to almost pelure; various watermarks; white and yellowish gum. Design: Laureated profile of Queen Victoria, to left, on ground of horizontal lines in double-lined circle, which in some specimens approaches more closely to the sides of the stamp than in others. Straight white labels above and below portrait, inscribed with coloured Roman capitals. Conventional foliate ornaments in the spandrels, which are of solid colour in the case of the One Penny, Two Pence, and Eight Pence; those of the Four Pence containing white perpendicular lines; small blocks with floreate ornaments in the four corners. Shape, upright rectangular. (*Illustration* 102.)

T. "VICTORIA." B. "ONE PENNY," "TWO PENCE," "FOUR PENCE," AND "EIGHT PENCE."

I. 1863. White and yellowish-white wove paper, varying in substance; watermark, double-lined numeral of value.

(a) *Imperf.*   4d., dull rose.

(b) *M.-Perf.* 12. (c) *M.-Perf.* 12½. (d) *M.-Perf.* 13.
    1d., green (shades). (1867.)
    4d., rose ,,

Errors.   1d., green; watermarked 4.
    2d., lilac   ,,   1.
    2d. ,,   ,,   4.

II. 1864. White and yellowish-white wove paper, varying in substance; watermark, single-lined numeral of value.

(a) *Imperf.*   1d., green.
    2d., slate.
    4d., dull rose.

(b) *M.-Perf.* 12. (c) *M.-Perf.* 12½. (d) *M.-Perf.* 13. (e) *M.-Perf. compound.*
    1d., bluish and yellow-green (shades).
    2d., violet, reddish-lilac, lilac, slate (shades).
    4d., carmine, rose, pink (shades).
    8d., orange-yellow (shades).

Errors.   1d., green; watermarked 4.
    1d. ,,   ,,   6.
    1d. ,,   ,,   8.
    1d. ,,   ,,   in letters, "SIXPENCE."
    2d., lilac   ,,   4.
    2d. ,,   ,,   6 (two varieties).
    2d. ,,   ,,   8.
    2d. ,,   ,,   in letters, "SIXPENCE."

III. 1867. Yellowish-white laid or wove paper. No watermark.
 (a) M.-Perf. 11½. (b) M.-Perf. 12. (c) M.-Perf. 12½. (d) M.-Perf. 13.
  (A) *On laid paper.*
   4d., rose (Moens).
  (B) *On wove paper.*
   1d., green (shades). | 2d., lilac (shades). | 4d., rose (shades).

IV. 1867–82. White, yellowish-white, lilac or pink, wove paper, varying in substance; watermark, "v" over Crown.
 (a) *Imperf.* 2d., lilac.
 (b) M.-Perf. 12. (c) M.-Perf. 12½. (d) M.-Perf. 13.
   1d., green (shades).
   2d., violet, lilac (shades).
   2d., lilac (shades), on lilac-tinted paper.
   4d., carmine, rose (shades).
   4d., bright rose-aniline colour. (October, 1881.)
   8d., red-brown (shades), on pink wove paper. (February, 1877.)
   8d. „ aniline colour „ „ „ (1883.)
 Error. 8d. „ watermarked 10.

Owing to the difficulties connected with the arrangement of these stamps, it has been considered advisable to give an alternative list in the form of a chronological table:

Issues.	Value and Colour.	Paper.	Watermark.	Perforation.
1863	4d., dull rose	White wove	Double-lined numeral 4	Mach. 12, 12½, 13.
	4d. ,,	,,	,, ,,	Imperf.
1864	1d., bluish and yellow-green (shades)	,, and yellowish, thick to very thin	Single-lined 1	Mach. 12, 12½, 13, and compound.
	2d., violet, reddish-lilac, lilac, slate (shades)	White wove ,,	,, 2	,, ,,
	4d., carmine, rose, pink (shades)	,, ,,	,, 4	,, ,,
	8d., or.-yellow (shades)	,, ,,	,, 8	,, ,,
	1d., green	,, ,,	,, 1	Imperf.
	2d., slate	,, ,,	,, 2	,,
	4d., dull rose	,, ,,	,, 4	,,
1867	1d., green (shades)	White wove	None	Mach. 11½, 12, 12½, 13.
	2d., lilac (,,)	,,	,,	,, ,,
	4d., rose (,,)	,,	,,	,, ,,
	4d. ,, (,,)	White laid. (See Remarks)	,,	,, 12½ (?).
1867–82	1d., green (,,)	White wove	Double-lined II	,, 12, 12½, 13.
	1d. ,, (,,)	,, hard and soft varying substances	Crown surmounted by the letter "v"	,, 12, 12½, 13.
	2d., lilac and violet in every variety of shade	White wove, hard and soft, and on lilac tinted	,, ,,	,, ,,
	4d., carmine, rose	White wove, hard and soft	,, ,,	,, ,,
	2d., lilac	,, ,,	,, ,,	Imperf.
1877–82	8d., red-brown (shades)	Pink wove	,, ,,	Mach. 13.
1881, Oct.	4d., bright rose-aniline colour	White wove	,, ,,	,, 12.
1883	8d., red-brown-aniline colour	Pink wove	,, ,,	,, 12.

VICTORIA.

ERRORS IN WATERMARK OF STAMPS OF TYPE XI.

Issues.	Values.	Watermark.	Perf.	Earliest Postmks. produced before the Society.
1867-68	2d., lilac (shades)	Double-lined numeral 2	Various	Feb., 1868.
	1d., green (,,)	,, ,, 4	,,	July, 1868.
	2d., lilac (,,)	,, ,, ,,	,,	March, 1868.
	1d., green (,,)	Single-lined ,, 4	,,	Feb., 1867.
	2d., lilac (,,)	,, ,, 4	,,	March, 1867.
	1d., green (,,)	,, ,, 6	,,	June, 1867.
	2d., lilac (,,)	Two varieties, single-lined numeral 6	,,	June, 1867.
	1d., green (,,)	Single-lined numeral 8	,,	Feb., 1867.
	2d., lilac (,,)	,, ,, ,,	,,	Jan., 1867.
	1d., green (,,)	In letters, "SIXPENCE"	,,	1867.
	2d., lilac (,,)	,, ,, ,,	,,	1867 (?).
1878	8d., red-brown (shades)	Single-lined numeral 10	13	March, 1878.

(B) *One value.* The One Penny, green, of Type XI., converted provisionally into a Half Penny value by surcharging the stamp in red, with the word "HALF" in Roman capitals above the original value, and with the numerals "½" on each side of the portrait. (*Illustration* 103.)

September, 1873.

½d., green, red surcharge; wmk. "v" over Crown; machine-perf. 12½, 13.

Remarks.—The variety Four Pence, on white laid paper, without watermark, is given on the authority of M. Moens; it is not known to the Society. In the marginal frames of the One Penny, Two Pence, and Four Pence there are noticeable irregularities, the outer lines being sometimes wholly or in part missing. In some specimens of the Two Pence there would seem to have been a slip in the printing of the value, which appears to be in double-lined lettering instead of in solid type. The perforations given in the table are found variously combined, but a detailed list of these is scarcely necessary.

Type XII.

(A) *Two values.* Engraved by Mr. Richards, of Sydney. Coloured impression on white and coloured wove paper, varying in substance; various watermarks; white gum. Design: Laureated profile of Queen Victoria, to left, on background of horizontal lines, enframed by double-lined oval, of the colour of the paper, which almost touches the top, bottom, and sides of the stamp, and is inscribed in the upper and lower curves with coloured Roman capitals. The two inscriptions are separated on either side by small double-lined ovals containing the Arabic numeral of value in colour. The pattern of the border is fluted, and there are small rectangular blocks of solid colour in each corner. The spandrels are filled in with a small arabesque ornament. Shape, upright rectangular. (*Illustration* 105.)

T. "VICTORIA." B. "SIX PENCE." "TEN PENCE." R. AND L. "6.6." "10.01."

I. 1865. White or pink wove paper, varying in substance; watermark, single-lined numeral of value.

(a) *M.-Perf.* 12. (b) *M.-Perf.* 12½. (c) *M.-Perf.* 13.
6d., blue (shades).
10d., slate-grey (shades).
10d., red-brown, brown (shades), on pink paper. (1866.)

Errors. (a) Watermark, single-lined numeral.
6d., blue; watermark, 4.
10d., slate-grey; watermark, 8.
(b) Watermark, double-lined numeral.
6d., blue; watermark, 2.
6d. ,, ,, 4.

VICTORIA.

II. 1867 (?). White wove paper, varying in substance; watermark, value in letters, "SIXPENCE."
   (a) *M.-Perf.* 12½.   (b) *M.-Perf.* 13.
             6d., blue (shades).
   Errors.   6d. „ watermarked "THREEPENCE."
           6d. „   „   "FOURPENCE."

III. (?)   White wove paper; no watermark. *M.-Perf.* 13.
             6d., blue.

IV. 1867.   White wove paper, varying in substance; watermark, "v" over Crown.
   (a) *M.-Perf.* 12.   (b) *M.-Perf.* 12½.   (c) *M.-Perf.* 13.
             6d., blue (shades).
             6d., ultramarine (shades). (1876.)

A chronological table is given for these two values, for the same reasons as for the stamps described under Type XI.:

Issues.	Value and Colour.	Paper.	Watermark.	Perf.
1865	6d., blue (shades)	Medium white wove	Single-lined numeral 6	Mach.12,12½, 13.
„	10d., slate-grey (shades)	„ „	„ „ 8	„ „
„	10d., „ („)	„ „	„ „ 10	„ „
1866	10d., red-brown, brown (shades)	Stoutish pink wove	„ „ 10	„ „
1867 (?)	6d., blue (shades)	Medium white „	Value in letters,"SIXPENCE"	„ „
1867	6d. „ („)	White wove, varying in substance	"V" over crown	Mach.12,12½, 13.
1876	6d., ultram. (shades)	„ „	„ „	„ „
(?)	6d., blue	Medium white wove	No watermark	„ 12½.

ERRORS IN WATERMARK.

Issues.	Values.	Watermark.	Perf.	Earliest Postmarks known to Society.
1865	6d., blue	Single-lined numeral 4	Various	
1867–70	6d. „ (shades)	Double-lined numeral II	„	1867.
	6d. „ („)	„ „ 4	„	1867.
	6d. „ („)	Value in letters, "THREEPENCE"	„	Early, 1870.
	6d. „ („)	„ "FOURPENCE"	„	Sept., 1870.

Remarks.—Specimens of the Ten Pence, apparently printed in greyish-brown on whitey-brown paper, and watermarked 10, were shown; but they were regarded with suspicion as being probably the result of chemical experiments upon the Ten Pence of 1866, or of some accidental discolouration.

There is the same reason for doubting the authenticity of the Ten Pence, grey on white paper; also watermarked 10.

(B) *One value.* This is the Ten Pence, Type XII., converted provisionally into a Nine Penny value by printing "NINE PENCE" in blue, Roman capitals, in a straight line across the bottom of the stamp and the numeral 9, in the same colour, over the original numeral 10 on either side of the oval. (*Illustration* 106.)

May, 1871.
9d., surcharged in blue on the 10d., red-brown on rose; wmk. 10; machine-perf. 12½.

Remarks.—Varieties may be found in the position of the surcharge. The stamp also exists with double surcharge.

Type XIII.

One value. Engraved in the colony. Coloured impression on stout coloured paper; white gum. Design: Laureated profile of Queen Victoria to left, on background of horizontal lines, enframed by a circular band of two inner and three outer lines inscribed in the upper and lower curves, with legends in Roman capitals. The two inscriptions are separated by small six-rayed stars on either side. The outline of the stamp is octagonal, but the lines of perforation are rectangular (*Illustration* 104.)

T. "VICTORIA." B. "ONE SHILLING."

1865.

1s., deep blue on blue wove paper; wmk. single-lined numeral 1; machine-perf. 12½.
1s. „ „ „ no watermark; machine-perf. 12½.

1875.

1s., deep blue on blue wove paper; wmk. "V" over Crown; machine-perf. 12½.

Type XIV.

(A) *One value.* Engraved in the colony. Coloured impression on medium white wove paper; various watermarks; white and yellowish gum. Design: Laureated profile of Queen Victoria to left, on ground of solid colour, within a double-lined white oval, which almost touches the borders of the stamp, and is inscribed in the upper and lower curves with coloured Roman capitals. The two inscriptions are separated by a small crown on either side. The spandrels are reticulated, and there is a rectangular double-lined white block in each of the four corners, with shaded and coloured Arabic numeral of value. The whole stamp is enframed by two plain outer lines. Shape, upright rectangular. (*Illustration* 107.)

T. "3 VICTORIA 3" (in shaded capitals). B. "3 THREE PENCE 3" (in plain Roman capitals).

October, 1866.

3d., dull lilac (shades); wmk. single-lined numeral 8; machine-perf. 13.

1867.

3d., dull and slatey (shades); wmk. double-lined numeral 1; machine-perf. 13.

1868.

3d., dull, reddish, and slatey (shades); wmk. "V" over Crown; machine-perf. 12½.

October, 1869.

3d., deep orange to yellow (shades); wmk. "V" over Crown; machine-perf. 12½.

(B) Same stamp, surcharged in blue, with the words "STAMP DUTY" in small block letters on each side of the portrait. (*Illustration* 108.)

L. "STAMP" reading upwards. R. "DUTY" reading downwards.

1885.

3d., yellow on medium white paper; wmk. "V" over Crown; machine-perf. 12½.

Remarks.—As the stamps of this type were never printed upon paper expressly set apart for them, the issues upon the paper watermarked with the numerals 8 and 1 have not been classed as errors.

Proofs on stoutish wove paper, without watermark, in pale lilac, are known. Various trials were made of this stamp in bi-colours and distinct self-colours for approbation. The former were produced by a paste and scissors operation, cutting out the oval containing the head, and gumming it on a border cut from a proof of another colour, and the latter were simply printed in self-colours. A list of these colours and combinations is beyond the scope of this catalogue.

Type XV.

One value. Engraved in the colony. Coloured impression on yellow and on white wove paper; white gum. Design: Laureated profile of Queen Victoria to left, on ground of solid colour, enframed by a plain circular band, inscribed in the upper and lower segments in coloured block letters. The two inscriptions are separated on either side by a small ring with a dot in the centre. Above the circle is a royal crown, and the whole is surrounded by arabesque and foliate ornaments. The shape of the design is an irregular seven-sided figure, but the stamp is perforated as a rectangle. (*Illustration* 110.)

T. "VICTORIA." B. "FIVE SHILLINGS."
January, 1868.
5s., Prussian-blue design, and inscriptions, on yellow wove paper; wmk. "V" over Crown; machine-perf. 12½.

July, 1868.
5s., Prussian-blue design, carmine crown inscription, on white wove paper; wmk. "V" over Crown; machine-perf. 12½.

1878.
5s., pale ultramarine, carmine crown inscription, on white wove paper; wmk. "V" over Crown; machine-perf. 12½.

1881.
5s., deep aniline-blue, scarlet crown, on white wove paper; wmk. "V" over Crown; machine-perf. 12.

Type XVI.

One value. Engraved and type-printed by De la Rue and Co. Coloured impression on white wove, slightly surfaced watermarked paper. Design: Diademed profile of Queen Victoria to left, on ground of horizontal lines within a double-lined white oval, which touches the borders of the stamp, and is inscribed in the upper and lower curves in coloured Roman capitals. The two inscriptions are separated on either side by a small circle of colour containing the minute Arabic numeral of value in white. The spandrels are filled in with arabesques, and the whole stamp is bordered by a plain outer line of colour. Shape, upright rectangular. (*Illustration* 109.)

T. "VICTORIA." B. "TWO PENCE."
January, 1870.
2d., rosy to grey shades of lilac; wmk. "V" over Crown; machine-perf. 12½.

Type XVII.

(A) *One value.* Engraved in the colony. Coloured impression on rose wove watermarked paper, white gum. Design: Profile to left of Queen Victoria with Gothic crown, on ground of horizontal lines, enframed in double-lined circle, with scalloped inner edge. Above and below the circle and following its outline are curved labels with notched ends, inscribed in coloured Roman capitals. The spandrels are of solid colour, and the borders consist of *fleurs-de-lis*-like ornaments. In each of the four corners is a small escutcheon, on the left upper and right lower of which is a Kangaroo, and on the left lower and right upper an Emu. Shape, upright rectangular. (*Illustration* 111.)

T. "VICTORIA." B. "NINE PENCE."
March, 1873.
9d., red-brown (shades); watermark, single-lined numeral 10; mach.-perf. 12½.

August, 1875.
9d., red-brown (shades); watermark, "V" over Crown; mach.-perf. 12 and 12½.

(B) This is Type XVII. (A) converted provisionally into an Eight Penny value, by surcharging the stamp in blue with the words "EIGHT PENCE," in Roman capitals, in a straight line above the original value, and with the value "8d." on each side of the portrait. (*Illustration* 112.)

August, 1876.

8d., red-brown, blue surcharge; watermark, "V" over Crown; mach.-perf. 12 and 12½.

Type XVIII.

One value. Engraved in the colony. Coloured impression on white and coloured wove watermarked papers, white gum. Design: Diademed profile of Queen Victoria to left, on ground of horizontal lines, within a single-lined oval, which touches the top, bottom, and sides of the stamp. The upper and lower curves of the oval are formed by two white labels—the first with convex, and the other with concave extremities—inscribed with coloured block letters. The sides of the oval, between the two inscribed labels, are filled in with a reticulated pattern, and the spandrels with Etruscan ornament. The whole stamp is bordered by a plain line of colour. Shape, upright rectangular. (*Illustration* 113.)

T. "VICTORIA." B. "TWO PENCE."

March, 1873.

2d., mauve (shades), on medium white wove paper; wmk. "V" over Crown; mach.-perf. 12½.

1878.

2d., mauve (shades), on medium green wove paper; wmk. "V" over Crown; mach.-perf. 12½.
2d.   „   „   „   buff   „   „   „   „

1879.

2d., mauve (shades), on medium white wove paper; wmk. "V" over Crown; mach.-perf. 12½.

Variety.—In 1879 the plate was altered, and the outer border of the oval, from being a thick single line, was changed to two fine ones.

Type XIX.

One value. Engraved in the colony. Coloured impression on white and coloured wove watermarked paper, white gum. Design: Diademed profile of Queen Victoria to left, on ground of horizontal lines, within a double-lined oval, which almost touches the sides of the stamps. Above and below the oval, following its outline, are white labels with pointed ends, inscribed with coloured block letters. The stamp is bordered by two lines of colour, which are broken at the four corners by circular coloured blocks with ½d. in white. The remainder of the stamp is filled in with reticulations. Shape, narrow, upright, rectangular. (*Illustration* 114.)

T. "½d. VICTORIA ½d." B. "½d. HALF PENNY ½d."

1874.

½d., carmine-lake, to rose (shades), white wove paper; wmk. "V" over Crown; perf. 11½, 12½.

1878.

½d., carmine, pink wove paper; watermark, "V" over Crown; perf. 12½.

1883.

½d., carmine, aniline colour on white paper; watermark, "V" over Crown; perf. 11½.

Remarks.—The watermark is spread over two stamps. The printing of this value, the Two Pence of Type XVIII., and the One Penny of the following type, upon coloured papers, seems to have been an experiment, which, judging from the speed with which it was abandoned, could hardly have afforded the results expected.

Type XX.

One value. Engraved in the colony. Coloured impression on white and coloured watermarked paper, white gum. Design: A barely three-quarter face of Queen Victoria to left, on ground of horizontal lines, within a white oval of two fine inner and outer lines, which touches the border of the stamp at top, bottom, and sides, and is inscribed in the upper and lower curves with coloured block letters. The two inscriptions are separated on either side by a conventional ornament. The spandrels are filled in with Etruscan ornament. In each of the two upper angles is a circle containing Geometric ornament, and in each of the lower ones a single-lined circle with fancy 1ᵈ· in colour. Shape, upright rectangular. (*Illustration* 115.)

T. "VICTORIA." B. "1d. PENNY 1d."

December, 1875.

1d., dull green (shades), on white wove paper; wmk. "V" over Crown; mach.-perf. 11½, 12½.

1878.

1d., dull green (shades), on yellow wove paper; wmk. "V" over Crown; mach.-perf. 12½.
1d.   „   „   drab   „   „   „   „

Type XXI.

(A) *One value.* Engraved in the colony. Coloured impression on stout coloured watermarked paper, white gum. Design: A diademed portrait of Queen Victoria, closely resembling that in Type XX., on ground of solid colour within double-lined circle. Scrolled labels above and below circle inscribed with block letters in hue of the paper. The border is formed of a heavy line of eccentric shape, and the rest of the stamp is filled in with reticulations. Shape, upright rectangular. (*Illustration* 116.)

T. "VICTORIA." B. "ONE SHILLING."

October 4th, 1876.

1s., blue (shades) upon a lighter blue wove paper; wmk., "V" over Crown; mach.-perf. 11½ and 12½.

(B) The same stamp, surcharged "STAMP DUTY" in black, similar to Type XIV. (B).

1885.

1s., blue upon a lighter blue wove paper; watermark, "V" over Crown; mach.-perf. 12½.

Type XXII.

One value. Engraved in the colony. Coloured impression on medium white wove watermarked paper, white gum. Design: Diademed profile of Queen Victoria to left, on ground of horizontal lines, enclosed by a single white oval line. Surrounding this and following the shape of the oval is an ornamental fancy frame, consisting of scrolled labels of solid colour, diminishing in width at the centre, above and below the oval, containing inscriptions in white block letters, also diminishing in height, like the labels, at the centre of the words. The remainder of the ornamental frame is made up on each side by a curved row of ten pearls and other ornamentation. The angles are filled in with irregularly shaped blocks and triangles. The small blocks in the corners are coloured, and bear a minute white letter "A.C." in the upper and "C.E." in the lower, most likely the initials of the engraver. The design is completed by a single outer line of colour. Shape, upright rectangular. (*Illustration* 117.)

VICTORIA.

T. "VICTORIA." B. "TWO PENCE."
January, 1881.
2d., brown (shades); wmk., "v" over Crown; machine-perf. 12½.
December 21st, 1883.
2d., mauve (shades); wmk., "v" over Crown; machine-perf. 12½.

Type XXIII.

(A) *One value*. Engraved in the colony. Coloured impression on stout coloured watermarked paper, white gum. Design: Similar to Type XX., except that the oval band enclosing the portrait is of solid colour, and has the block letters in the hue of the paper. The conventional ornaments separating the two inscriptions are also a little different. The circles in the corners are replaced by an irregular pentagon, bearing "2s." in colour. Shape, upright rectangular. (*Illustration* 118.)

T. "2S. VICTORIA 2S." B. "2S. TWO SHILLINGS 2S."
June (?), 1881.
2s., blue upon a light green wove paper; wmk., "v" over Crown; mach.-perf. 12½.

(B) The same stamp, surcharged "STAMP DUTY" in black, similar to Type XIV. (B).
1885.
2s., blue upon a green light wove paper; wmk., "v" over Crown; mach.-perf. 12½.

Type XXIV.

(A) *One value*. Engraved in the colony. Coloured impression on medium white wove watermarked paper; white gum. Design: Diademed profile of Queen Victoria to left (similar to Type XXII.), on ground of horizontal lines, enclosed by a single white oval line. Surrounding this and following the shape of the oval is an ornamental fluted frame, containing two scrolled labels above and below the oval. These labels, though rather smaller, are similar in shape to those of Type XXII., and are similarly inscribed with white block letters. The spandrels and corners are filled in with branching portions of the ornamental frame, and under the "F" and "E" of "FOUR PENCE" are small coloured circles, containing minute letters—"c" in the left, and "A" in the right. The design is completed by a double outer line of colour. Shape, upright rectangular. (*Illustration* 119.)

T. "VICTORIA." B. "FOUR PENCE."
Jan., 1882. 4d., carmine-rose; wmk. "v" over Crown; machine-perf. 12½.
(?) 4d., „ (aniline colour) „ „ „

(B) The same stamp surcharged "STAMP DUTY" in blue, similar to Type XIV. (B)
1885. 4d., carmine-rose; watermark "v" over Crown; machine-perf. 12½.

Type XXV.

One value. Engraved in the colony. Coloured impression on medium white wove watermarked paper; white gum. Design: Diademed head of Queen Victoria, nearly three-quarter face, to left, on background of horizontal lines, enclosed by a linear oval band, which touches the top, bottom, and sides of the stamp, and is inscribed, in coloured block letters, with the name of the colony and the value. The upper portion of the inscription is separated from the lower by an arabesque ornament on either side. The four corners contain small white circles, enclosed by a single coloured line, containing in the two upper circles a species of linear Maltese cross, in the centre of which is a minute letter—"c" in the left corner, and "H" in the right. The two lower circles contain the value "1d." The design is completed by a double outer line of colour. Shape, upright rectangular. (*Illustration* 120.)

T. "VICTORIA." B. "1d. VICTORIA 1d."
29th October, 1883.
1d., green and emerald-green (shades); wmk. "v" over Crown; machine-perf. 12½.

Type XXVI.

One value. Engraved in the colony. Coloured impression on medium white wove watermarked paper; white gum. Design: Diademed profile of Queen Victoria to left, on background of solid colour, enclosed by a white oval band, which touches the top, bottom, and sides of the stamp, and is inscribed, in coloured block letters, with the name of the colony and the value. The two inscriptions are separated by arabesque ornamentation. The two upper corners are filled in with arabesque ornaments, and with two curved labels of solid colour, containing in the left the word "STAMP," reading upwards, and in the right "DUTY," reading downwards, both words being in small block letters. The lower corners contain two rectangular linear blocks, impinged upon by the oval band, and bearing the value "½" expressed in white figures. On the inner side of the figures there are two white semicircles. The design is completed by a single outer line of colour. Shape, upright rectangular. (*Illustration* 121.)

T. "STAMP. VICTORIA. DUTY." B. "½ HALF-PENNY ½."

1884. ½d., rose (shades), aniline colour; wmk. "v" over Crown; mach.-perf. 12½.

Type XXVII.

Three values. Engraved in the colony. Coloured impression on medium white wove watermarked paper; white gum. Design: Diademed profile of Queen Victoria to left (similar to Type XXVI.), on ground of horizontal lines, enclosed by a single white-lined oval. Surrounding this and following the shape of the oval is an ornamental fancy frame, consisting of scrolled labels of solid colour above and below the oval. The labels diminish in width at the centre, and bear the name of the colony and value in block letters. At either side is a small linear label, inscribed in white block letters—L. "STAMP," reading upwards, and R. "DUTY," reading downwards. The upper corners are filled in with floral ornaments, and the lower with small, irregularly-shaped linear blocks. The design is completed by a single coloured line. Shape, upright rectangular. (*Illustration* 122.)

T. "VICTORIA." B. "ONE PENNY," "THREE PENCE," "SIX PENCE."

1884. 1d., yellowish-green to green (shades); wmk. "v" over Crown; mach.-perf. 12½.
  3d., bistre   "   "   "   "
  6d., ultramarine "   "   "   "

Type XXVIII.

Two values. Engraved in the colony. Coloured impression on medium white or coloured wove watermarked paper; white gum. Design: Diademed profile of Queen Victoria to left (similar to Type XXVI.), on ground of solid colour, enclosed by a plain white circular line. Above and below, and following the shape of the circle, are two plain white labels, inscribed with the name of the colony and value. The bottom label of the One Shilling bears the value in the hue of the paper, upon a linear ground. At either side is a small circle, which touches the side of the stamp, and impinges upon the circle containing the head. The circles on the

Two Pence contain the numeral of value upon a white ground, while those on the One Shilling bear the numeral in the hue of the paper upon a ground of solid colour. In the bottom corners are two small curved linear labels, with "STAMP" to left and "DUTY" to right in block letters. The upper corners are filled in with conventional ornaments. The remainder of the design is completed by fancy fancy framework, and by an outer line of colour. Shape, upright rectangular. (*Illustrations* 123, 124.)

T. "VICTORIA." B. "STAMP. TWO PENCE. DUTY," "STAMP. ONE SHILLING. DUTY."

1884.

2d., violet, mauve, rose-violet (shades) on white wove paper; wmk. "v" over Crown; machine-perf. 12½.

1885.

1s., blue, on light yellow wove paper; wmk. "v" over Crown; machine-perf. 12½.

Type XXIX.

One value. Engraved in the colony. Coloured impression on medium white wove watermarked paper, white gum. Design: Diademed profile of Queen Victoria to left (similar to Type XXVI.), on ground of solid colour, enclosed within a narrow white circular line. Curved linear labels above and below. The upper one inscribed with the name of the colony, and the lower with the value in full in white Roman capitals. In the left upper corner is "STAMP," and in the right "DUTY," both in thin coloured block letters; and the two lower corners contain the numeral of value. The design is completed with conventional ornaments, irregularly shaped blocks, and an eccentric outer line of colour. Shape, upright rectangular. (*Illustration* 125.)

T. "STAMP. VICTORIA. DUTY." B. "4 FOUR PENCE 4."

1884. 4d., puce; watermark, "v" over Crown; machine-perf. 12½.

Type XXX.

Two values. Engraved in the colony. Coloured impression on medium coloured wove watermarked paper, white gum. Design: Diademed profile of Queen Victoria to left (similar to Type XXVI.), on ground of horizontal lines, enclosed within an irregular octagon, the frame of which is composed of dented ornamentation. The frame is broken at the top and bottom by two small plain labels with rounded ends. The upper one is inscribed "STAMP," and the lower "DUTY," both in coloured block letters. Above and below these are two straight labels of solid colour, of the width of the stamp, the first bearing the name of the colony, and the second the value in full, in plain Roman capitals. At either side is the numeral of value upon a diamond of solid colour. The spandrels are filled in with conventional ornaments, and along each side is a key pattern border. The whole design is enclosed within a single outer line of colour. Shape, upright rectangular. (*Illustration* 126.)

T. "VICTORIA STAMP." B. "DUTY EIGHT PENCE." "DUTY TWO SHILLINGS."

1884.

8d., rose on a lighter rose coloured paper; wmk., "v" over Crown; mach.-perf. 12½.

1886.

2s., olive-green on light green coloured paper; wmk., "v" over Crown; mach.-perf. 12½.

Type XXXI.

One value. Engraved in the colony. Coloured impression on thin white wove watermarked paper, white gum. Design: Diademed profile of Queen Victoria to left, on ground of horizontal lines within a double-lined circle, the inner line of which is notched. Above the circle is a curved white label with pointed ends, inscribed with the name of the colony in coloured fancy capitals. Straight white label below the circle bearing the value in full in coloured block letters. Both labels extend the whole width of the stamp. On either side of the circle, between two rows of six white pearls, are two small white labels, inscribed, in thin block letters, "STAMP" to left and "DUTY" to right. Below these are two white upright labels, with the upper ends rounded. They rest upon the bottom label of value, and are inscribed "$\frac{1}{2}$" in coloured numerals. The remainder of the stamp is filled in with conventional ornaments, and a narrow fancy border along the top and sides, and the design is completed by a double outer line of colour. Shape, oblong rectangular. (*Illustration* 127.)

T. "VICTORIA." B. "$\frac{1}{2}$ HALFPENNY $\frac{1}{2}$."

1886. $\frac{1}{2}$d., dull lilac; wmk., "V" over Crown, placed sideways; mach.-perf. 12$\frac{1}{2}$.

Type XXXII.

One value. Engraved in the colony. Coloured impression on thin white wove watermarked paper; white gum. Design: Same head of Her Majesty as the preceding type, but somewhat larger in size, upon ground of horizontal lines, within an upright rectangle, the upper portion of which is rounded. Above, on a straight white label, is the name of the colony, and crossing the bottom is a white arched scroll bearing the value in full, both inscriptions being in coloured block letters. The scroll passes round the sides of the oblong, and the ends are straight, and are inscribed in small thin block letters "STAMP" to left, and "DUTY" to right. Conventional ornaments and two outer lines of colour, the inner one of which is notched, complete the design. Shape, upright rectangular. (*Illustration* 128.)

T. "VICTORIA." B. "STAMP DUTY. ONE PENNY."

1886. 1d., yellow-green; wmk. "V" over Crown; machine-perf. 12$\frac{1}{2}$.

Type XXXIII.

One value. Engraved in the colony. Coloured impression on thin white wove watermarked paper; white gum. Design: Same head of Her Majesty as the previous type, upon ground of horizontal lines, within a toothed circle, broken at the top by a curved label of solid colour, inscribed with the name of the colony in white block letters, and at the bottom by two straight labels, one resting upon the other. The upper of the two is white with rounded ends, and bears the words "STAMP DUTY" in small coloured block letters. The lower one is of solid colour, and is inscribed with the value in full in white block letters. A royal crown surmounts the label with the name of the colony. The upper spandrels are filled in with radiating lines grouped in couples, and along the bottom of the stamp there is a key pattern border. The design is completed by a double outer line of colour. Shape, upright rectangular. (*Illustration* 129.)

T. "VICTORIA." B. "STAMP DUTY. SIX PENCE."

1886. 6d., ultramarine; wmk. "V" over Crown; machine-perf. 12$\frac{1}{2}$.

ENVELOPES.

Issue I. November 1st, 1869.

One value. On white or blue laid paper, varying in substance. In the right upper corner of the envelope is a stamp engraved by Messrs. De la Rue and Co. The die was probably printed from in the colony. Coloured impression. Design: Embossed diademed profile of Queen Victoria to left, on ground of solid colour, enclosed by a white embossed beaded oval. Surrounding this is a white embossed reticulated oval band, inscribed T. "POSTAGE TWO PENCE," B. "VICTORIA," in coloured block letters, the two inscriptions being separated by star-shaped ornaments. A single outer oval line of colour completes the design. Shape, upright oval. (*Illustration* 131.)

Sizes. (A) 4¾ × 2¾ inches or 120 × 67 mm.
(B) 5½ × 3 „ 132 × 80 mm.
(C) 5¾ × 3½ „ 145 × 88 mm.
(D) 8¾ × 3¾ „ 222 × 97 mm.

2d., pale rose, dull rose-lilac, bright rose (slight shades).

Remarks.—Specimens are known with a double impression of the stamp on the face, the second being without colour. The flaps are found pointed and rounded with several varieties in shape of the latter. There are also numerous varieties of the *tresse* impressed upon the flap. The following "note" is taken from Major Evans's *Catalogue:* "The above sizes are those given in the *Postal Guide of Victoria,* and I am informed that envelopes in these four sizes are to be purchased at the Post Office. Various ornaments are to be found on the flaps (I possess eighteen varieties besides each size with plain flap); but these can hardly be considered of any official significance, as the envelopes as a rule are purchased by the Government ready made, and the stamp is impressed upon them afterwards. I find two specimens which are apparently exceptions to this—one of the smallest size with a fancy "V" on the flap, the stamp on which was evidently embossed before it was made up; the other size 5¾ × 3½ inches, with a crown enclosed in a garter, inscribed "VICTORIA" on the flap, stamped after it was made up, but the envelope of colonial manufacture. The foolscap envelope of thin wove paper may have been printed to order, as I am informed are all blue or coloured envelopes." The varieties of the size, *tresse,* and flap, of this and the succeeding issues do not seem to the Society to merit the separate classification devoted to them in some catalogues.

Issue II. 1878.

One value. Engraved by Messrs. De la Rue and Co., and printed in the colony. The stamp is impressed in the right upper corner of the envelope. Design: Embossed diademed profile of Queen Victoria to left, on solid ground, within a beaded oval. Surrounding this is a coloured oval band, inscribed, in the upper portion, "ONE PENNY," in white block letters. The lower portion is filled with an inner semi-oval reticulated band, inscribed "VICTORIA," in coloured block letters. Star-shaped ornament at each end of "VICTORIA." The design is completed by an oval outer line of colour. Shape, upright oval. (*Illustration* 132.)

1d., yellow-green.

Remarks.—Major Evans says: "I am informed that the One Penny envelopes are not on sale at the Post Office in Victoria, but are printed to order only, as in the case of the English envelopes of higher values. I have seen this type upon white, blue, and buff envelopes, and upon a wrapper."

VICTORIA.

Issue III. 1882.

One value. Engraved by Messrs. De la Rue and Co., and printed in the colony. The stamp is impressed in the right upper corner of the envelope. Design: Same as that of the Two Penny stamp of 1869, previously described, except in one or two unimportant details. The head is slightly larger. The reticulations of the oval band are coarser, and the letters of the inscriptions are smaller and thicker. Shape, upright oval. (*Illustration* 133.)

T. "ONE PENNY." B. "VICTORIA."
Various sizes and papers made to order.
1d., yellow-green.

Remarks.—Specimens are known with a double impression of the stamp on the face of the envelope, the second being without colour. These envelopes were also made to order; and the same observations apply to the varieties of size, paper, tresse, &c., as to the previous issues.

Issue IV. January 1st, 1885.

Two values. Engraved and printed in the colony. The stamp is impressed in the right upper corner of the envelope. Designs: Same as those of the adhesives, Types XXVII. and XXVIII.; various sizes (eight are given by M. Moens for the Two Pence, and one for the One Penny). Shape, rectangular. (*Illustrations* 122, 123.)

1d., green. | 2d., mauve, violet.

These two stamps, like the others, were doubtless impressed to order upon envelopes of the various sizes, though among them are found the four quasi-official sizes of the first issue.

Issue V. 1885.

Two values. Same as the types of Issues I. and III., but the words "STAMP DUTY" have been added to the die, in small block letters; "STAMP" to left reading downwards, and "DUTY" to right reading upwards. Various sizes and papers. (*Illustration* 134.)

1d., green (shades). | 2d., light mauve (shades).

Issue VI. 1886.

One value. Same as Type XXXII. of adhesive. The stamp is impressed in the right upper corner. Various sizes and papers. (*Illustration* 128.)

1d., yellow-green.

OFFICIAL ENVELOPES.

Issue 1865.

These are hand-stamped envelopes used by different officials and departments, and are similar in character to those previously described for Tasmania. The handstamps are printed in red, black, or blue, upon variously-sized and coloured envelopes. The following are given by M. Moens: "Attorney-General; Chief Secretary (4 types); Colonel-Commandant of Volunteers; Commandant of Local Forces; Commandant of Volunteers; Commander of H.M. Land Forces; Commander of H.M. Sea Forces; Commander Royal Artillery; Commissariat Staff; Commissioner of Crown Lands and Survey; Commissioner of Public Works; Commissioner of Railways and Roads; Commissioner of Trade and Customs; Governor of Victoria; Minister of Justice; Minister of Mines; Minister of Public Works; Postmaster-General (3 types); Solicitor-General; the Treasury." (*Illustration* 130.)

A detailed list of the varieties would possess but little interest.

REGISTRATION ENVELOPES.
Issue I. 1881.

One value. These envelopes are made of stout white laid paper. The face and back of the envelope are divided into four equal compartments by two lines which cross at right angles, and are continued from the face to the back of the envelope. On the face in the upper part is an inscription in two lines—"THIS LETTER MUST BE GIVEN TO AN OFFICER OF THE POST-OFFICE TO BE REGISTERED, AND A RECEIPT OBTAINED FOR IT"—in thin block capitals. The vertical crossing line falls between the words "OFFICER OF" and "RECEIPT OBTAINED" in the two lines of inscription. In the left upper compartment, below the lines of direction, is the word "REGISTERED" in thick block capitals, enclosed in an oblong single-lined frame. In the right upper compartment is a single-lined rectangle. The whole printed in vermilion. Pointed flap with white gum, impressed with a stamp in mauve, engraved and printed in the colony. Design: Embossed diademed profile of Queen Victoria to left, on solid ground, enclosed by a beaded oval. Surrounding this is an embossed reticulated oval band inscribed in block letters, the two inscriptions being separated by star-shaped ornaments. The design is completed by an outer oval line of colour. Shape, upright oval. (*Illustration* 135.)

T. "REGISTERED." B. "FOUR PENCE."

Sizes. (A) $5\frac{3}{10} \times 3$ inches or 135×78 mm.
(B) $5\frac{7}{10} \times 3\frac{2}{3}$ „ 145×88 mm.

4d., mauve.

Issue II. January 1st, 1885.

One value. Same paper, sizes, inscriptions, &c., as the preceding; but the stamp on the flap is the same as the adhesive (Type XXIX.) On the smaller sized envelope, $5\frac{3}{10} \times 3$ inches, the directions—"THIS LETTER MUST BE GIVEN," &c.—are printed in smaller capitals closer together, thus shortening the length of the inscriptions. (*Illustration* 125.)

Sizes. (A) $5\frac{3}{10} \times 3$ inches or 135×78 mm.
(B) $5\frac{7}{10} \times 3\frac{2}{3}$ „ 145×88 mm.

4d., puce.

Issue III. 1886.

One value. Similar in every respect to the envelope of Issue I., but the stamp is surcharged "STAMP DUTY." Sizes and paper, &c., as before.

4d., mauve, with mauve surcharge.

Remarks.—This envelope is unknown to the Society.

WRAPPERS.
Issue I. September, 1869.

One value. On white wove watermarked paper. Size, $10\frac{9}{10} \times 4\frac{1}{2}$ inches. The watermark is placed vertically, and consists of a crown, beneath which is "ONE PENNY—VICTORIA," in two lines, in double-lined block letters, the first letter of each word being slightly larger than the other letters. The stamp, type of adhesive 1864, is impressed about two inches from the top in the centre. The wrappers throughout all the issues are ungummed. (*Illustration* 102.)

1d., pale green.

Issue II. July, 1873.

One value. Similar to last issue, but the width of the wrapper is reduced to $4\frac{1}{4}$ inches, and the stamp is impressed in the right upper angle, about $\frac{3}{4}$ inch from the top. On either side and at the top of the wrapper is a coloured border, consisting of two straight lines, the outer one being considerably thicker than the inner. The wrappers on the sheet are rouletted on lines of colour at the top and sides to facilitate separation. (*Illustration* 102.)

    1d., green.

Varieties. (A) The side borders are distant $4\frac{3}{10}$ inches from each other.
    (B)   „   „   „ $4\frac{7}{10}$ „   „   „

Issue III. September (?), 1873.

One value. Same as last. The stamp is surcharged "$\frac{1}{2}$" on either side of the head, and "HALF" in Roman capitals above the original value, similar to adhesive Type XI. (B). (*Illustration* 103.)

    $\frac{1}{2}$d., red surcharge on 1d., green.
    $\frac{1}{2}$d., black   „   „   „
    Varieties. (A) and (B) as above.

Remarks.—The Half Penny with black surcharge has been chronicled, but is unknown to the Society.

Issue IV. End 1882.

One value. Same as last issue, but the stamp is replaced by Type XX. of the adhesives. (*Illustration* 115.)

    1d., green, dark green.
    Varieties. (A) and (B) as above.

Issue V.

One value.—Both types of the One Penny envelope—*i.e.* Issues II. and III.—have been impressed on paper sent in by the public, without regard to make and size. (*Illustrations* 132, 133.)

    1d., green (Type I).
    1d.   „   („ II).

Issue VI. July, 1883.

One value. Similar to Issue IV., but with stamp Type XIX. of the adhesives in the right upper corner, and there is no border to the wrapper. (*Illustration* 114.)

    $\frac{1}{2}$d., rose.

Issue VII. January 1st, 1885.

Two values. Same as Issue IV. Stamps, type of adhesives issue January 1st, 1885, are impressed to right, about two inches from the top. The side borders are distant $4\frac{1}{4}$ inches on the Half Penny. Varieties (A) and (B) as before for the One Penny. (*Illustrations* 121, 122.)

    (A) *On white wove watermarked paper.*
        $\frac{1}{2}$d., rose (shades).
        1d., sage-green, green (shades).
    (B) *On white wove unwatermarked paper.*
        $\frac{1}{2}$d., rose.
        1d., green.
    (C) *On coloured wove unwatermarked paper.*
        $\frac{1}{2}$d., rose, on green paper.
        1d., yellow-green, on buff paper.
        1d.   „   on blue   „

138   VICTORIA.

Issue VIII. 1885.

One value. Similar to last issue, but impressed upon thin greenish wove paper, watermarked "N.S.W." in single-lined block letters, repeated fifty times, within a single-line frame, outside of which, at top and bottom, is "NEW SOUTH WALES" and on either side "STAMP DUTY" in double-lined block letters. The whole watermark extends over about 2½ wrappers. This paper was obtained many years ago from the Sydney Post Office, but was found unsuitable at the time. It has only lately been used up. (*Illustration* 121.)

     ½d., rose, on greenish wove paper.
     ½d., „ white „ no watermark.

Varieties. (A) Without the coloured border at the sides, and not rouletted; wmk. as above.
     ½d., rose, on greenish wove paper.

  (B) Two stamps, impressed side by side; wmk. of the maker's name of paper only.
     ½d. + ½d. rose, on white wove paper.

Issue IX. 1885.

Two values. The Half Penny wrapper, Issue VI., and the One Penny wrapper, Issue IV., surcharged in blue "STAMP DUTY," similar to the Three Pence adhesive, Type XIV. (B).

    ½d., rose. | 1d., green.

Varieties. (A) With double surcharge.
     1d., green.

  (B) With the word "STAMP" misspelt "STAM.," and the word "DUTY" lower down than the word "STAM."
     1d., green.

Issue X. 1886.

Two values. On unwatermarked wove paper. Same size as the preceding issue, and with a similar border. The stamps, which are the same as the adhesive Type XXXI. for the Half Penny and XXXII. for the One Penny, are placed about two inches from the top at the right-hand side. (*Illustrations* 127, 128.)

  (A) *With border, and rouletted on lines of colour.*
    ½d., dull lilac-mauve, on white paper.
    1d., yellow-green „ „

  (B) *Without border, and imperforate; unofficial (?).*
    ½d., dull lilac, on light blue paper.
    ½d. „ yellow „
    1d., yellow-green on light blue „
    1d. „ yellow „

POST CARDS.

Issue I. July 1st, 1876.

One value. Designed and printed in the colony upon white or straw-coloured card, varying in substance. Size 4¾ × 3½ inches. The inscription is at the top of the card in the centre, and is in two lines—first, "POST CARD," in fancy capitals, with the Royal Arms directly beneath; second, "THE ADDRESS ONLY TO BE WRITTEN ON THIS SIDE," in block letters. Lower down to left is the word "*To*," in script type. The stamp is in the right upper corner, and is of the same type as the One Penny adhesive issue, 1864. The design of the card is completed by a twisted or cable pattern border. Size 4⅞ × 3 inches. (*Illustration* 136.)

    1d., pale to deep lilac, on straw.

Varieties. (A) With two imperfectly shaped dots after the word "SIDE."
    1d., lilac (shades), on straw.

(B) Without period after the word "SIDE."
    1d., lilac (shades), on straw.
    1d. „ „ on white.

Issue II. November 1st, 1876.

One value. Designed and printed in the colony upon straw-coloured card, varying much in substance. Size 4¾ × 3 inches. At the top of the card in the centre is a plain scroll with shaded ends, inscribed with the words "POST CARD" in fancy capitals. Beneath the scroll are the Royal Arms with the word "*droit*" misspelt "*drot*," and lower down, in a straight line, is "The Address only to be written on this side," in lower-case type. Below this to left is the word "*To*," in script type. The stamp, type of the One Penny adhesive issue, 1875, is in the right upper corner. The design of the card is completed by a frame composed of *fleurs-de-lis* between two thin lines, with other fancy star-like ornaments at the corners. Size 4 × 2½ inches. (*Illustration* 137.)

    1d., red-lilac (shades).

Varieties. (A) With small dash of ½ mm. in length after the word "CARD" in place of period.
    1d., red-lilac.

(B) With dash of 1 mm. in length; otherwise the same as variety (A).
    1d., red-lilac, mauve (shades).

Issue III. 1878.

One value. Similar to variety (B) of the preceding issue, but the frame is reset. The lines are more regular, and the outer one is much thicker. The dimensions also are slightly increased. The Royal Arms (still bearing the error "*drot*") are 1⅓ mm. nearer the stamp, and the word "*To*" is 1½ mm. further from the frame than in the last issue.

    1d., mauve on straw.
    1d., red-lilac on light buff surfaced card.

Issue IV. 1882.

One value. Precisely the same as the last issue, except that the Royal Arms are smaller, and the shield is enclosed within an upright instead of a transverse oval. The error "*drot*" is corrected to "*droit*."

    1d., lilac, on light buff surfaced card.

Issue V. November, 1883.

One value. Designed and printed in the colony upon light buff surfaced card. Size 4⅞ × 3 3/16 inches. The inscription consists of two lines at the top of the card. First, "POST CARD," in fancy shaded capitals, with the royal arms between the two words; second, "THE ADDRESS ONLY TO BE WRITTEN ON THIS SIDE," in block letters. The stamp, type of the One Penny adhesive issue, October, 1883, is in the right upper corner. The design of the card is completed by a frame formed of a plain line crossed at the four corners like an Oxford frame. Size 4¾ × 3 1/16 inches. (*Illustration* 138.)

    1d., rose.

Issue VI. January 1st, 1885.

One value. Designed and printed in the colony. The inscription and arms are the same as those on the preceding issue, and they are similarly disposed. The type employed is different. The words "POST" and "CARD" are in fancy, and "THE ADDRESS ONLY," &c., in italic capitals. The stamp type of the One Penny adhesive issue of the same date is in the right upper corner. The design of the card is completed by a fancy frame with cross-like ornaments at the four corners. Size, $4\frac{5}{8} \times 3$ inches. Size of card, $4\frac{7}{8} \times 3\frac{1}{4}$ inches. (*Illustration* 139.)

(A) *On light buff surfaced card.*
  1d., rose (shades).

(B) *On yellowish buff surfaced card.*
  1d., rose (shades).

(C) *On white surfaced card.*
  1d., rose (shades).

(D) *On bluish-white surfaced card.*
  1d., rose (shades).

Issue VII. 1886.

One value. Designed and printed in the colony upon light buff card. Size, $4\frac{7}{8} \times 3\frac{1}{4}$ inches. The inscription at the top of the card is in five lines—First, "POST CARD" in Roman capitals, with the royal arms between the two words; second, third, and fourth, "☞ Note.—On affixing an additional One Penny stamp to this Card, it may pass through—the Post to any of the following Colonies, viz. :—New South Wales, South Australia—Queensland, Western Australia, Tasmania, New Zealand, and Fiji," in small type; fifth, "THE ADDRESS ONLY TO BE WRITTEN ON THIS SIDE," in Roman capitals. There is a short ornamental line between the fourth and fifth lines of inscription. The stamp type of the One Penny adhesive of the same date is in the right upper corner. The card is without frame.

  1d., pale red-brown.

REPLY PAID CARDS.
Issue I. 1883.

One value. Designed and printed in the colony upon stout light buff card. Size, $4\frac{7}{16} \times 2\frac{11}{16}$ inches. At the top in the centre of the first half is the word "VICTORIAN," in tall thin block letters, and below this "POST CARD," in fancy capitals. Lower down to left, in small block letters, is, "THE ADDRESS ONLY TO BE WRITTEN ON THIS SIDE." Below this is the word "*To*" in script type, and two long and one short dotted lines for the address. In the left lower corner is, "THE ATTACHED CARD IS FOR THE REPLY," in thin block letters. The stamp, type of the One Penny adhesive issue, October, 1883, is placed in the right upper corner. The second half has the word "REPLY" in fancy capitals, within brackets, beneath "POST CARD," and the two lines of inscription—"THE ADDRESS ONLY," &c., and "THE ATTACHED CARD," &c.—are omitted. The cards have no frame, and are folded along the top. The design is impressed on the first and fourth pages, and the two halves are inverted to each other. (*Illustration* 140.)

  1d. + 1d., violet (shades).

VICTORIA.

Issue II. January 1st, 1885.

One value. Precisely similar to the preceding issue, except that the stamp on each half is surcharged "STAMP DUTY" in the same way as the Three Pence adhesive. (Type XIV. B.)

1d. + 1d., violet, surcharged in violet.

OFFICIAL CARDS.

Most of the Government Departments issue cards which are used for official correspondence. There are a large number of varieties, but they all have the official handstamp in the right upper corner of the card, struck in blue or in black. As in the case of Tasmania no detailed list is given, for the reasons there stated. (*Illustration* 130.)

FISCAL STAMPS USED FOR POSTAGE.

From January, 1884, all the fiscal stamps have been available for postage. Following the rule adopted for the other colonies, no detailed list is given of the varieties so used, although large numbers of them have been and are legitimately employed to defray postage.

WESTERN AUSTRALIA.

Issue I. 1855-60.

Four values. Lithographic transfers from dies engraved on steel by Messrs. Perkins, Bacon, and Co., of London; printed in colour upon white and coloured paper, varying in substance; brownish gum; watermark, a swan: imperforate. Design: In the centre of each value is a swan, swimming to left. In the Two Penny and Six Penny values there is an addition of reeds on either side of the swan in the vignettes. In the Two Penny value the background is plain; the border is octagonal, of solid colour, and inscribed in white block letters. In the Four Pence the background is reticulated; the border octagonal, of solid colour, and inscribed in similar type. In the Six Penny value there is an addition of reeds on either side of the swan in the vignette; the background is striped; the border octagonal, of solid colour, and inscribed in white block letters. The One Shilling has a reticulated background, and an oval border of solid colour, inscribed in white block letters. Shape, oblong octagonal, except the One Shilling, which is a transverse oval.

The Two Pence, Four Pence, and Six Pence are inscribed: T. "POSTAGE." B. "TWO," "FOUR," and "SIX PENCE." L. "WESTERN." R. "AUSTRALIA." The One Shilling is inscribed: T. "POSTAGE . W. AUSTRALIA." B. "ONE SHILLING," the upper and lower inscriptions being separated by small cross-like ornaments. (*Illustrations* 142, 143, 144, 145.)

The four values were issued in the following order: Two Pence and Six Pence, 1855; Four Pence and One Shilling, 1858.

 2d., brown, on red and orange paper.
 4d., blue (deep, light, and nearly slate-), on white and yellowish paper.
 6d., coppery- to golden-bronze, on white and yellowish paper.
 1s., deep and pale red-brown, deep and pale bistre, on white and yellowish paper.

Varieties.—The Four Pence exists with the central vignette inverted in the frame. The Two Pence is found printed on both sides, not merely having a reversed impression, owing to one wet sheet being laid on the top of another.

Die proofs on India paper, in black, of the Four Pence and One Shilling are known, and presumably existed for the other values.

Remarks.—In the case of the Four Pence, as M. Schmidt de Wilde has pointed out, there are numerous varieties of type in the lettering of the octagonal band. It seems probable that the frames were separately prepared and placed on the stone, the swan and the centre portion of the design being the result of a second operation. Several different frames evidently were drawn, in which the size of the lettering differs. In the absence of an entire sheet, it is impossible to say how many distinct varieties exist, though it is beyond doubt that only a limited number of different frames were employed, and that consequently there are *not* as many varieties as there were stamps to the sheet. By this theory the error with the swan inverted, which was evidently speedily corrected, is fully accounted for. The whole question is difficult, and needs fuller investigation. The sheet consisted of 240 stamps, divided into four panes or blocks, each containing ten horizontal rows of six stamps. It is not known whether similar variations occur in the other values, though this is far from improbable.

In 1861 the above four values were rouletted, probably unofficially. The following varieties are known to the Society:

(A) 2d., brown; rouletted 9.
4d., blue ,, ,,
6d., bronze ,, ,,
1s., bistre ,, ,,
(B) 1s. ,, ,, 12½.
(C) 2d., brown ,, 13.
(D) 2d. ,, ,, 14.
4d., blue ,, ,,
6d., bronze ,, ,,
1s., bistre ,, ,,
(E) 4d., blue ,, 17 (a kind of pin-prick perf.)
(F) 4d. ,, pin perf. 14.

Considerable differences exist in the sizes of the swans in the watermark.

Issue II. 1860-61.

Four values. Engraved on steel by William Humphreys, and printed by Perkins, Bacon, and Co. Coloured impression upon thinnish white paper, verging, in some specimens of the Two Penny value, to pelure; yellowish gum; watermark, a swan. Design: A swan swimming to left on reticulated background. Border formed of four straight reticulated labels, separated in the corners by floreate ornaments, and inscribed in white block letters. The One Penny value preceded the others by about a year. Shape, oblong rectangular. T. "POSTAGE." B. "ONE PENNY," "TWO PENCE," "FOUR PENCE," and "SIX PENCE." L. "WESTERN." R. "AUSTRALIA." Unperforated. (*Illustration* 141.)

1d., black.
2d., orange-vermilion (shades).
4d., deep blue.
6d., sap-green.

Remarks.—The Four Penny value is very seldom met with in a cancelled state, although beyond doubt a limited number were used for postage.

Varieties.—All the values except the Four Pence, which has not been met with in this condition, exist unofficially perforated. The following varieties are known to the Society:

(A) 1d., black; rouletted 9½.
2d., orange-vermilion; rouletted 9½.
6d., sap-green ,, ,,
(B) 1d., black ,, 12¼.
2d., orange-vermilion ,, ,,
6d., sap-green ,, ,,
(C) 1d., black; perf. 13½ (square holes).
2d., orange-vermilion; perf. 13½ (square holes).

Proofs in black, on plate paper, of all the values exist.

Issue III. 1862-64.

Five values. Engraved on steel by Perkins, Bacon, and Co. Coloured impression upon stoutish white paper; whitish gum; watermark, a swan. Same design and inscriptions as in preceding issue. Machine-perforated 16, 15½, 15, 14½, 14, 13. In most, if not all the values, the perforations are compound. All the values, except the One Shilling (which alone is perforated 16, *true*), are found with an all-round perforation of 14. (*Illustration* 141.)

    1d., deep rose (shades, verging upon lake).
    2d., blue (dark and light).
    4d., vermilion.
    6d., purple-brown.
    1s., bright green.

Remarks.—Specimens of the One Penny and Two Pence are to be met with with their respective values and a crown, printed upon the reverse side, in red. This is the control mark.

Varieties.—The One Penny, Two Pence, and Six Pence are known imperforate, and are probably in this state to be considered as proofs, although specimens of the One Penny, imperforate, seem to have passed through the post. The Six Pence is found upon paper blued by the acid action of the printing ink employed.

Issue IV. 1864.

Five values. Same type as preceding issue, but without watermark; various perforations. (*Illustration* 141.)

    1d., lake, carmine to deep dull red; machine-perf. 13.
    2d., deep blue; machine-perf. 15, and 14 to 16 compound.
    4d., carmine   „   „   „   „
    6d., violet   „   „ 15½ „   „
    1s., deep green „   „ 15½ „   „

Variety.—The Six Pence, violet, upon paper blued like the previous issue.

Issue V. 1865-80.

Five values. Same type as preceding issue. With this issue the printing of the stamps of Western Australia by Messrs. De la Rue and Co. seems to have commenced, for the watermark is changed to "CC" and Crown. Machine-perf. 12½, and latterly 14. (*Illustration* 141.)

1d., bistre.	4d., carmine.
1d., yellow-ochre.	6d., violet (deep to pale).
2d., chrome-yellow.	1s., bright green, dull deep green.
2d., pale violet.	1s., bistre.

Remarks.—The One Penny, bistre, and the One Shilling, green, of this issue are catalogued by M. Moens as existing watermarked with the swan instead of "CC" and Crown. The President has seen the One Penny, bistre, so watermarked, in the collection of Dr. Legrand; but the specimen is imperforate, and of a distinct shade of bistre to that met with in the ordinary perforated stamps of that value. Therefore it would appear probable that this label is only a proof struck upon paper, watermarked with the swan, which had passed into the possession of the new printers, together with Messrs. Perkins, Bacon, and Co.'s dies. The One Shilling stamp so watermarked appears to be a myth.

The One Shilling, bistre, is an error, printed by mistake in the colour of the One Penny some time towards the end of 1869.

The Two Pence, pale violet, is an error, having been printed by mistake, towards the end of 1877, in the colour of the Six Pence. A die of the Two Pence was by mistake inserted when preparing the plate to print off the Six Pence.

A specimen of the One Penny exists printed in the exact colour of the Two Pence. Whether this is an error or a variety of shade is not known.

Varieties.—Printed as proofs:

        1d., deep bistre; imperforate.
        2d., yellow   „
        6d., deep purple   „
        1s., green   „

Issue VI. 1871.

One value. Type-printed by Messrs. De la Rue and Co. in colour upon medium white glazed paper, white gum; watermark, "CC" and Crown. Design: A black swan swimming to left, upon ground of horizontal lines, within double-lined oval; straight white labels at top and bottom of stamp, inscribed with coloured block letters upon white; sides and spandrels ornamented with bullrushes. The whole enframed by a border of double lines. Shape, oblong rectangular. Machine-perf. 14. (*Illustration* 146.)

        3d., reddish-brown.

Remark.—The swan, portrayed so faithfully on this vignette, is the indigenous black swan of the Australian continent, most appropriately introduced as an emblem of the colony.

Issue VII. March, 1875.

One value. Owing to the temporary exhaustion of the stock of One Penny stamps, a makeshift was extemporised by surcharging the current Two Pence with "ONE PENNY" in Roman capitals, the initial letters of each word being larger than the others. (*Illustration* 147.)

        1d., surcharged in green, on 2d., chrome-yellow.

    Varieties. (A) With treble surcharge.
           (B) With inverted surcharge.
           (C) With black surcharge.

Remarks.—In the last variety the letters "O" and "P" of the surcharge are the same in size as the other letters, and there is a period after the word "PENNY."

Issue VIII. End of 1882.

Five values. Same types as those of Issues V. and VI., but the watermark is changed to Crown and "CA"; machine-perf. 14. (*Illustration* 141.)

        1d., yellow-bistre.
        2d., chrome-yellow.
        3d., reddish-brown.
        4d., carmine.
        6d., mauve (1885).

Issue IX. 1884.

One value. Same type, surcharged ½d., in figures measuring 10 mm. in height. Watermark, Crown and "CA"; machine-perf. 12. (*Illustration* 148.)

        ½d., surcharged in red, on 1d., yellow-bistre.

Issue X. 1885.

One value. Engraved and printed by Messrs. De la Rue and Co., in colour, upon medium, white glazed paper; white gum; watermark, "CA" and Crown. Design: Similar to that of the Three Pence of 1871. The sides are composed of perpendicular bands of colour, each containing eight white oval ornaments. The spandrels are filled in with arabesque ornamentation, and the inscriptions above and below are in rather smaller block capitals. In other respects the stamps are the same. Shape, oblong; machine-perf. 14. (*Illustration* 149.)

½d., green.

Issue XI. 1885.

One value. Same type as the issue of 1871, surcharged "**1d.**" Watermark Crown and "CC"; machine-perf. 14. (*Illustration* 150.)

1d., surcharged in green on 3d., reddish brown.

Remarks.—There are two varieties of the numeral "**1**" of the surcharge. In one the figure has a straight top; in the other it is slanting, and the down stroke is thicker.

STAMPS EMPLOYED FOR OFFICIAL CORRESPONDENCE.

Most of the stamps already enumerated are to be found with a circular hole, varying in size, punched as nearly through the centre of the label as possible. In the early days of stamp collecting a superstition was current to the effect that these stamps were supplied to convicts, serving their sentences of transportation in Western Australia, and distinguished their correspondence from that of the rest of the community. As a matter of fact, these mutilated stamps were employed to frank and to particularize official correspondence. There were two distinct sizes of punch in use—the earlier (A) cutting a hole about 3, and the later (B) one of 4 mm. in diameter. The following varieties are known to the Society:

	Issue I.	Varieties of holes.
4d., blue	imperf. and rouletted	A and B
6d., bronze	imperf.	B
1s., brown	imperf. and rouletted	A

	Issue II.	
2d., orange	imperf.	A and B
6d., green	imperf.	A and B

	Issue III. & IV.	
1d., deep rose	perf. 15½	A and B
2d., blue	perf. 15	A and B
4d., vermilion and carmine	perf. 14–16, shades and varieties of perf.	A and B
6d., violet	perf. 13	A and B
6d., violet, blued paper		A
1s., green	perf. 14–16	A

	Issue V.	
1d., bistre and yellow-ochre		A and B
2d., chrome-yellow		A and B
4d., carmine	perf. 12½, shades.	A and B
6d., violet		A and B
1s., green		A and B

WESTERN AUSTRALIA.

	Issue VI.	Varieties of holes.
3d., reddish brown		A and B
	Issue VII.	
1d., chrome and green		A and B

Varieties.—Some of the above values may be found with two and even three holes in them, showing both varieties on the same stamp. This system of puncturing the stamps has now ceased.

POST CARDS.
Issued May, 1879.

Two values. Type-printed in colour by Messrs. De la Rue and Co., of London. Two lines of inscription: first, "POST CARD," in Roman capitals, the two words being separated by the Royal Arms and supporters; second, "THE ADDRESS ONLY TO BE WRITTEN ON THIS SIDE," in block letters. The stamp is in the right upper corner, and the design comprises the black swan, of the same type as in the Three Penny adhesive, with a frame varying for each value. In the Half Penny card the swan is in an oval, on ground of horizontal lines. Above and beneath the oval are white double-lined straight labels, inscribed in coloured block letters, "WESTERN AUSTRALIA" and "POSTAGE ONE HALFPENNY." The side labels are filled in with floreate ornaments, and the spandrels with conventional arabesques. In the One Penny card the swan, on ground of horizontal lines, is enframed in a double-lined octagon of irregular shape, resembling that of the first Four Penny adhesive. The top and bottom labels are the same as in the Half Penny card, and the lower one is inscribed "POSTAGE ONE PENNY." The side labels are filled in with lozenge-shaped ornaments, with a *fleur de lis* in the centre of each. The spandrels have conventional arabesque ornaments. Both cards have the same key-patterned border, and the reverse side is plain. (*Illustration* 151.)

½d., red-brown on stout rosy-buff card
1d., blue   „   bluish white card   } Size 4⅜ × 2$\frac{9}{10}$ inches.

FISCALS USED POSTALLY.

In 1882 the One Penny, yellow-ochre, of the type previously described, was converted into a fiscal stamp by means of a surcharge "I.R." in Roman capitals, and two parallel bars obliterating the word "POSTAGE." The surcharge was printed in green, and specimens are known that have been used for postal purposes.

The One Penny telegraph stamp is also catalogued by M. Moens as having been similarly used. Since these specimens were catalogued a decree of the Postmaster, dated October 25th, 1886, has been issued, officially authorizing the use of this stamp for postage during the exhaustion of the stock of the ordinary One Penny adhesive.

CORRECTIONS AND ADDENDA.

Page 73. STAMPS FOR OFFICIAL CORRESPONDENCE. II. *Surcharged in red.*—Add to (c)—(1) *Perf.* 12½:

    2d., blue (Type of 1871). | 6d., lilac (Type of 1882).

Page 91. ISSUE I.—To the *Varieties* add: The One Shilling may be found printed in purplish-blue instead of in its normal colour, orange. This stamp seems to have been an error, printed by mistake in the colour of the Six Pence.

Page 115. TYPE I.—Add to the *Remarks:* Proof impressions, in black, upon thick white card, of the Two Pence (state A) are known.

Page 115. TYPE II.—Add to the *Remarks:* Mr. David H. Hill, of Melbourne, informs us that the plate was engraved by Thomas Ham, of Melbourne, whose name it bears at foot, and that it was not copper, but steel.

    In the plan of the lettering of the sheet, at the bottom of the page, No. 18 should read "S W," not "S N."

Page 117. TYPE III.—Strike out the date 1862 above the 6d., black, and substitute August, 1861 (?)

    Add to the *Remarks:* The Six Pence, black, has been seen on an envelope postmarked "WARNAMBOOL, VICTORIA, AUGUST 21st, 1861," and "MELBOURNE, AUGUST 23rd, 1861." The envelope bearing this stamp, as well as the one described for Type VI., has been sent to the Society by Mr. J. Walker, of Edinburgh.

Page 119. TYPE VI.—Strike out the date April, 1861, for the 6d., and substitute June, 1859 (?). After the *Varieties* add:

    Remarks.—The Six Pence has been seen on an envelope postmarked "WARNAMBOOL, JUNE 7th, 1859," and "MELBOURNE, JUNE 10th, 1859."

Page 143. ISSUE I.—Add to the list of rouletted stamps:

    4d., blue, rouletted horizontally; imperforate vertically.

Page 144. ISSUE III.—Add to *Remarks:* Complete imperforate sheets of all the values exist at Somerset House, with swan watermark, and bearing the official approval, dated 13th December, 1860. The colours are as follows:

    1d., carmine. | 2d., blue. | 4d., rose.
    6d., deep red. | 1s., pale green.

    The sheet of the One Penny consists of 240 stamps, in twelve horizontal rows of twenty; while the sheets of the other four values have half that number of stamps, arranged in ten horizontal rows of twelve.

www.ingramcontent.com/pod-product-compliance
Lightning Source LLC
Chambersburg PA
CBHW020817230426
43666CB00007B/1044